Dietrich Bonhoeffer

Dietrich Bonhoeffer

An Evangelical Reassessment

Georg Huntemann

Translated by Todd Huizinga

Baker Books
A Division of Baker Book House Co
Grand Rapids, Michigan 49516

Der Andere Bonhoeffer © 1989 R. Brockhaus Verlag Wuppertal und Zürich

First English cloth edition, *The Other Bonhoeffer: An Evangelical Reassessment of Dietrich Bonhoeffer*, © 1993 by Baker Book House
First English paperback edition © 1996 by Baker Book House

Published by Baker Books
a division of Baker Book House Company
P.O. Box 6287, Grand Rapids, Michigan 49516-6287

ISBN 0-8010-2070-0

Printed in the United States of America

Contents

Part 6 *Christian Existence as Concrete Truth*

Part 7 *Bonhoeffer's Ethics of Order*

Part 8 *Bonhoeffer in the Resistance*

Part 9 *Bonhoeffer and the Established Protestant Church*

Part 10 *Unity in the Church and Peace in the World*

Note to the Reader

In this English edition, all quotes from the six-volume *Gesammelte Schriften (GS)*, published by Chr. Kaiser, München, were translated from the original German.

The following English editions of Bonhoeffer's works are cited:

The Cost of Discipleship. New York: Macmillan, 1963.
Ethics. New York: Macmillan, 1986.
Letters and Papers from Prison. New York: Macmillan, 1972.
Life Together. New York: Harper and Row, 1954.

Introduction

They are called "evangelicals," these Bible-believing, reformational (sometimes more pietistic), revivalist Christians—Christians who hold to conservative values and therefore live in basic opposition to their times. They are irritated when they hear the name "Bonhoeffer." They generally do not know what to make of the man who is perhaps the most widely read German-speaking theologian in the twentieth century. To be sure, the prayers from *Letters and Papers from Prison* often hang in church foyers and prayer rooms, framed or as posters. There is even a very famous revivalist hymn that contains a prayer from Bonhoeffer. A sentence or two from *The Cost of Discipleship* is appreciatively accepted.

Nevertheless, Bonhoeffer's legacy as a whole provokes perplexity and a sense of helplessness more than anything else.

After all, did Bonhoeffer not dirty himself with politics more than is necessary for a Christian? Did he not have very disturbing things to say about the "powerlessness of God"? Did he not say that "mankind come of age" would have to live without the "God hypothesis"—as if God did not exist?

Did he not think that the era of religion was now over for mankind come of age and that we have to face the otherworldliness of God in this world? Did he not utter sympathetic words on behalf of the archheretic Rudolf Bultmann, and even write that Bultmann had not been radical enough?

When a group of evangelical theologians was asked once whether Bonhoeffer had not been a heterodox theologian who deviated from right belief, an approving murmur of agreement went through their ranks.

When in the 1960s the protest meetings of the confessional movement calling itself "No Other Gospel" filled the largest halls and auditoriums in West Germany; when modernism after two decades of a false postwar restoration of traditional values once again boldly raised its critical-revolutionary head in Germany; when the populist Anglican bishop John A. T. Robinson categorized Bonhoeffer as one of the numerous rising progressives—when all of these things happened the "religionless" Bonhoeffer fell under grave suspicion. Since that time Bonhoeffer has been viewed by most German evangelicals exclusively in the dark shadow of postwar modernism.

At least partly, I also fell for modern theology's "creative abuse" of Bonhoeffer, as G. Krause put it in the *Theologische Realenzyklopädie*. My copy of *Letters and Papers from Prison* is stamped as having been acquired in 1951, and I read *Ethics* in 1956. For a long time I tried to internalize Bonhoeffer. I was stirred by the realism and the dynamic totality of his theology. But in the final analysis I was also one of those among the evangelicals who was irritated and disconcerted by Bonhoeffer, and I even wrote a number of things against Bonhoeffer's theology that a man from Stuttgart by the name of Rainer Mayer read. A very surprising letter from him—surprising because it was unusually polite and kind for a letter from a theologian—and his book *Christuswirklichkeit—Grundlagen, Entwicklungen und Konsequenzen der Theologie Dietrich Bonhoeffers* [*Christ Reality: Bases, Developments, and Consequences of Dietrich Bonhoeffer's Theology*] (2d ed., 1980) brought about my eventual change of heart. Therefore, I studied all of Bonhoeffer's work once again, and the result is this book.

Mayer's book, originally a doctoral dissertation, has already interacted thoroughly with the creative-modernist Bonhoeffer speculation. I will not therefore redo here what Mayer has already done. The amount of literature on Bonhoeffer (more has been written in English than in any other language) has become incredibly immense anyhow, and a *History of Dietrich Bonhoeffer Research* analogous to Albert Schweitzer's *The Quest of the Historical Jesus* is not yet available. I am happy not to have to reveal the conceptual abysses that Mayer has already brought to light in his book. Rather, what I have done is draw conclusions—not only theological conclusions, but above all conclusions that relate to intellectual history and a critique of the times in which we live.

It has occurred to me that Bonhoeffer's struggle against National Socialist ideology can readily be carried over to our day. The patriarchal figure Bonhoeffer, for whom the assigned place of the woman was the household of her husband and to whom it was crucial that the wife be subject to the husband, this Bonhoeffer, who fought for an ethos "from above" and for a governmental authority "by God's grace"—this Bonhoeffer was no comrade of the Nazis nor fitting contemporary of his times. Neither does he fit the spirit of our times. On the contrary, this consciously "Christian Westerner" is a witness against our times. Furthermore—and this is a very important aspect of this book for me—all of the anti-Christian elements of the Nazi period continue to be at work precisely among those who count themselves, often with such careless disregard of history, part of the progressive or left-wing scene. This is the case in spite of the fact that these anti-Christian elements appear in a different conceptual raiment than the garments they wore during National Socialism. The more or less matriarchal, socially utopian, and merely selectively biblical theology in Germany (and not only in Germany) cannot appeal to Bonhoeffer to support its claims. Moreover, it stands in complete contradiction to that which Bonhoeffer wanted to accomplish through his thought and his life.

Because the partly consciously produced historical forgetfulness of our day obscures both present and past and therefore time itself, the main purpose of this book is to remind the reader of all that really happened when Dietrich Bonhoeffer had to go it largely alone in his struggle against theological and political contemporaries and so-called national comrades.

Bonhoeffer was conservative. He was a conservative as an ethicist advocating rule and order on the basis of revelation (how little the moderns among the theologians esteemed his thought on ethics!). He was enough of a conservative in his interaction with the Bible that people talked of "naive biblicism" (E. Bethge) or of an "almost antimodernist foundation" (G. Krause) when they pondered Bonhoeffer's biblical exegesis. But as a "conservative" Bonhoeffer was also the man who called for a turning back, a conversion. He broke through the mental dead end of modern schools of theological thought with his dialectical-dynamic and multidimensional outlook. This theologian of the "historical turning-point," in whom the heritage of the Reformation (more Reformed than Lutheran, by the way) nevertheless remained alive, this theologian who saw the demise of the form of Christendom that we still experience in our state Protestant churches in Germany—this witness against our time is no less than a theologian of a wholly other time. He is a theologian of an era that has not yet begun in theology or the church. Above all, he is a challenger of modernism.

The religionless Christ-mystic Bonhoeffer (an aim of this book is to show that Bonhoeffer was a Christ-mystic) is very close in spirit to the evangelicals, for whom this book was chiefly written. He will be their church father in the future—or else the evangelicals will have no future. Bonhoeffer is in fact so similar to the evangelicals that it will become uncomfortable for them. For Bonhoeffer's theology could bring the necessary catharsis for the "evangelicals of all lands"—and that catharsis will quite certainly hurt. Many will therefore experience cleansing pain while reading this book. But this pain will be followed by much joy.

At the end of his short life, while in prison, Bonhoeffer read Dilthey. From the intellectual historian Dilthey, we have learned what it means "to understand." It is something different than "to comprehend." In this book, I will attempt to understand Bonhoeffer in the context of his time and against his time, for our time and against our time.

Basel, in the spring of 1989
Georg Huntemann

PART 1

Bonhoeffer's Life
and Thought

1

Challenged by a Revolution

At the end of his short life Dietrich Bonhoeffer knew that the hitherto existing character of Christianity would pass away. That was what he experienced in his lifetime as a Christian from 1906 to 1945, from the cradle in an elevated bourgeois family until his death on the gallows. Yet at the beginning everything looked very peaceful and stable. Bonhoeffer was born on February 4, 1906, in Breslau as the sixth of eight children, a son of a professor of psychiatry and neurology and of his wife Paula, nee von Hase. Bonhoeffer's death by hanging—after a nighttime court martial in the Flossenbürg concentration camp—occurred on the morning of April 9, 1945, between 5 and 6 o'clock. But this Protestant theologian was destined to be a sensitive witness of the first half of the twentieth century with its two World Wars, two defeats of Germany, and two revolutions—one a Marxist-socialist revolution and the other a National Socialist one. This dramatic time brought forth a dramatic life with a dramatic theology, which as a whole was not systematic but impressionist—a theology provoked by painful impressions.

The year 1906 was imbedded in the politically peaceful time of the German Reich between 1871 and 1914. But already then many signals of the coming storm were apparent to those who looked deeper. The German parliament rang with bitter debate over the increasing rearmament, above all that of the navy. That led to the dissolution of par-

liament while in the same year Chancellor von Bülow was already
warning of the threatening encirclement of Germany. In the year 1906
the so-called Crisis of Tangier revealed that the influence of the German Empire in North Africa was being stopped by a concerted effort
of all the other major powers of the time. The political and military
encirclement of the German Empire and its defeat in an ever more
probable war loomed on the horizon. But only a few thoughtful people saw the danger of a war. Most people were much more concerned
about a nominal (by modern standards) tax increase that had come
about because of a recent tax reform.

When Kaiser Wilhelm II celebrated his silver wedding anniversary
in that year of 1906, the world seemed whole, stable, and in the best
of order. For many, the rumblings of Socialists and Democrats, who
were sounding rather sinister cries, were much more alarming than
the seemingly far-off danger of war. In Russia the first Duma failed and
with it the attempt at bourgeois democracy. Czar Nicholas I had to dissolve the Duma. The fear of a violent upheaval from below, of an
uprising of the revolutionary masses, haunted Europe like a specter.

Bonhoeffer experienced the First World War as a youth; and then
as a young man (student, instructor, and pastor) he experienced the
years before Hitler's seizure of power in 1933 as ominous phases in the
dissolution of an intact and safe bourgeois world that was disappear-
ing under the fractious shadows of revolutionary uprising.

This time of uprising in Germany, which sensitized Bonhoeffer to
the extreme, was in substance the time of an antifather revolution. In
1944, one year before his death, Bonhoeffer wrote the following to his
fiancée, Maria von Wedemeyer:

> This severity in the relationship of the father to the son is a sign of great
> strength and inner assurance. . . . The people of today are for the most
> part too weak-kneed. They are afraid to lose the love of their children
> and degrade themselves to comrades and friends of their children. That
> is precisely how they end up making themselves superfluous as parents.
> This kind of upbringing, which is no upbringing, is dreadful to me. I
> believe that the parents who brought us up have similar opinions.[1]

1. Letter of January 22, 1944, in Eberhard Bethge, *Dietrich Bonhoeffer*, 1967, p. 38.

A year after Bonhoeffer's birth, in 1907, Sigmund Freud's essay "Zwangshandlungen und Religionsübungen" ["Compulsive Acts and Religious Exercises"] appeared. In this essay Freud revealed the father hatred that he later openly admitted. According to Freud religion is connected with fear of the father, father hatred, and patricide. Already in 1910 Freud wrote the following about religion: "Psychoanalysis has taught us to recognize the intimate connection between the father complex and belief in God. It has shown us that a personal God is psychologically speaking nothing other than an exalted father, and it demonstrates to us daily how young people lose religious faith as soon as the authority of their father breaks down. In this way we recognize in the parental complex the roots of the religious urge."[2] Thus religion becomes in Freud's view a human compulsive neurosis that arises out of the Oedipus complex, a transitory adolescent phase in the development of humankind that must be overcome by any means. Freud brought his thoughts on religion to a final conclusion in the year 1939, just when the antifather revolution gave vent to itself in the form of the Second World War, in his book *Moses and Monotheism*.

When Bonhoeffer was born, the paternal lover of orderliness who feared nothing more than having chaos within or around himself, Hitler had just turned seventeen years old. He traveled to Vienna, visited museums, went to operas (above all the Wagnerian operas that Bonhoeffer hated), and admired the magnificent architecture of the capitol of the Austro-Hungarian Empire. Hitler, the "mama's boy" who was at the same time a "rebellious and disrespectful pupil" who often missed school (apparently he finally had to leave school because of blasphemy against the Eucharist), began at this time to live a disorderly life—liberated from the authority of his father who had died in 1903.[3] In the year in which Bonhoeffer was born, Vladimir Ilyich Lenin, who had just fled his Russian fatherland once again, was also busy carving out his place in history. He was preparing the 1907 London Congress of the Russian Socialist party, in which three hundred revolutionaries later participated. Among those present at this congress in the Church of Brotherhood on Southgate Road were Maxim Gorky, Rosa Luxemburg, Josef Stalin, and Leo Trotsky. From the pul-

2. In *Sigmund Freud—Studienausgabe*, ed. A. Mitscherlich, 1969– , p. 580.
3. See W. Maser, *Adolf Hitler*, 7th ed., 1978, pp. 70ff.

pit of this indescribably ugly church, which was later destroyed during the air raids of World War II, Lenin, a man who had been driven out of his fatherland and who hated the patriarchal structures of Russia mainly because of the death sentence that had been carried out against his brother, proclaimed the revolution of the proletariat against the patriarchal and feudal Eastern world.

The year of Bonhoeffer's birth, therefore, was a year in which the groundwork was laid for the European catastrophes that would in 1945 claim Bonhoeffer himself as one of their many victims.

In the year 1906, when Bonhoeffer was born, the German Reich shone in its splendor and magnificence. In the year 1945 this empire perished for all time. After the German offensive in the Ardennes had collapsed on January 3 under the British-American pincer attack, while in the east the Red Army had crossed the Vistula and in course of the following weeks had reached East Prussia, Silesia, and Pomerania, the total defeat of the German Empire was sealed. As this was happening Bonhoeffer sat in the cellar of the Gestapo headquarters on Prinz Albrecht Street in Berlin, from where he was taken to the Buchenwald concentration camp and then via Regensburg and Schönberg to the Flossenbürg concentration camp. There, in Flossenbürg, he was hanged to the death on April 9, 1945. On that day Königsberg, the birthplace of the German philosopher Immanuel Kant, surrendered. Five days later the United States Army reached the Elbe, and on April 25, American and Soviet troops met at Torgau and exchanged their famous handshake. Three weeks after Bonhoeffer's execution, on April 30, 1945, Hitler committed suicide. Bonhoeffer, who had originally been arrested and indicted on charges of subversion of the armed forces and treason, did not experience the end of the Third Reich. It outlived him by one month. Bonhoeffer, one of the first theologians in Germany to recognize the coming revolution against fatherhood and order, became the victim of that very revolution.

Amid the Ruins of Protestantism

Bonhoeffer lived in a Protestant household that, although belonging to the church, was indifferent to it. What kind of a church was it? Already at the end of the nineteenth century the Christian social politician Adolf Stöcker, former court preacher for Kaiser Wilhelm I and

Kaiser Wilhelm II, felt compelled to recognize that German Protestantism was no longer capable of doing or accomplishing anything. Already, the Protestant Church in Germany had slowly but surely lost its identity.

The industrial working class had become radically estranged from this church. The large cities of northern Germany were already completely secularized. Christianity there was at best a Christian-bourgeois facade. Religion, as Rudolf Otto outlined it in 1917 in his book *The Idea of the Holy,* with its elements of pious reserve, reverence for the wholly other, and humility over against the sublime, was evaporating in the industrial landscape of the German North and West. Bonhoeffer would sensitively comprehend this process and draw theological conclusions from it. The downfall of religious Christianity was not an invention of a writer at his desk. By the time Bonhoeffer was born, it was already a reality. Not only the working class but also the nobility and the bourgeoisie experienced Christianity as a setting, slowly extinguishing sun. Already in 1853 the German novelist Theodore Fontane wrote what would become common knowledge by 1906:

> I can't help it, all of history is antiquated and the trouble is that there is nothing new. The efforts of the orthodox are boundless and yet they are suspended in mid-air. It's just simply a fact that the people have lost their Christian faith, and baptism, confirmation, the Lord's supper as well as all other outer manifestations of this faith are nothing more than habit or obedience to the authorities. The momentary victory of the so-called pious hypocrites is in reality their fiasco.[4]

More and more, Christian belief had been driven out of the general consciousness of modern man. Bonhoeffer not only understood this, he also said it openly: "God is allowing himself to be pushed out of the world." Both the factory owner and the worker, the "master and the servant," saw themselves by the beginning of the twentieth century as autonomous human beings come of age who could neither think religiously nor feel religious feelings. The relevant political forces from the right as well as the left, the Conservatives and the

---

4. Theodore Fontane, *Von Dreißig bis Achtzig. Sein Leben in Briefen,* 1970, p. 99.

Social Democrats, but also the National Liberals and the middle-of-the-road Democrats, no longer included any Christian content in their political ideas. Socialism, nationalism, imperialism, and economic liberalism as well as natural science and historical theory all existed *si deus non daretur,* as if God did not exist. The most horrifying thing about this, however, was that a kind of Christian sauce was still poured out over everything—more so in the case of the bourgeois and conservative parties and a little or not at all in the case of the Fourth Estate and socialists.

The Christianization of the world had been transformed into a secularization of Christianity. "Cheap grace" ruled in the Protestant Church. This was what Bonhoeffer, in the 1930s, saw as the true catastrophe in the Protestant Church. People lived under the myth of the "dear God" who spreads out the cloak of love over everything. This myth of the dear God fell apart in the disastrous events of two World Wars. The God of cheap grace and the superficial Christianity of an elderly and feeble Christian tradition became unworthy of belief.

One has to have experienced and suffered through this secularization of Christianity as Bonhoeffer did in order to understand the commonality of struggle between him and Karl Barth. Exactly eight years after Bonhoeffer's birth, Barth had challenged the "And-Also-Christianity" (culturally overfriendly Christianity) to battle with his *Epistle to the Romans,* and later he took a stand against the secularization of Christianity with his firm "No!" to those who would accommodate to and join with the spirit of the day. This struggle against cultural Protestantism was the struggle against the sermons taken from Schiller and Goethe rather than from the Bible, against the quasi-Christian liberalism that led to the total accommodation to bourgeois culture of Christianity. Already before World War I, Protestant Christendom's willingness to adapt seemed boundless. Adolf von Harnack, who later was a teacher of Bonhoeffer and in whose seminar Bonhoeffer even became class spokesman, drew up the war manifesto for Kaiser Wilhelm II at the outbreak of World War I. The manifesto was so bristlingly militant that Wilhelm II had to rework it in order to tone it down. Later, von Harnack, now as a "common-sense advocate of the republican form of government," made his peace with the democratic and social-democratic Weimar Republic. Protestant Christianity was in a life-threatening identity crisis and allowed itself to fall for any type of political manipulation. Thus the accommodation of Protestantism to the Nazi ideology that would occur in the 1930s was pre-programmed. It was precisely this identity crisis that Bonhoeffer suffered through, lived through, and thought through in his theology.

While in the Netherlands of the previous century there was a "miracle of the 19th century,"[5] an awakening of a Reformed-Calvinistic lifestyle that also radiated forth into the political sphere, nineteenth-century Germany remained without a comparable ecclesiastical revival to leave its stamp on the German situation. While in the Netherlands new churches arose by splitting off and founded institutions of higher learning with a Reformed character—even if this was accompanied by the pain of church schism—the established Protestant churches in Germany remained "intact." For all practical purposes their reconciliation with the existing Wilhelminian culture was perfect.

When this is taken into account it is not surprising that these established state churches—apart from some exceptions—also came to a reconciliation with Nazi ideology and adopted many anti-Christian elements of Nazi doctrine: racism (Aryan article of law forbidding Jews to hold church office); the leader principle (*Führerprinzip*); the "doctrine of decadence" (denial of the traditional understanding of original sin and atonement); a Neo-Darwinist ethos (militarization of the soul); and on and on. To be sure, not all Protestants were enthusiastic participants in all of this. Many sought half-hearted accommodation, even neutrality. Many tried to retreat into private spirituality or the liturgy. After all, Lutheranism offered a political evasion maneuver with its doctrine of the two kingdoms, which could be used to maintain that Christ did not play a role in the "inherent laws" of the political realm and that Romans 13 (being subject to the authorities) should be applied to every authority, thus also to Hitler.

From the very beginning Bonhoeffer rejected this tendency. On February 20, 1933 (which was, after all, subsequent to Hitler's coming to power on January 30, 1933), he said during the end-of-the-semester service in the *Dreifaltigkeitskirche* (Church of the Trinity) in Berlin:

In the church we have only one altar, and that is the altar of the Most High, the one true God, the Lord, who alone deserves honor and wor-

5. See H. Algra, *Het Wonder van de 19e Eeuw*, 4th ed., 1976.

ship! We have no secondary altars for the veneration of man. The worship of God, not the worship of man, takes place here at the altar of the
church. . . . We also have in the church only one pulpit and from this
pulpit we speak of belief in God. We speak of no other belief than this,
and of no other will than God's will, regardless of how good that will
may appear to be.[6]

Basically, however, only a minority really ever took up the opposition against the Nazi regime's ideological infiltration of the church.
The Stuttgart Confession of Guilt of October 19, 1945, was obliged
sadly to look back to the so-called time of struggle: "It is true that we
have struggled in the name of Jesus Christ through many long years
against the spirit that found its terrible expression in the National
Socialist terror regime. However, we charge ourselves with not having
confessed our faith more courageously, not having prayed more faithfully, not having believed more joyously and loved more ardently."
Above all, the great message of Bonhoeffer was passed over in this
struggle with and in the totalitarian Nazi state: Bonhoeffer not only
wanted the church to survive and to rescue itself and its doctrine; he
also wanted the commandment of God to be heard through the
church's preaching and through its struggle within society to defend
order, beat back chaos, and make possible a worthy human existence.

Against Contemporary Currents

Bonhoeffer was neither a National Socialist comrade nor a friend of
the times. His life and thought flowed totally against the contemporary currents. Herein lies the ultimate cause of his martyrdom. Against
nationalism he took a stand for the cause of ecumenicity. Against the
voices of nationalistic, pro-German theologians such as P. Althaus and
E. Hirsch, Bonhoeffer was an advocate and member of the movement
that sought Christian community over and above all political borders.
He stood against those German theologians who accused the ecumenical movement of the 1920s of a "superficial jargon of international
understanding"[7] and maintained that understanding among churches
of different nations was impossible as long as the consequences of the

---

6. Sermon on Gideon (Judg. 6:15), in GS, 4:110.
7. See Bethge, Bonhoeffer, p. 188.

ignominious dictate of Versailles, as many Germans called the treaty that ended World War I, weighed upon Germany.

Against Hitler's dictatorship as well as his pretension to the right to leadership, Bonhoeffer wrote a powerful essay for a radio broadcast in 1933. In what was probably the most profound essay to be written by a theologian at that time, Bonhoeffer contrasted dictatorship and authority, the mandate of the masses and the mandate of God. Against the militarization of the German soul in books, films, heroic epics, and later by means of a ubiquitous propaganda machine, Bonhoeffer took a stand for peace. Against militarism he advocated pacifism. And against the racism that drove men of the Jewish race out of church offices, Bonhoeffer wanted to repudiate the Aryan Laws and anti-Semitism by means of a *status confessionis,* a basic confession, of the church.

Very early on, Bonhoeffer had a consciousness of the crisis into which church and society had fallen. On July 31, 1930, in his inaugural lecture in the auditorium of the University of Berlin entitled "Die Frage nach dem Menschen in der gegenwärtigen Philosophie und Theologie" ["The Issue of Humanity in Current Philosophy and Theology"], the twenty-five-year-old Bonhoeffer said: "Today one sees old ideologies collapse and is obliged to fear that mankind will be buried with them. One sees a new spiritual reality arise in which man is overtaken by forces and demons, and yet is not willing to relinquish himself to them."[8] Bonhoeffer had the gift of sensitively discerning realities—political, social, and spiritual. He brought—and this is what he actually expected of all Christians—the "*sensorium* of God," a sense of God's own perception, into his experience of the world in order to suffer in the world and then, through the suffering, to recognize and live truth as a Christian. Bonhoeffer did nothing less than undergo inwardly the times he lived in. He totally immersed himself in the abundance of countervailing tensions of his day: "Quite suddenly, and for no apparent physical or psychological reason, the peace and composure that were supporting one are jarred, and the heart becomes, in Jeremiah's expressive phrase, 'deceitful above all things, and desperately corrupt; who can understand it?' It feels like an invasion from outside, as if by evil powers trying to rob one of what is

8. *GS*, 3:64.

most vital."[9] One has to admit unabashedly that this was Bonhoeffer's greatness—to have first suffered through the spirits of his times, both the constructive and the destructive, and then to have reflected upon it and worked it through in his thought.

Throughout his life, Bonhoeffer suffered *acedia* and *tristitia*—the affliction with resignation and sadness that was well known to medieval theology. Yet he did not suffer simply because of individually experienced depressions. On the contrary, he all too often was afflicted through the experience of powerlessness over against the immense monstrosity that befell him and his times. Thus Bonhoeffer did not suffer because of himself, but rather because of the challenges of his times that he had to bear. For Bonhoeffer—a powerful, athletic, robust, and strong man who in many ways symbolized "Germanicness"—was anything but a neurotic. Humorously, Barth saw something akin to a Germanic archetype, a realization of the ideal of the "Nordic race" in this strapping youth with blue eyes. Neither was Bonhoeffer a man who avoided the world. By no means was he a frustrated "drop-out." Rather, he was a person who was open to the world and to life. He could enjoy life intensely—whenever there was an opportunity to do so. His man-of-the-world lifestyle, which was obviously genuine rather than affected, allowed him to experience and recognize realities in the midst of the world rather than at a desk. In Bonhoeffer's case, the experience of a sensitive man preceded theological reflection. He fulfilled the basic rule of theological existence: *pectus facit theologum*, the heart makes the theologian.

Sensitive people often live lonely lives because they need the protective wall of solitude to guard their sensitivity. In that sense, Bonhoeffer was also a lonely person. However, precisely for that reason he understood that he had to live in community with others. His reserved, aristocratic manner and respect for discretion forbade him to invade the privacy of others. It has often been said that Bonhoeffer was an aristocratic person. He was authoritative—precisely because he was paternal. For this reason G. Th. Rothuizen was justified in entitling his book about Bonhoeffer *Aristokratisch Christendom—Over Dietrich Bonhoeffer* [*Aristocratic Christianity—A Study of Dietrich Bonhoeffer*]. In this book Rothuizen quotes the impression van Ruler had

---

9. Letter of May 15, 1943, in *Letters and Papers from Prison*, p. 39.

when he reflected on Bonhoeffer: "I sense there is something domineering and constraining, something haughty in his work."[10] But it was not a syrupy aristocratic attitude that distinguished Bonhoeffer, but rather a genuine vitality that characterized his life and work. The wife of the bishop of Chichester, Henriette Bell, recalled Bonhoeffer's time in London (1933–35) with the comment that he radiated "an enormous Germanic vitality."[11]

However, it was his cause—the struggle for his church—that led to Bonhoeffer's isolation. Very soon he was forced to acknowledge that he was alone even in the Confessing Church that was forming in response and opposition to the rising tide of nazism. He was alone in the resoluteness of his stand in the struggle against National Socialist ideology, and especially in his opposition to the Aryan Laws. Thus he wrote the following to Barth on October 24, 1933: "I felt as if I were suddenly and incomprehensibly in radical opposition to all my friends. I became more and more isolated in my views on this matter."[12] The twenty-seven-year-old theologian who was an instructor in the Department of Theology at the University of Berlin, a young man with good prospects of making an impressive career for himself, turned and went into the isolation of a foreign pastorate in London. Just as there were symbolic acts on the part of the prophets, there were also symbolic life circumstances and signs in Bonhoeffer's life. The end of his life was a tiny prison cell. It was there that he wrote in a morning prayer at Christmas 1943:

> In me there is darkness,
> But with you there is light;
> I am lonely, but you do not leave me;
> I am feeble in heart, but with you there is help.[13]

That Bonhoeffer was a man of order and inner discipline is important. For it was precisely the lack of order and discipline that comprised the threat of the revolution in which he lived. It is well known that dictatorship can exist without order, that drill may destroy rather

10. G. Th. Rothuizen, *Aristocratisch Christendom—Over Dietrich Bonhoeffer*, 1969, p. 20.
11. Ibid., p. 56.
12. Bethge, *Bonhoeffer*, p. 379.
13. *Letters and Papers from Prison*, p. 139.

than nurture discipline. That is why Bonhoeffer is precisely the man who stands opposed to the permissiveness of the pleasure principle that characterizes our time. Otto Dudzus writes about Bonhoeffer: "The smallest infringement of order hurt him. For the sake of the order that had in large part been destroyed, he became a revolutionary."[14] Because of the destruction of order and the annihilation of justice Bonhoeffer became a rebel. That constitutes the profound dialectic of his existence, the wealth of countervailing tensions with which he lived. His understanding of discipline and order did not allow self-pity or whininess. When Bonhoeffer suffered, he usually dealt with it alone. Even in the extreme situation of incarceration in a prison cell, he practiced spiritual and athletic discipline and kept the aristocratic *contenance* that meant so much to him and cannot be translated simply as "bearing" or "inner poise."

Bonhoeffer exemplifies the exact antithesis of the permissiveness of today's matriarchal-feminist era. The paternal Dietrich Bonhoeffer set personalization and individuation over against lasciviousness and permissiveness. He set responsibility over against the pleasure principle. Discipline and order, like justice, are certainly not—as is sometimes mistakenly suggested—elements of a protofascist lifestyle. Bonhoeffer understood Nazi ideology as an uprising of the mob, a revolution from below. He did not misunderstand the National Socialist revolution as a conservative, rightist revolution.

The above-mentioned *contenance* also kept Bonhoeffer from bringing Christianity down to a sentimental level: "there is a kind of weakness that Christianity does not hold with, but which people insist on claiming as Christian, and then sling mud at it. So we must take care that the contours do not get blurred."[15] Throughout his life, Bonhoeffer opposed the whininess apparent in much Christian piety, seeing it as a sign of the degeneration of Christianity. Bonhoeffer's piety was manly, bracing, and rugged in every way.

---

14. See *Dietrich-Bonhoeffer-Lesebuch*, 1958, p. 11: "Bonhoeffer was afraid of nothing more than he was afraid of inner chaos. He knew that a simple fall into inner chaos is deeply connected with the fall into chaos in general, with our susceptibility to chaos, our powerlessness against chaos. And above all he knew that the most effective aid against inner as well as outer chaos consists of the patient, faithful, listening to God's word and of doing his will."

15. Letter of February 2, 1944, in *Letters and Papers from Prison*, p. 205.

2

Concern with the "Big Picture"

Christianity in the Modern World

In grade school Bonhoeffer read the works of Friedrich Naumann, who had gone from being a liberal pastor to being a liberal politician. In his book *Jesus der Volksmann* [*Jesus the Man of the People*] Naumann championed the opinion that the love-ethos of Jesus of Nazareth could be realized through Christian social engagement. After a trip to Palestine he returned disenchanted. He could now no longer understand how Kaiser Wilhelm II's naval program and the industrialization and power politics of Europe at the end of the nineteenth century could be brought into relation to Jesus of Nazareth's eternal kingdom of God. In modern industrial society—so thought Naumann—Jesus remained meaningful only for the "inner life." Christianity no longer had anything to do with the political shaping of the world. For Naumann, the God of the Christians could no longer be found in the world of the nineteenth century.

But Bonhoeffer also read this in Naumann: "For all intents and purposes, many are merchants with the right hand and benefactors of the poor with the left hand. . . . All of the moods of the gospel just float like distant white clouds of longing above all tangible activity of our time."[1]

---

1. Friedrich Naumann, *Briefe über Religion*, 1917, p. 16. In the postscript to Bonhoeffer's lecture course of the winter semester 1931–32 on the history of the systematic theology of the twentieth century, Bonhoeffer writes in regard to Naumann of the "conscious capitulation of Christian ethics to the inherent laws of the world." Further on, we read: "If Christian and human purpose can be clearly distinguished, then it is really over for our Christianity." See *GS*, 5:212ff.

Naumann, however, no longer even dreamt of evaluating or shaping modern industrial society according to the standards of the biblical ethos, which for him represented the world of preindustrial Palestine. This is precisely what brought forth Bonhoeffer's opposition. His understanding of Christianity in this world was entirely characterized by totality and radicality. The division of the world into one reality in which Christianity was valid and another reality in which Christianity was not valid remained unacceptable to Bonhoeffer throughout his entire life. In this type of thinking Bonhoeffer cannily sensed the capitulation of theology and the Christian faith to the perceived reality of the modern world. From the very beginning, Bonhoeffer's way was opposed to that of Naumann.

Christianity was not to be relegated to the periphery of this world, as it were a secondary altar of inwardliness having nothing to do with world events. Bonhoeffer's conviction was rather that Christ was Lord of all creation and of the entire cosmos. In this way Bonhoeffer sought to depict the Christian life very concretely for his time and in his time. His foremost concern was to make Christianity concrete and tangible. He wanted to make clear what "Christ [means] for us today." Naumann was not the only example of how the Christian God was forced out of this world. The theology dominant in Germany at that time offered several possibilities of how Christianity could be put in its place.

First of all, there was Lutheranism with its doctrine of the two kingdoms. This doctrine came to the fore especially during the 1920s as a result of the work of Paul Althaus. The kingdom of grace, love, reconciliation, salvation, and the church stood opposite the kingdom of the world, of politics, and of the natural disposition of the common people. What was valid in one kingdom did not necessarily have to be valid in the other. The church was relegated to the sphere of inwardliness and bliss, the sphere of personal salvation. The church had little or nothing at all to do with economics or politics. In the abusive application of this doctrine of the two kingdoms, the political sphere was left more and more to its "autonomous laws."

Second, liberal theology had reduced Christianity to the ethical sphere alone. The Christian was a person renewed through faith who lived by the love and grace of God. All metaphysics and dogma were rejected; all statements about nature, the saving acts of Christ, and the beginning and end of the world were ruled out. Here Immanuel Kant, who wanted to see "religion within the bounds of reason," was the great church father. He inspired opposition to the "false wealth" of theology and the desire for a return to the "essence of Christianity." But here the ethos of love and justice was formalized, because it was more or less detached from any reference to reality as a whole. The ethos of liberal theology became a private ethos perhaps still lived out within the family but no longer having any meaning in the world of politics and industry.

Third, there was pietism, which had retreated completely into inwardliness. Here the concern was personal salvation. The world was left to itself. This type of pietism could even develop into a kind of dualistic disassociation from the world in which one lived in the belief that it was no longer worthwhile to be concerned about the events of this vile world, since it was quickly approaching its end anyway.

Bonhoeffer fought against all of these theologies of retreat. On June 8, 1944, he clearly delineated the reductionistic impulse of liberal theology: "The weakness of liberal theology was that it conceded to the world the right to determine Christ's place in the world; in the conflict between the church and the world it accepted the comparatively easy terms of peace that the world dictated. Its strength was that it did not try to put the clock back, and that it genuinely accepted the battle (Troeltsch), even though this ended with its defeat."[2] In his ethics, Bonhoeffer fought passionately against the notion of the autonomy of the political and economic spheres. Here he was in complete agreement with Article 2 of the Barmen Declaration of May 1934: "We reject the false doctrine that there are areas of our life in which we belong not to Jesus Christ, but to other lords; areas in which we do not need justification and sanctification."

When Bonhoeffer began work on his *Ethics* in 1939–40, the fact that Christ had been forced out of the arts, science, and politics was clear to him. Beyond that, the totalitarian state had laid its seemingly all-powerful hand upon every sphere of reality. But in this ultimate challenge thrown up by the totalitarian state, Bonhoeffer also saw how reason, education, humanity, and tolerance were again surging back toward a Christian point of view: "The children of the Church, who

2. *Letters and Papers from Prison*, p. 327.

had become independent, now in the hour of danger returned to their mother."[3] To the very end, Bonhoeffer never capitulated; he was never intellectually willing to exempt any sphere of reality from the rulership of Christ. He never accepted some preassigned or limited role for Christianity.

Amid Countervailing Tensions

Many interpretations of Bonhoeffer assume that he experienced a profound break in his theological thought in the spring of 1944. The new guiding phrases such as "world come of age," "religionless Christianity," the "powerlessness of God," and living in the world "as if God did not exist" were, according to these interpreters, completely new themes with completely new answers. The general attempt was made to isolate several separate phases in Bonhoeffer's life's work: the Discipleship period, the Ethics period, the Letters from Prison period, perhaps also before that a liberal period, and finally the confessional period. This selective method can lead to a relativizing of Bonhoeffer's statements, since they are each assigned to only one period of his life. These incomplete statements then become practically meaningless when they are thus isolated by such analysis of Bonhoeffer's life. This interpretation of Bonhoeffer is completely wrong. What Martin Heidegger once said proves to be true also of Bonhoeffer: "Every person has but one dominant thought." Whoever, like Bonhoeffer, has lived not a boring life, but rather a stormy, highly dramatic, and adventurous life will not be free of corners, hooks, turns, heights, and depths in his thought. In Bonhoeffer's case there is change, long-range development, growth, drama, struggle—but never a fundamental break with what went before.

Bonhoeffer appropriated and reflected upon each of his experiences with his Christian faith as the reference point. His theology as a whole consists of nothing but testimonies. But these testimonies must be understood synoptically as the single testimony of a single journey through life and not be picked apart analytically. On April 11, 1944, Bonhoeffer wrote: "I'm firmly convinced—however strange it may seem—that my life has followed a straight and unbroken course. . . . If I were to end my life here in these conditions, that would have

3. *Ethics*, p. 56.

a meaning that I think I could understand." Here it is clear that Bonhoeffer understood his life as a unity. To be sure his life was a process of turning away from the idiomatic to actual reality, "It has been an uninterrupted enrichment of experience."[4] The crucial factor for him is that one does not lose sight of the totality. He was certain of the continuity and consistency of his life, and he professed to be "travelling with gratitude and cheerfulness along the road where I'm being led."[5]

These statements alone give us cause to see primarily the core unity of his life rather than the abundance of tensions that pulled at him. Bonhoeffer's life and thought consist of a single testimony. There may be several notes—happy and sad, high and low—but there is just one song. In fact, even Bonhoeffer's theology cannot be merely thought about. Rather, it must first be personally experienced, for in Bonhoeffer a new form and manner of thinking theologically has entered the world.

4. *Letters and Papers from Prison*, p. 272.
5. Letter of August 23, 1944, in *Letters and Papers from Prison*, p. 393.

3

Breaking Out of the Closed System

Christianity in Captivity to the System

Bonhoeffer's theology actually consists only of a bundle of fragments. Even *The Cost of Discipleship* and *Life Together* are only fragments. Bonhoeffer did not leave a theological system behind, nor did he intend to. What Bonhoeffer left behind was a bundle of perspectives that in themselves consist of paradoxical formulations.

After all, the second commandment, which forbids us to make any graven images or likenesses of God, means that we may not force God into a system, nor into a worldview. In a view, or image, of God we do not meet God but only ourselves. Images of God are products of our unrestrained fantasy, our needs, our fears—images of God are religion. Bonhoeffer often called attention to the fact that we should read the Bible not for ourselves, but *against* ourselves. The Bible brings our thought and our religiosity into question. Whoever proceeds the opposite way and reads the Bible for himself, thereby bringing God into his worldview, makes an idol which—as Feuerbach expounded—expresses a projection of man and the longing for a superman. In reality, God—as Barth called to the attention of twentieth-century theology—is the wholly "Other" who speaks to us through his Word but does not admit of reduction to a collection of concepts.

The so-called later Heidegger, whom Rudolf Bultmann never understood, saw the transgression of "being" precisely in the fact that in Western philosophy access to being was supposed to occur by forcing being into an image, a system. He traced *cogitare* (to think) back to *cogere* (to force), and saw the era of the worldview as the attempt to force being into an image.

But God, the Creator of heaven and earth, is free over against creation and cannot be understood or recognized by means of creation, or from creation, or even according to the likeness of creation. Paul professes that all things are from him, through him, and to him, but also that there is no human being who has known the mind of the Lord or acted as his counselor (Rom. 11:36). Therefore God may never become simply a "God of the gaps" in a system that man feels he more or less understands, apart from the "gaps." Then God would be assigned a place in a metaphysical system of man's making. It was precisely against such a move that Bonhoeffer revolted: the God of the Bible is neither a God of metaphysics nor a "God of the gaps."

Modern theology is, however, by and large a theology of the worldview in which space and time became comprehensible. Time became comprehended time; salvation history became historically-critically comprehended secular history. The action of God in this world was forced into a conceptual paradigm of the world. Saving acts, creation, miracles, God's lordship over the world, and the endtimes had no place in this paradigm, because all of these things would be unknown quantities in a paradigm that allows only knowable concepts in finite space and finite time. In this way, God's acts came to be seen merely as a part of the whole. God himself was to be made comprehensible. But God was also made "comprehensible" in so-called special theology, in the doctrine of God. He was made tangible as the God of love. The wrath of God, evil, the satanic, sin—these realities with all of their biblical radicality were removed from this one-dimensional paradigm or, at best, remained as derived quantities.

Bonhoeffer experienced the demonic power of conceptuality in European theology at harrowingly close range in his interaction with colleagues and his seminary students. At the seminary in Finkenwalde where he taught, Bonhoeffer implored his pupils:

> The greatest danger to the pastor comes from his theology. He knows everything that a human being can know about sin and forgiveness. He knows what right belief is and tells himself what it is for so long that he one day no longer abides in belief, but rather in his thinking about belief. . . . Knowledge reveals its demonic nature. It drives one further

and further into what is in effect unbelief. When that point has been reached, we no longer experience belief. Our only experience is intellectual reflection about belief. . . . But it is truly serious when it no longer unsettles us that our experience remains so far behind the Word—when we become pleasing to ourselves perhaps even in the role of martyr, who in renouncing his own experience brings himself to speak a Word that is strange to him. . . . In this case one cannot believe because one does not want to believe. The conscience has been lulled to sleep. Theology becomes a scholarly discipline within which one has learned to excuse everything and to justify everything. . . . The theologian knows that he cannot be deposed by any other theologian. He is righteous in everything that has to do with his theology. That is the curse of theology. All of these things cannot be said without fear and embarrassment. We must have theology and cannot simply do away with it. However, an adaption of Matthew 16:25, "Whoever loses his life for my sake will find it," bears heeding here . . . Whoever has once begun to justify himself with the help of theology has fallen into Satan's clutches. Naturally, be a good theologian! But keep your theological knowledge at arm's length![1]

The paradoxical salvation statements in the Bible about the wrath and the love of God, his revenge and his reconciliation, dying and resurrecting, death and eternity, freedom and the predestination of salvation—all of these statements were nicely straightened so as to conform to a thought system. They were thereby robbed of the content conveyed by the various biblical statements.

Bonhoeffer's theology is completely different. It is dialectical in the sense that it takes up the biblical paradoxes in unbroken form. A few examples: The believer is obedient; and only the obedient believe (against the ethical and fideistic dissolution of biblical paradox). He who cannot bear solitude should beware of community; and he who can do without community should beware of being alone (against both bourgeois hyperindividualistic salvation as well as idolatrous overemphasis on community). He who is justified is made holy; and he who has been made holy will be saved through the fire of judgment against holiness-perfectionism, on the one hand, and blithely counting on Christ's merits to cover one's own willful sinning, on the other.

1. From notes on the lecture course on pastoral care at the seminary at Finkenwalde and later at the Sammelvikariat between 1935 and 1939, in *GS*, 5:404ff.

Nothing happens against God's will; but also nothing happens without God's will (against the one-dimensional, naive desire to derive everything that happens in the world directly from God's good providence—the unsatisfactory flippant answer sometimes given to the question: How can one believe in God after Auschwitz?). Before God and with God we live without God; and God is powerless, thus he is with us and helps us (against the idea of a linear upward mobility via interaction with the love of God).

Whoever evades or relativizes these paradoxes in Bonhoeffer's thought even for a moment makes Bonhoeffer into a church father of a modernist theology. Bonhoeffer's theology is not to be re-rationalized when it is precisely his theology that breaks out of the Egyptian captivity of a rational worldview.

Bonhoeffer was very much aware of the dialectic involved in his mode of expression. When speaking of how to make belief possible he said: "We have to get people out of their one-track minds."[2] On May 29, 1944, he wrote that belief in God makes possible "a multidimensional life." Already in his lectures of the 1931–32 winter semester he clearly articulated this opinion: "We must never speak one-dimensionally of God, but rather in terms of statement and rejoinder, or point-counterpoint. For we must remember that God can absolutely never be captured even in the grasp of a dialectical mode of expression. Real dialectic is humble. It contrasts statement with rejoinder and knows that the truth lies beyond this mode of expression in the imperceptible center. God remains free in relation to the dialectic." In these same winter lectures, Bonhoeffer said, during a discussion of the latest publications in systematic theology: "Therefore everything has to be said once again from the other side: God and not-God, revelation and the non-revelatory, ego and non-ego. All my discourse can be nothing more than a reference to the imperceptible center."[3]

Bonhoeffer's theology can be understood only in the context of a new type of thinking that transcends systematic thought. Only in this way does it become clear that there are no ruptures in Bonhoeffer's theology, although this theology itself represents a break within modern theology and church history. Bonhoeffer's theology is a theology

2. *Letters and Papers from Prison,* p. 311.
3. *GS,* 5:221, 303.

of paradoxes. It clearly recognizes that revelation "cannot be interpreted by means of concepts arising out of our intuitive notions of
time and space or cause and effect"—as Fritjof Capra expresses it in
his book about contemporary thinking.[4] Modern thought knows
about the "principle of indeterminacy," to which all theology must
stay alert if it is not to end in a systematic-speculative "positivism of
revelation." What Thomas Kuhn wrote about the "structure of scientific revolutions"[5] may be said in part about Bonhoeffer's theology as
well. It represents a new structure of theological revolution that is at
the same time radically biblical.

After all, Bonhoeffer not only brought about a revolution in the
structure of theological thought; he also lived out and aspired to a
Christian "anticulture" in connection with his theology. His statements about university theology in the early 1930s already suggest
something akin to Krishnamurti's program of *Freedom from the Known*
(the title of Krishnamurti's book).[6] Bonhoeffer directed his gaze
toward India at a time when today's disciples of the New Age were not
yet even born. But he remained a Western theologian. He revolution-
ized the rational system of Western metaphysical theology, but not in
order to immerse himself in the myths of Asiatic religiosity, but rather
in order to testify to the freedom of the Word of God. Capra's question, "How can one transcend thought without being unfaithful to science?" and the "role of the paradoxical in mystical traditions"[7] were
already preoccupations of Bonhoeffer in the 1930s, at a time when
there was talk of a turning point in thought only in the areas of theo-
retical physics and in the philosophy of Karl Popper and Ludwig Witt-
genstein—at a time when Protestant theology struggled to preserve a
place for its God within the worldviews of the nineteenth century.

Bonhoeffer recognized and refused to accept the mental "dead-end"

4. See Fritjof Capara, *Das neue Denken*, 1987, p. 17. Of course, the quotation of passages from
this book does not mean agreement with the program of the so-called new age that it advocates.
5. See Thomas S. Kuhn, *The Structure of Scientific Revolutions*, 2d ed. (Chicago: University
of Chicago Press, 1970).
6. See J. Krishnamurti, *Einbruch in die Freiheit*, 1969. In this context we are not interested
in the Far Eastern manner of meditative thought advocated in this book, which in the final analysis is, as always, totally one-dimensional. Of relevance to our discussion is the protest against
the fragmentation brought about by one-sidedly analytical European thought that is caught up
in conceptual constraints and necessarily fails to gain access to biblical revelation.
7. Capra, *Das neue Denken*, p. 30.

into which above all German theology had been led by means of the rationalist rape of biblical revelation. The multidimensional thinking that Bonhoeffer calls for in view of biblical revelation sees reality as a "fabric of connections."[8] Bonhoeffer's *The Cost of Discipleship,* his letters, and above all his *Ethics,* which today is frequently passed over in silence, remain unintelligible if one is controlled by the firm belief that "all knowledge must have a solid foundation."[9] It is only possible to understand Bonhoeffer, from his pacifist sermon in Fanö in 1934 to his joining the militant resistance group called the Kreisauer Circle during World War II, if one realizes, as Heisenberg expressed it, "that every word or every concept, regardless of how dear it may seem to us to be, nevertheless possesses a limited sphere of applicability."[10] In reading Bonhoeffer, one senses in every line that theology is always an approach toward revelation, and never the rational prison in which revelation itself can successfully be held captive.

The various statements of Bonhoeffer from the different phases in his life and thought cannot and must not be selected out analytically in "source critical" fashion. Rather, they must be looked at together multidimensionally as parts of an interwoven tapestry. Certainly, Bonhoeffer himself gave notice of the dynamic and processual nature of his theology in his motif of the ultimate and penultimate. With this motif the Christ-mystic Bonhoeffer (see below) led theology out of its captivity to modern European cultural consciousness.

> Do you understand now, when I refuse to relinquish at any point the Bible as the Word of God that is alien to man, that I am asking with all the strength within me what God wants to say to us here? Every other place outside of the Bible has become too uncertain for me. I am afraid that anywhere outside of the Bible I will encounter a divine double of myself . . . and now I would like to say very personally: Since I have learned to read the Bible in this way—and that was not very long ago at all—it is becoming more wonderful to me every day . . . but you wouldn't believe how happy one is when one has left the false paths of so much of theology and found his way back to these primitive things.[11]

8. Ibid.
9. Ibid., p. 69.
10. Ibid., p. 71.
11. Bethge, *Bonhoeffer,* p. 250.

In this letter of April 1936 to his brother-in-law Rüdiger Schleicher, who was later condemned to death because of his involvement in the resistance against Hitler, one notices Bonhoeffer's desire to break out of the rationalist paradigms of theological biblical criticism. Already in 1932, in a lecture to students on discipleship, Bonhoeffer said: "Discipleship stands exclusively on simple faith, and faith is true only in the context of discipleship."[12] For Bonhoeffer, theology and existence form an inseparable unity.

Mystery and Fragment

Bonhoeffer's life is symbolic. It is symptomatic of his theology: no wholeness in life, no wholeness in thought. Bonhoeffer was aware of the sporadic nature of his theological thought, and he sensed that he would not live his life to a natural end, that he would probably only live to be thirty-eight years old. Bonhoeffer's life was in fact not lived out to a natural end. He died at the age of thirty-nine. When Barth was that age, he wrote his *Christian Dogmatics*, which was only a first draft of the "church dogmatics" that followed.

Generally speaking, Bonhoeffer was of the opinion that the time of the great "life systems" was past. On February 23, 1944, he wrote: "we feel how fragmentary our lives are, compared with those of our parents. . . . Where is there an intellectual *magnum opus* today? Where are the collecting, assimilating, and sorting of material necessary for producing such a work? Where is there today the combination of fine *abandon* and large-scale planning that goes with such a life?"[13] In Bonhoeffer's existence, "the constant danger to which nearly all of us are at present exposed in one way or another provides a wonderful incentive to use the present moment, 'making the most of the time.'"[14] His thoughts about religionless Christianity and the world come of age were never thought out to their conclusion.

The ineffable mystery of God has great significance for Bonhoeffer. He was always clearly aware of the fact that God cannot be incorporated into an image, a concept, or a system. When we speak of God, we speak of that which we do not know. It is the revelation of "the

12. Ibid., p. 253.
13. *Letters and Papers from Prison*, p. 219.
14. Ibid., p. 223.

wholly other" God. Our lot is one of faith, not of unrestricted sight. Thus Bonhoeffer clearly saw the limits of theological reflection. He wrote in a letter on July 21, 1944: "These theological thoughts are, in fact, always occupying my mind; but there are times when I am just content to live the life of faith without worrying about its problems. At those times I simply take pleasure in the day's readings."[15] The dialectic of speaking and being silent already begins to play a role in Bonhoeffer's lectures on Christology in the summer semester of 1932: "To speak of Christ means to be silent, to be silent about Christ means to speak." And on May 17, 1934, he said in a sermon on 1 Corinthians 2:7ff. ("we are speaking of the mysterious, hidden wisdom of God") that the world bears an unmistakable sign of its blindness to the mystery of God: the cross of Jesus Christ. "It is a mystery because God on the cross became poor, lowly, inferior, and weak out of love for humanity; because God became a human being like us so that we might become divine; because he came to us that we might come to him. God as the one who became lowly for our sakes, God in Jesus of Nazareth—that is the mysterious, hidden wisdom that no eye has seen nor ear heard and that has never entered the heart of any human being." Revelation does not remove the mystery because the incarnation itself is a mystery. We will never comprehend why God acted as he did. The prophets, Christ, and the apostles never explained God's acts, but only described them. That is why theology should also allow itself to be reminded that it does not fix revelation, but at best describes revelation—and does so incompletely, because the ultimate, the mystery, is ineffable.

"Hidden" was a key word for Bonhoeffer, not only in relation to his personal life, but also in regard to revelation. Whoever knows about the mystery will recognize that the mystery is incomprehensible. Bonhoeffer also never spoke of the mystery of his conversion. He could be silent. In other words, he cultivated a virtue that is very rare among theologians. He probably never even told his best friends everything. Both the theology and the life of Bonhoeffer will always remain partly shrouded in mystery.

15. Ibid., p. 369.

PART 2

Bonhoeffer's Church

4

Bonhoeffer as Antirevolutionary

In 1923, when Bonhoeffer began to study theology in Tübingen, France occupied the Ruhr area and Hitler attempted his Beer Hall Putsch in Bavaria. Radical socialist governments were deposed in Saxony and Thuringia with the help of the Imperial German army, and the Soviet Union ratified its first constitution. Chaim Weizmann became president of the World Zionist Organization and inflation reached its high point in Germany with single bank-notes of one trillion marks. In 1923, Sigmund Freud published his depth-psychological *The Ego and the Id,* and Albert Schweitzer wrote his work of cultural criticism, *The Decay and the Restoration of Civilization.* Karl Barth's *Epistle to the Romans* had already excited a new generation of theologians, and the world's first radio broadcast took place in Berlin.

The seven years in which Bonhoeffer studied, ending in 1930 with his second theological examination before the church of the old-Prussian union and finally rounded off with his dissertation presented before the theological faculty in Berlin, were politically, intellectually, and ecclesiastically stirring years—for Germany more so than for any other country in Europe. When Bonhoeffer attained formal academic rank in 1930 with the treatise *Akt und Sein,* Alfred Rosenberg, the chief ideologue of the National Socialist German Workers party and managing editor of the National Socialist party newspaper *Völkischer*

Beobachter, published the book *Der Mythos des 20. Jahrhunderts,* in which the racial religion of an Aryan Jesus was proclaimed. In this book, the entire Old Testament as well as the second coming of Christ, his atoning death on the cross, his miracles, his incarnation as the Son of God, and the resurrection of the dead were all dismissed as Jewish.

The year 1930 also saw the forced resignation of Reichschancellor Brüning and with it the end of parliamentary democracy in the German Reich.

In the Weimar Republic of these days, people lived without an intellectual or spiritual center. The Christian traditions, especially in the Protestant part of Germany, had crumbled more than in any other European country. In regard to the process of de-Christianization Germany was a highly modern nation, more "progressive" than all other European nations. How would this country, and the church in this country, the very "national churches," react to a political catastrophe in the form of war or revolutionary violence? Germany was intellectually and spiritually an empty space, a vacuum, which any possible type of anti-intellectual or antispiritual ideology could fill.

Bonhoeffer saw through the situation early on. In 1931, just after he had been ordained as a pastor by the general superintendent in the Church of St. Matthew in Potsdam Square in Berlin, Bonhoeffer asked prophetically: "Will our church survive another catastrophe? Will that mean the final end, unless we change immediately?"[1] That nothing changed in the church weighed heavily on Bonhoeffer until his death. For that matter it would still weigh him down today, were he to experience current conditions in the German Protestant church.

Although the 1920s and 1930s were characterized by political troubles, intellectual and spiritual adventurism of all kinds, and economic and political instability, through all of this a single, unified, sweeping, and fundamental process came to maturity in the German Reich more than anywhere else: the secularization of the German "soul," the collapse of Christianity as the "religion of public life." Christianity in its Protestant form had no answer to the challenge of the time.

Already in the last third of the nineteenth century, a dissolution of Christian ways of life had taken place to an extent that was unparalleled in the rest of the world. This was especially noticeable in North

---

1. Bethge, *Bonhoeffer,* p. 269.

Germany, with its tendencies toward secularization that were so strong that they were downright reminiscent of Babylon. Already in 1875, Adolf Stöcker, the court pastor who had been called to Berlin by Kaiser Wilhelm I, said the following about the religious situation in the capitol city of Berlin:

> That which no one, not even the worst pessimist, had expected, happened. In the new year 1875 it came out with horrifying statistical conclusiveness. For every 100 legally performed marriages here in Berlin, only about 18 or 19 were performed in the church; for every 100 children born, only about 52 were baptized. And so it remained for almost a decade, until church life rallied and took measures to resist this trend.[2]

But this "rallying" and "resistance" brought only a small pause for breath in the ecclesiastical disintegration in Germany. The World War of 1914 to 1918 would bring only at its very beginning something akin to a—at any rate very questionable—"reawakening of religious enthusiasm." The collapse of the German Empire in 1918 tore apart the synthesis of throne and altar not only in its political, but also in its religious bankruptcy. Repentance, conversion, or revival were just as rare in Germany in 1918 as in 1945.

Theologians, though probably few others, began to reflect upon this identity crisis in Protestantism. The 1920s and 1930s brought something like a brief flowering of Protestant theology. Theologians such as P. Althaus and W. Elert led the way to a reevaluation of Reformation theology within the framework of Lutheranism. In Tübingen Heim and Schlatter, each with very different emphases, brought a biblicism to the fore that did not avoid confrontation with the spirit of the times. Karl Barth—at that time still considered to be some kind of a theological monster—destroyed the sand castles of cultural Protestantism and called for a return to the revelation of the wholly other God. These are only a few examples of an unprecedented flowering of German-language theology that was, however, often categorized in other countries as a "quasi-orthodoxy." For with a wary view to these developments in German theology, many other theologians, such as

---

2. D. von Oertzen, *Adolf Stöcker*, 1910, 1:107. Stöcker was installed as court pastor in October 1874 in Berlin.

those in the Calvinist Netherlands, considered the German developments to amount to a mediating or compromising theology whose answers to the problems of the time did not arise from the center of biblical revelation. In addition, this flowering of German-language theology stood completely outside of the daily church life of the laypeople. It hardly had an influence on congregational life and was completely insignificant on the political scene. The little bit of "Christian-German nationalist" here or "religious-socially conscious" there never gathered any political momentum.

Astutely, Hitler had recognized early on that the churches, especially the Protestant theologians, would not try to set substantial limits on his aspiration to political power.

In prison at Tegel in 1943 it became clear to Bonhoeffer how little the afflictions of the Second World War challenged "man come of age" to "overcome" his crises "through religion." On April 30, 1944, he wrote:

> What is bothering me incessantly is the question what Christianity really is, or indeed who Christ really is, for us today. The time when people could be told everything by means of words, whether theological or pious, is over, and so is the time of inwardness and conscience—and that means the time of religion in general. We are moving towards a completely religionless time. . . . (else how is it, for example, that this war, in contrast to all previous ones, is not calling forth any "religious" reaction?).[3]

Nevertheless, the ecclesiastical apparatus kept on functioning undisturbed then as it does today, administering the bustle of official acts that were still in demand among the population. In the 1920s the general superintendent of Brandenburg, Otto Dibelius, could even triumphally write a book about the century of the church,[4] although his book was sharply contradicted by Barth. It was as clear to Bonhoeffer as it was to Barth, at that time a professor of dogmatics in Bonn, that Christianity in Germany had fallen into the most decisive crisis in its history. And German theology, which like no other theology in

---

3. *Letters and Papers from Prison*, pp. 279–80.
4. The first edition of Otto Dibelius' *Das Jahrhundert der Kirche* appeared in 1926. The second edition was published in 1928—sensational for a book with the word "church" in its title.

Europe at that time wanted to be and had to be contemporary theology, wanted to take on this crisis with all the resoluteness it could muster. That situation led to that typical kind of determined German theologian who passed himself off as infallible and was certain he could find the solutions to all the problems he faced. The sometimes so penetrating, sly, and self-assured manner of German theologians in particular is a compensation for their insecurity in the face of the crisis of Christianity as it was experienced in Germany and as it took place and still takes place today in the innermost regions of the hearts of all German theologians.

The course that this German theology chose, its so-called plan of action to rescue Christianity as Bonhoeffer came to know it, was to resort to reductionism. Bonhoeffer would later condemn Bultmann too as a reductionist theologian. At least, thought the German theologians, a safe place for Christianity should be set aside within the pervasive dominion of secularized life. According to many German theologians, Christianity no longer fit into the framework of a secularized, "scientific" understanding of the world, nature, history, and society. Christianity would have to be smoothed out, stripped, and scaled down. It would have to be reduced until what remained was capable of survival over against the modern understanding of the world. An unfilled space would have to be found (a place for the "God of the gaps") in order to salvage the God of old. Later this plan of action, which Bonhoeffer recognized from the beginning as reductionist theology, would be called "demythologization."

It was above all National Socialist ideology that was intent on pushing Christianity out of political and social life. Bonhoeffer struggled passionately against this lockout of Christianity from the world. Bonhoeffer's engagement for the one reality does not entail the one-dimensionality of modern theology with its horizontalization of Christianity (no God and no heaven and no God in heaven). Rather, Bonhoeffer's engagement for this reality understands itself as a protest against the notion that the rulership of the triune God should be rendered ineffectual in any sphere of reality. Bonhoeffer recognized the tendency of Nazi ideology to relegate Christianity as well as Judaism to a ghetto, to balkanize it and thereby nullify its social presence.

It is here, therefore, that the conflict with Nazi ideology begins, because it was a totalitarian movement that intended to permeate all areas of public life, eliminating all competition. To be sure, the attitude toward Christianity within the Nazi party, especially toward Protestant Christianity, was at first glance by no means clear-cut. Martin Niemöller thought, as did many other members of the Confessing Church that was forming at the time, that he had "the better, genuine National Socialists" on his side. After all, Germany had never before experienced such an inundation of totalitarian ideology. How could Protestant theology recognize the full significance of this challenge when this very theology itself was in such a state of doctrinal chaos that it was impossible for it to reach an agreement as to what Christianity actually is?

Nevertheless, point 24 of the National Socialist German Workers party platform was abundantly clear in one key respect. It placed the value of race above the value of religion. Point 24 reads:

> We demand the freedom of all religious confessions within the state, as long as they do not endanger the existence of the state or violate the moral and ethical sense of the Germanic race. The party as such advocates the viewpoint of a positive Christianity without binding itself to a specific confession. The party actively opposes the Jewish-materialist spirit within and outside of us and is convinced that lasting healing of our people can occur only from within on this foundation: public before private welfare.

This item in the party platform was crystal clear: the final standard was the moral and ethical sense of the Germanic race. "Positive Christianity" could mean nothing other than a Christianity of action. And the reference to the "Jewish-materialist spirit" could be interpreted in such a way that with it all the saving acts and hopes of salvation contained in biblical revelation were denied—just as did in fact happen. And that the public interest should come before the private interest proves unequivocally the socialist component of National Socialism in that it put the collective before the individual.[5]

---

5. Alfred Rosenberg conceived of this point of the party platform as dynamic-revolutionary: "The only thought that is capable of uniting all classes and confessions in the German people is the new and ancient racial (*völkisch*) worldview. . . . This worldview today is called National Socialism." Thus, the "racialists" around Rosenberg quite unequivocally insisted on a change, namely, the Aryanization of Christianity. On this point, see K. Scholder, *Die Kirche und das Dritte Reich*, 1977, 1:107.

Now the common, as well as officially disclosed, opinion was that the major Christian confessions, thus also the Protestants, fulfilled this "Aryan requirement" in doctrine, worship, and religious life. After all, the Protestants, especially the large Lutheran state churches, had their Luther. He had written bluntly and unmistakably against the Jews and their "lies," and had from the beginning brought a hefty dose of anti-Judaism into German Lutheran theology.[6]

Bonhoeffer's Role in the Resistance

The life of Bonhoeffer would have been unique apart from his imprisonment and execution for the simple reason that Bonhoeffer, as a twenty-six-year-old theologian at the beginning of his career, recognized more clearly than almost any other German theologian the "political" challenge that the Nazi regime presented to Christianity. This challenge occurred most importantly in two fundamental areas: (1) in its totalitarian claim to leadership from below (i.e., by appeal to the masses); and (2) in the struggle against Judaism and therefore ultimately against biblical revelation and Christianity itself.

On February 1, 1933, two days after Hitler's so-called seizure of power on January 30, Bonhoeffer gave a radio lecture on the subject

---

In contrast to Rosenberg's view, which was actually obsolete already in the 1930s, many National Socialists quite logically saw the total incompatibility of Christianity and Nazi ideology. One of these National Socialists was von Leers, the training leader of the National Socialist Student Federation. As Reich youth leader, Baldur von Schirach also expressed similar views, at least in the 1930s. See Scholder, *Die Kirche*, 1:671.

In the final analysis, the radical Christians in Thuringia, led by the pastors Leffler and Leutheuser, for whom Hitler was "the mouth of a Savior" and National Socialism "the new body of Christ," had also been overtaken by the course of events—even though they professed that "Hitler has brought us to Christ; we do not bring Christ to Hitler." It is significant in this connection that the racial Christians placed unity above truth. Thus, Christianity was to be unified beyond all confessional limits by a racial-ideological superstructure. For Bible-believing theology, the greatest caution is thus advisable wherever such a high premium is placed on unity.

6. Luther's 1542 treatise, "Von den Juden und ihren Lügen" ["On the Jews and Their Lies"], often served as the prime example of a "legitimate" Christian anti-Semitism. For the Jewish point of view on this point, see R. Lewin, *Luthers Stellung zu den Juden*, 1911; and Carl Cohen, *Die Juden und Martin Luther*, in *Archiv für die Reformationsgeschichte*, no. 1, 1963. The thesis of the Jewish infiltration of early Christianity with Paul as the "main guilty party" runs from the eighteenth century, from Hermann Samuel Reimarus, one of the earliest fathers of historical criticism, to J. G. Fichte and Paul de Lagarde, up to contemporary feminism. Investigations of anti-Semitic motives in the so-called historical-critical method as practiced on the Old and New Testaments in the eighteenth century up to the present remain to be done.

of the *Führer* and the individual in the young generation.[7] The broadcast of this lecture was cut off before its conclusion. The content of
this lecture and the circumstances surrounding it show Bonhoeffer as
a man of the conservative political opposition from the very beginning. We know that he remained so until the end. Meanwhile, the
masses left the socialist parties, the Communist party, and the Social-
Democratic party in droves. In Berlin in particular SA-storm troop bri-
gades took in "converted" communists (for example, SA-storm troop
Brigade No. 5 named after the Nazi martyr Horst Wessel). While all of
this was happening, the actual opposition to Hitler's socialist system
("You are nothing, your people is everything") was taking shape as a
conservative opposition. It was this conservative opposition, including Bonhoeffer, which later planned and carried out the uprising of
July 20, 1944. To claim Bonhoeffer today as a political leftist is a part
of the theater of the absurd characteristic of modern contemporary
theology.[8]

7. *GS*, 2:22ff. Later, the broadcast lecture was expanded into a lecture presented at the German College of Politics in March 1933.

8. The National Socialist movement was a youthful movement that was rebelling against the
patriarchal world. The average age of party members between 1930 and 1933 is estimated at
twenty-five to twenty-six years of age. By way of comparison, not even 8 percent of the party
members of the Social Democratic party (SPD) were under twenty-five in 1930. (On this point,
see Scholder, *Die Kirche*, p. 166.) As a youthful movement, National Socialism's ideology was
anticonservative, antipatriarchal, and socialist. (On this point, see J. Goebbels, *Der Nazi-Sozi*.
This work, published in 1929, was both anti-Semitic and antibourgeois.)

In 1929 Paul Löbe used the expression "outline of totalitarianism" to describe both the
NSDAP and the KPD (German Communist party). The reactionary conservative Alfred Hugen-
berg, founder of the Harzburg Front and the father of the cooperation between German national
"conservatives" and National Socialists, harbored no illusions about the socialism of the National Socialist movement. (On this point, see E. Nolte, *Der europäische Bürgerkrieg 1917–1945. Na-
tionalsozialismus und Bolschewismus*, 1987.) Crucial speeches given during the war, such as
Hitler's antilawyer speech of April 26, 1940, and Goebbels' call to total war on February 18,
1943, were effective among the working population mainly because of their purposefully socialistic emphases.

Nolte (pp. 308ff.) has given many examples of an ideological affair between Stalinist
national-communism and Hilterist National Socialism, especially after the nonaggression pact
of August 1939. At that time Nazi Foreign Minister von Ribbentrop thought that especially the
"simple people" in Germany would understand the pact (p. 311). But the affinity between National Socialism and communism is much deeper. In the summer of 1933, the Comintern was
already in a state of near panic about "the masses of workers streaming to fascism" (p. 214). The
old, traditional working-class strongholds were not a safe refuge for communist functionaries
after Hitler's so-called seizure of power. Hitler became especially popular among the working
masses, and many Communists streamed into the SA of Ernst Röhm, who wanted the revolution
to go even further—above all, against the "Jewish-capitalist world" (p. 228).

It is significant that the interrupted radio lecture, which was in effect a conservative proclamation against the Nazi regime, was published shortly afterward on February 25. It appeared with only a very few abridgments in the most conservative weekly in Germany at the time, the *Kreuz-Zeitung*. In this astonishingly apt conservative depiction of a political dictatorship, Bonhoeffer contrasted political office as bestowed from above—the structure of authority within the conservative, Occidental rule of law—with the *Führer* as the dictator from below. He contrasted authority that derives its legitimacy from the command of God with the dictatorship of the masses. Bonhoeffer wrote:

> The *Führer* has authority from below, derived from those he leads. True political office has authority from above. The authority of the *Führer* derives from his person, but the authority of true political office supersedes the personal. Authority from below is the self-justification of the people, but the authority of true political office is acknowledgment of the legitimacy of law. Authority from below is borrowed authority, but the authority of true political office is authority that is derived from its true source. . . . There is a decisive difference between the authority of the father, the teacher, the judge, and the statesman on the one hand and the authority of the *Führer* on the other hand. The former have authority because of their office and only when carrying out their duties as holders of their office. The *Führer*, however, has authority because of his person. The authority of the former can be infringed upon or violated, but it nevertheless remains valid. The

---

At the same time the SA, just as the NSDAP and the KPD, was fascinating to youth, whose glorification the conservative Bonhoeffer consciously opposed. Youth organizations were the crucial and significant subdivisions of both the NSDAP and the Soviet Communist party. The percentage of young workers and apprentices in the Nazi youth movements up to 1933 was approximately 70 percent (pp. 377ff.).

All in all, Hitlerist socialism was more dynamic—and for the German soul—more romantic and vital than the traditional, more intellectually oriented Marxist socialism. In addition, the Nazis borrowed many communist working-class themes, adding a text to them that was often barely changed from the original. Also, the National Socialist movement made May 1, the holiday of socialism, into a state holiday. "Comrade" remained the common form of address in Hitler's form of socialism, even if the word *Volk* was added at the beginning of the word so that former "comrades" were called "*Volk*-comrades." The annexation propaganda of the Nazi movement in Austria up to 1938 shows that National Socialism cannot simply be identified with fascism. This propaganda was able to fascinate the Austrian masses of the Austro-fascist "class state" with its socialist agenda.

authority of the *Führer*, however, is totally at stake at every moment. This authority lies in the hands of the followers. I choose my *Führer*, but I cannot choose my father or my teacher.[9]

According to Bonhoeffer the revolutionary *Führer* is merely a function of a totally unpredictable, unregulated mob that is able to do away with traditional values and put new "social arrangements" ("life systems") in place. True office as meant by Bonhoeffer, however, is connected to the order instituted by God. A good part of Bonhoeffer's rejection of National Socialism rests upon justified primal fear of this kind of uprising of the masses, which threatened like a tidal wave to wash away all order of law and God-ordained values. According to Bonhoeffer, the masses have no real way of connecting to a social will. Rather, the apparent expressions of will are as it were mechanical, mindless forces in reaction to stimuli. The masses comprise a unity that is not based on the separateness of the individual person. Therefore it cannot last very long. It is the simplest social entity and brings forth the most powerful experiences of unity. How much these "experiences of unity" became a part of daily life and what it means when a mob reacts to stimuli—these became the bitter and painful experiences of the twelve years from 1933 to 1945.

Thus the twenty-six-year-old Bonhoeffer hit upon the nerve of the conflict between socialist dictatorship and conservative-Christian-Western rule of law. Bonhoeffer saw the downfall of the individual and his responsibility under the crushing power of the collective.

Only in the context of the disintegration of the Christian ethos of order could the reciprocal relationship among office, authority, and law be destroyed and the individual be robbed of his responsibility over against this absolute law. Only in this tragic context could the rule of law be ruined. From that hour on Bonhoeffer was aware of the necessity of a Christian political ethic. Until his death, he struggled to outline the contours of such an ethic. Under the constraints of the circumstances he could leave behind no more than a fragment of this ethic. As we will see, it was an ethic of order—a Christian-Occidental ethic of order—and this alone suffices to render ridiculous any attempt at a modernist, left-wing interpretation of Bonhoeffer.

9. On this point, see n. 7.

In addition to its totalitarian claim to leadership from below, there is a second point that Bonhoeffer detected in the ideological challenge presented by nazism to Christian-Occidental culture. Nazi ideology was anti-Jewish. Why, really? The answer is simple, but one hardly ever hears it. Because Nazi ideology was an antipatriarchal ideology it functioned anti-Semitically. The God of the Bible is a God who reveals himself patriarchally. He is a Father God who places his order and his authority against any uprising from below. The archenemy of Old Testament revelation is Baalism, the struggle for the golden calf, through which the deification of the fertility of nature and thus also the worship of blood and race are played out against the revealed will of God.[10] The Nazi dictatorship wanted to be rooted in the masses. It did not desire the authority of the father, but the authority of the id, the manipulated unconscious. It was precisely this "stimulation" of the mob, this mechanization of motivational forces, that was the central issue in this as in any other mass movement. The people were put in the place of God, and the *Führer* in the place of the father. The youthful hero committed patricide, and revelation was replaced with the "prophecy" of the thousand-year Reich.

Whoever sees National Socialism in the context of the authoritarianism of premodern, conservative Germany, has not understood nazism. The struggle of National Socialism against Judaism was the struggle against the Father God of the Bible. We will see that the paternally minded Bonhoeffer was able to see through this more accurately than perhaps any other theologian.

Because of its identity crisis, the Protestant Church fell into a situation that forced it to accommodate itself to nazism, although the anti-Semitism of the National Socialist movement was ultimately anti-Christian. The struggle against Judaism within the church, the lock-out of Christian Jews from the office of pastor, and finally the refusal

10. In a treatise of 1938 based on lectures he gave during his period of emigration, my former teacher H. J. Schoeps referred to the Nazi movement as a "Baalization" against which the Old Testament prophets had fought. This treatise, which is now almost nowhere to be found, is entitled *Der moderne Mensch und die Verkündigung der Religionen*. A Prussian Jew, Schoeps recognized the anti-Jewish and at the same time anti-Christian naturalism of the Nazi movement. In many books about Prussia, he brought out, just as Bonhoeffer, the radical contrast between the conservative heritage of Prussia and the racist-socialist ideology of the Nazi movement. It was a tragedy, not only for Germany but also for all of Europe, that Nazi ideology was misinterpreted as a reactionary or conservative movement.

to allow Jewish Christians to participate in the sacraments of baptism and communion were all part of the program of the "people's church" in Germany, a church whose colors were getting closer and closer to Nazi-brown. In opposition to this, Bonhoeffer pithily demanded the following in a pamphlet written in August 1933: "The exclusion of Jewish Christians from the church community destroys the substance of the church of Christ. . . . Race and blood are classifications that the church recognizes, but it may never be allowed to become a criterion for belonging to the church. This criterion is solely the Word of God and faith." Bonhoeffer saw and drew the consequences: "It may be that the church will fail to win millions for the sake of the thousand believing Jewish Christians whom she may not sacrifice. But what would the gain of even millions of souls be worth, if it had to be traded for one individual soul at the cost of truth and love?"[11]

For Bonhoeffer, the church could not be limited racially, ethnically, or nationally. Bonhoeffer was "ecumenical." He wanted a Christianity that went beyond all national and ethnic borders. But Bonhoeffer was also—and above all—a man who held to conservative Occidental values. For him, the unity of the Christian West was much more significant than the nation: "Between the cliffs of nationalism and internationalism, ecumenical Christendom calls out to its Lord and asks for his guidance. Nationalism and internationalism are questions of political necessity and possibility. But the ecumenical movement does not inquire after these questions, but after the commandments of God. And it proclaims these commandments right into the midst of the world without regard to other considerations."[12] The ecumenical movement at that time, as Bonhoeffer experienced it, cannot be compared with the ecumenical movement as we experience it today. As an ecumenical, Bonhoeffer advocated conservative, Occidental order of law against the uprising from the people. What Bonhoeffer wanted was a call to struggle against the racial state as well as against the racial church in which he lived. For the established church was becoming more and more a racial church. And although this may grate on the nerves of all third world-oriented liberation theologians,

11. The pamphlet, "Der Arierparagraph in der Kirche," was drafted by Bonhoeffer in August 1933. See *GS*, 2:62ff.

12. *GS*, 1:461.

Bonhoeffer was consciously and until his death a man of the Christian West. In the fragment of his *Ethics* we read: "Jesus Christ has made of the west a historical unit. . . . The form of Christ is the unity of the western nations. . . . What is intended is rather a discussion of the way in which in this western world the form of Christ takes form. . . . western history is, by God's will, indissolubly linked with the people of Israel, not only genetically but also in a genuine uninterrupted encounter."[13]

An Ecumenical Witness for the Christian Occident

For Bonhoeffer Western understanding of law and freedom took precedence over the nation. In this he stood completely within the conservative Prussian tradition. The conservative state of Prussia had always placed rule of law above nationality. During the Second World War, the conservative Prussian Bonhoeffer wrote the following in his *Ethics:*

> Prussia had a sound instinctive sense of the revolutionary implications of the notion of nationhood, and refused to accept them. In nationalism Prussiandom was combatting the revolution of the *grande nation* and resisting its encroachment into Germany. Nationalism evokes the countermovement of internationalism. The two are equally revolutionary. To both of these movements Prussia opposed the state. Prussia wished to be neither nationalistic nor international. In this respect its thought was more western than was that of the Revolution.[14]

Of course, the ecumenical Bonhoeffer was not a World Council of Churches-type bureaucrat like we often see nowadays, the result of an unpleasant synthesis of pragmatism and socialism. Bonhoeffer fought on two fronts. On the one hand, he wanted to see the church of Christ throughout the world move toward a clear confession rather than focus on ecclesiastical-political pragmatism. He did not place pragmatism above the truth. On the other hand he clearly saw the political ruin that was on the horizon for Europe, Germany, and the Protestant Church in Germany. The consequences of secularization in Europe— not only in Germany—deeply troubled him. The aristocratic Bonhoef-

13. *Ethics*, pp. 92, 87, 89.
14. Ibid., p. 101.

fer was horrified at the militant columns of brown-shirted marchers who were pouring onto the streets of Berlin. He realized the significance of this uprising of the masses, this growth within organized plebeianism of a lifestyle totally cut off from tradition. His struggle for ecumenism was quite decidedly also an appeal to the Christian-Occidental conscience to resist this rising terror. And here he pressed for the quickest, clearest, and most binding statements possible.

Thus Bonhoeffer swam completely against the current of his day. Against the militarization of public life that reached from the Hitler youth to the SA, Bonhoeffer advocated the struggle for peace. In fighting this losing battle for peace he was nearly alone in his own church. Every word in his *The Cost of Discipleship* was a word against "total mobilization," against the "adventurous life," against living in "lust for the heat of battle."[15] Bonhoeffer preached peace at a time when the movie theaters, the radios, the schools, the mass demonstrations, and the newspapers were all filled with praise for the heroic warrior. Bonhoeffer was not an absolute pacifist, but as a believer in the Occidental ideal of the state governed by law and order he refused to ride the coattails of the uprising of the father-killers, with their cult of the heroic warrior. Because he was not a hanger-on, a coattail rider, he was alone—alone enough to have to face the bitter experience of powerlessness. The conservative Bonhoeffer experienced in the Germany of the 1930s and above all of the 1940s what the "powerlessness of God" means.

---

15. Ernst Jünger, an author who was very popular at that time, wrote in the style of this inner mobilization. The titles of some of his books speak for themselves: *In Stahlgewittern* (1919); *Krieg als inneres Erlebnis* (1920); *Feuer und Blut* (1925); *Totale Mobilmachung* (1931); and *Der Arbeiter* (1933). These books, whose titles were catchphrases in the 1920s for the coming German revolution, bring the "feeling of life" of this "new era" concentratedly and comprehensively to expression. Everything about Bonhoeffer stood in contrast to this "feeling of life."

5

Modernist Theology's Claim to Bonhoeffer's Thought

The Argument of Religionlessness

Since the 1960s, Bonhoeffer's experiences of and thoughts about the powerlessness of God have been interpreted in such a way that Bonhoeffer appears to have all the earmarks of a true church father of progressive theology. A flood of literature and secondary literature in almost all of the languages of this planet has laid hold of Bonhoeffer. His letters from prison became the charter documents of a new understanding of Christianity. "Religionless Christianity" in the modern world became the foremost plan of action of a revolutionary-minded semblance of Christianity and a "liberation theology."

Pietists, who had read Bonhoeffer's *The Cost of Discipleship* and *Life Together* like a prayer book, stiffened in paralysis when they learned what this man said later on in his life about Bultmann, the Bible critic above all other critics. Did Bonhoeffer, in 1942, not extol the intellectual pureness and integrity of Bultmann and send Bultmann's books to his students in the barracks and at the front? When Bonhoeffer spoke of the "one reality" did the belief in the one God outside of the one humanly perceptible reality not have to be denied? Did Bonhoeffer not desire the end of metaphysics (God "without the time-condi-

tioned presuppositions of metaphysics"), which would require that a
God in heaven who is "behind nature" or—in other words—who is
above the one world reality does not exist? Did Bonhoeffer not claim
in his letters from prison that a new autonomous mankind come of
age could quite adequately deal with himself, even without having to
take recourse to the "'working hypothesis' called God"? Had he not
even written that "everything gets along without 'God'—and, in fact,
just as well as before,"[1] and that God, just as in the sphere of science,
was also being pushed back farther and farther in the everyday realm
of human life, losing more and more ground all the time? Would that
not mean the end of belief in God the Father, the Almighty Creator of
heaven and earth?

Had Bonhoeffer not clearly held that the "attack by Christian apologetic on the adulthood of the world" were "pointless," "ignoble," and
"unchristian," because this was a cunning game that sought to
"exploit man's weakness" and because "it confuse[d] Christ with one
particular stage in man's religiousness, i.e. with a human law"?[2] Did
Bonhoeffer not wage war against Barth's 'positivism of revelation' and
say in remembrance of the *Kirchenkampf*, a struggle in which Bonhoeffer himself had taken up arms as a right-winger, that it was no
longer a matter of believing in the faith of the church, but rather of
living one's personal faith?[3] Did Bonhoeffer not even say that there
were "only a few 'last survivors of the age of chivalry,' or a few intellectually dishonest people" on whom one could still successfully
"descend as 'religious,'" pouncing on "a few unfortunate people in
their hour of need," doing violence to them with religious fervor?[4]
Did Bonhoeffer not even confess of himself that he had once had
much richer times "spiritually," but that he had reached a point at
which he felt how the resistance within himself against everything
"religious" was growing, "often reaching the level of an instinctive
loathing"? ("But I can feel the resistance growing within me against
everything religious. Often to the point of an instinctive loathing—
which certainly is not good either."[5])

---

1. *Letters and Papers from Prison*, pp. 325, 326.
2. Ibid., p. 327.
3. Ibid., pp. 328, 280.
4. Ibid., p. 280.
5. April 25, 1942, in *GS*, 2:420ff.

Was Bonhoeffer's Theology Atheistic?

Does the phrase that is so important to modern theologians—*etsi deus non daretur*, as if God did not exist—come from Bonhoeffer? Did he not write that we have to live as those who can deal with life without God?[6]

The key statements of Bonhoeffer for modernist theology, the ones that are probably most frequently quoted, come from a letter of May 5, 1944. In this letter we read the following: "It is not with the beyond that we are concerned, but with this world as created and preserved, subjected to laws, reconciled, and restored. What is above this world is, in the gospel, intended to exist *for* this world; I mean that, not in the anthropocentric sense of liberal, mystic pietistic, ethical theology, but in the biblical sense of the creation and of the incarnation, crucifixion, and resurrection of Jesus Christ."[7]

Does this mean that Bonhoeffer's theology represents the end of theistic theology? Is not Bonhoeffer in the final analysis the great initiator of the "God-is-dead-theology" after all? When Bonhoeffer said that human receptivity to religious matters was a question of individual predisposition, did he not thereby deny the possibility of religious access to God and with it, everything connected to reverence, anticipation, fear, grandeur—in other words, everything connected to the experience of the holiness of God? After all, he did say that "to build the knowledge of God upon such [religious] experiences is comparable to basing it on musical talent. There are people who are not musical, and people who do not have any clearly religious experiences."[8]

Bonhoeffer was concerned with the question "How can Christ be Lord of the religionless also?" and thus with the question "Who really is Christ for us today?" Did he mean by this a Christianity adapted to modern man?

When Bonhoeffer was condemned to death by "court martial" in Flossenbürg on April 9, 1945, and then hanged, he was thirty-nine years old. But the question arises whether that which he wrote in the last months of his life could not be seen as a legacy for modernist the-

6. *Letters and Papers from Prison*, pp. 325–26.
7. Ibid., p. 286.
8. On this point, see ibid., pp. 278–82; and *GS*, 2:420ff.

ology and the gospel of social liberation. In one of his last letters, written on August 3, 1944, Bonhoeffer writes:

> Encounter with Jesus Christ. The experience that a transformation of all human life is given in the fact that "Jesus is there only for others." His "being there for others" is the experience of transcendence. It is only this "being there for others," maintained till death, that is the ground of his omnipotence, omniscience, and omnipresence. Faith is participation in this being of Jesus . . . not infinite and unattainable tasks, but the neighbour who is within reach in any given situation. God in human form![9]

Does this not reduce Christianity to horizontal human relationships? Can the theology centered on fellow man not thus lay complete claim to Bonhoeffer on behalf of a socialistic Christianity? Is Christianity not reduced here to a social humanism of "living for others"? Does prayer as a concrete way of bringing requests to God still make any sense in this nonreligious Christianity of "the one reality"? Does God not have to be reduced to a "God of the gaps" when Christians in this life wait for their prayers to be heard and fulfilled? In the 1960s John A. T. Robinson, in his best-seller *Honest to God*, contributed quite decisively to the popularization of Bonhoeffer's theology along the lines of theological modernism.[10]

A "Socially Rewritten Christianity"

Bonhoeffer's statements about Christians "being there for others" were understood by the ethicist Robinson in such a way that there no longer existed an absolute God-revealed ethical standard. Only that which arises out of love, which people live and experience for the sake of other people, is good: "Love alone, because, as it were, it has a built-in moral compass, enabling it to 'home' intuitively upon the deepest need of the other, can allow itself to be directed completely by the sit-

---

9. *Letters and Papers from Prison*, p. 381.

10. Today no Bonhoeffer interpreter doubts that Robinson's *Honest to God* was a trivialization of Bonhoeffer's insights. Unfortunately, however, it led especially in the 1960s to a very misleading and negative view of Bonhoeffer, above all among evangelicals. This view continues to be influential today. Because of this influence, it is necessary to take Robinson's shallow yet symptomatic interpretation of Bonhoeffer seriously. Robinson's book appeared at a time in which the "No Other Gospel" confessional movement began to hold its large conventions.

uation."[11] Robinson thus sees the legitimate interpretation of the Bonhoefferian imitation of Christ in the situational ethics of Paul Tillich or Joseph Fletcher: "For nothing can of itself always be labelled as 'wrong.'"[12] Therefore modern theology can remain unperturbed or even react with disinterest when it is reminded of the commandments, the law of the Old Testament. By means of love expressed in "being there for others" the entire biblical ethos can be unhinged. What love is and what love means are determined by the *kairos,* the glorified moment in the life of society or the individual. Love and ethos are reinterpreted each time in the light of momentary expectations and needs.

Thus the question arises: Is Bonhoeffer not in the final analysis the church father of modernist, socialist theology? Wolfgang Huber, at one time the president of the German Protestant Church Conference, emphasizes that the social dimension was present in Bonhoeffer's work from the very beginning. Already in Bonhoeffer's doctoral dissertation the statement appears that Christ was the man for others: "Life, death and resurrection of Jesus are thus valid not only for me, but for us." Huber believes that in Bonhoeffer the substitutionary ministry of Jesus Christ on earth has been "written socially."[13]

If the church is the "church for others," if it is precisely those in distress and the poor who are sisters and brothers in a special way, if the church according to Bonhoeffer should divest itself of its possessions, and if through that Christian behavior becomes exemplary for the world—then does present-day Christian socialism's program of the social redistribution of wealth not lay at the heart of Bonhoeffer's theology? If the church should be the church for the poor, then is it not the church of the third-world proletariat? Are the poor not then the bearers of salvation for a new, Christian age?

"Christ existing as the body of believers," as the young Bonhoeffer said—does this not mean in the final analysis that Christ exists in the form of socialism or even communism?

Cannot the God-is-dead-theology also confidently rely on Bonhoeffer? After all, for Bonhoeffer religion was a historical and temporary

---

11. John A. T. Robinson, *Honest to God* (Philadelphia: Westminster Press, 1963), p. 115.
12. Ibid., p. 118.
13. Wolfgang Huber, *Folgen christlicher Freiheit,* 1983, p. 173.

"clothing" of Christianity. Is "dereligionized" Christianity not in the end nothing more than atheistic Christianity? Huber expressed his opinion on this subject in the following way:

> Bonhoeffer does not advocate a systematic but rather a historical concept of religion. For this reason he could characterize religion as a historically conditioned and fleeting form of human expression. In Bonhoeffer's view, the following elements are particularly characteristic of this historical garment of religion: a spacially conceived transcendence of God (the world beyond as God's location), the immediacy of the human relationship to God; the partiality of the human notion of God (God as stopgap and working hypothesis); finally, inwardliness, understood as detached from the outside world, as the sphere of religion.[14]

In other words, this means that in Huber's opinion Bonhoeffer did not believe in a God who exists outside of the realm of reality experienced by humans, and that the individual as individual (apart from the "social condition" of community) cannot by any means have any type of personal, individual relationship with this God. Thus the questions arise once again: Is there no God outside of the reality of this world? Is God just a code word for human interpersonal relationships? Has God become nothing more than a symbol of socialization for a human race aimlessly drifting toward global socialization as a substitute for salvation?

Does mankind in this view not finally become a substitute for God? Does Christ not become a symbol of interpersonal relationship in devotion to others, and the church a community held together by socialistic solidarity? Does the feminist theologian Dorothee Sölle not then have the explicit right to appeal to Bonhoeffer with her conception of substitution (man as the player of God's role)? Finally, isn't she denying, in unison with the martyr Bonhoeffer, modernist liberal theology that bans the God of Hebrew and Christian tradition from the scene? After all, she writes:

> If the radically critical content of the proposition "God is dead" is understood correctly, a content that at the same time opens up new possibilities for liberation, then it is no longer very far removed from

14. Ibid., p. 193.

the proposition "God is red." . . . God can be red only when people become the active agents of their own history. We ourselves are the active agents of liberation, and every theological incursion by a wholly other God contradicts not only the Marxist assumption that it is precisely man who is of highest essential importance for man, but also contradicts the gospel of the liberation of man for man. In this sense a nontheistic theology is preparation for a socialist theology.[15]

Are Bonhoeffer and Marx now to be understood as fraternal exemplary figures for a new Christo-Marxist world-and-life order?

This complex of questions will more or less accompany the development of the ideas in this book. In this main section we will make do for now with provisional answers. Undoubtedly, Bonhoeffer's letters as theological fragments have become "stopgaps" and a deus ex machina for a progressive theology that seeks in Bonhoeffer its martyr, its predecessor, and its basis in honorable tradition. Modernist theology deals with Bonhoeffer in the same way it always did with the biblical tradition: tradition as it actually presents itself is undone. The pieces of rubble that are left after the tradition has been analyzed to death are then put together to construct a new tradition. In Bonhoeffer's case the *Letters and Papers from Prison* were separated from the rest of his life's work just as the apostle Paul's letters from prison were detached, according to the long-standing historical-critical fashion, from the other Pauline letters. The exegesis of Bonhoeffer could and still can take its bearing from the long preparatory schooling of decades of cunning critical theology. The task of the upcoming larger sections of this book will be not only to correct this "left-wing" invasion and occupation of Bonhoeffer's thought, but also to articulate the significance of Bonhoeffer's message regarding the proper understanding of Christian faith precisely for our time.

15. Dorothee Sölle and Klaus Schmidt, *Christen für den Sozialismus*, 1975, 1:7ff., 14ff.

6

Bonhoeffer as Christ-Mystic

My thesis, that Bonhoeffer was a Christ-mystic, brings forth the question: What is Christ-mysticism? There is no better answer to this question than the answer to the first question of the Heidelberg Catechism. This passage from the Reformed catechism shows that Christ-mysticism means a life in, with, and through Christ. Because these crucial words of the Heidelberg Catechism are no longer widely known, I will quote them here:

> That I belong—body and soul, in life and in death—not to myself but to my faithful Savior, Jesus Christ, who at the cost of his own blood has fully paid for all my sins and has completely freed me from the dominion of the devil; that he protects me so well that without the will of my Father in heaven not a hair can fall from my head; indeed, that everything must fit his purpose for my salvation. Therefore, by his Holy Spirit, he also assures me of eternal life and makes me wholeheartedly willing and ready from now on to live for him.

But before Bonhoeffer is introduced as a Christ-mystic, it is of utmost importance that the following be taken into account.

The Other Reality

In order to do justice to Bonhoeffer, one must read all of his work from beginning to end or from end to beginning. In Bonhoeffer's the-

64

ology there are refinements and changes in emphasis, but there is no break—not even, contrary to many interpreters, in the spring of 1944. The last letters from prison bring new and deeper, undoubtedly radical insights, but they stand completely in the same line of development as his previous thoughts and writings. It bears repeating: Bonhoeffer's theology is a seamless whole with no dramatic breaks. This theology is multifaceted. It is expressed in paradoxes and formulated in dialectical statements. It is anchored in deep and genuine experiences of a dramatic time and exhibits above all the will to be honest and, in its own way, concrete and radical. It is difficult to understand Bonhoeffer. It is still more difficult to integrate Bonhoeffer's thought into one's own thinking. But Bonhoeffer was more concrete than his interpreters, with their Bonhoeffer-reconstructions, suspect or want to admit.

Beyond that, his theology—and this was a part of the challenge of a time dominated by ideologies—was a theology formed in struggle, and in the end a theology of resistance until death. Throughout his entire life, Bonhoeffer rejected all speculative theology removed from life, which plays conceptual games and revolves around itself. It was precisely concreteness that Bonhoeffer endeavored to realize. That is why he always saw the writing of a work on ethics as his main task in life. He wanted to articulate the concrete significance of Christian faith for living the Christian life in his day.

It is the intent of the following sections of this book to make clear that Bonhoeffer's theology and his ethics were a theology of revelation and an ethics of order—until the end. Nothing of this changed in Bonhoeffer's life or theological work.

The last recorded words of Bonhoeffer, shortly before being taken to his execution at Flossenbürg, were as follows: "This is the end—for me, the beginning of life."[1] The camp doctor at Flossenbürg, who was present at Bonhoeffer's execution on April 9, 1945, wrote about this event ten years later: "Through the half-opened door of a room in the barracks I saw Pastor Bonhoeffer, before taking off his prison uniform, kneeling in fervent prayer to his Lord God. The devoted manner and faithful certainty that characterized the praying of this extraordinarily likable man shook me to the depths of my being. Even at the place of

---

1. Bethge, *Bonhoeffer*, p. 1037.

execution itself he said another short prayer and then courageously and calmly climbed the steps to the gallows. He died within a few seconds. In my nearly fifteen years as a doctor I hardly ever saw a man die so devoted to God."[2] This concentration camp doctor's undoubtedly "religious" manner of expression reveals more clearly what the God who really exists as a person meant to Bonhoeffer than the concept-shamanism of modern theology could ever express it.

Bonhoeffer died in the belief in another reality—in the reality of the other life, an eternal life with God. He did not dispute the existence of this other reality. He simply resolutely denied that that other reality of God should be condemned to a reinterpretation as part of this reality and exiled to the metaphysical no man's land of our this-worldly existence. For one-and-a-half years, from April 1943 to October 1944, Bonhoeffer was in the military prison in Tegel awaiting trial. Then, until the spring of 1945, he was in the infamous cellar of the main office of state security on Prinz-Albrecht Street in Berlin. All of the statements he made during this time, including the letters he wrote from prison, are statements made in the context of a desperate situation.

In this situation it was no longer the faith of the church that was decisive for Bonhoeffer, but his own personal faith. He witnessed his Christianity being thrown back to the beginnings of understanding— a beginning that was not a break, but a deepening. In the world that was now surrounding him, Bonhoeffer prayed before God and with God without God. He lived with God in a cell that had to become a symbol for him of a world whose God was weak indeed. That was not God-is-dead theology; it was the experience of a man who out of his existence as a Christian could only express his Christian experience— although with surprising clarity and freedom—paradoxically, or to say it as a theologian would, dialectically: "with God . . . without God."[3] In the powerlessness of his existence, he saw himself borne along by God. God bore his powerlessness. When Bonhoeffer spoke of the powerlessness of God, he meant the omnipotence of God that also bears the powerlessness of him who was despised and rejected by all, so that the Pauline confession "dying, and yet we live on" (2 Cor.

2. Ibid., p. 1038.
3. *Letters and Papers from Prison*, p. 360.

6:9) resounds. In Bonhoeffer's processual thought, formed and molded in times of great change, God's power and powerlessness are not opposites that exclude each other, but rather relationships, part of the reality of salvation history, which are actually experienced in the life of a Christian.

The imprisoned Bonhoeffer witnessed the collapse of Reich, Occident, and Christendom. He experienced the once-and-for-all dissolution of traditional Christianity in the former "Christian world." In the powerlessness that he really experienced, he experienced also the powerlessness of God—not the death of God: "God would have us know that we must live as men who manage our lives without him. The God who is with us is the God who forsakes us (Mark 15:34). The God who lets us live in the world without the working hypothesis of God is the God before whom we stand continually. Before God and with God we live without God."[4] These sentences will be thoroughly considered in the following sections of this book. For the time being I would simply like to remind the reader of the structure of Bonhoeffer's processual, Christ-mystical thought. Notice especially the dialectic of this statement of Bonhoeffer: the suffering God helps; the powerless God clears a space; strength to overcome grows in suffering. God is not summoned in order to fill the gap in his lordship over the world, a gap that suffering has made obvious. He is not summoned to come to a place where he has never been. Bonhoeffer rejected this religious appeal to the power of God, which is exercised through religious rites and temporary outpourings of piety, as a "false conception of God" that is unbiblical. In his Christ-mysticism[5] he took on the suffering, the cruciform structure of the world. He experienced the messianic labor pains, the birth pangs of the kingdom of God, because it is through suffering and the experience of powerlessness that one walks the path of redemption. Bonhoeffer's Christ-mysticism rejects the deistic religiosity of a static worldview. It rejects the view of a God who stands at the edge and does not act in the midst of life. The dynamic, processual thought of a dramatic Christ-mysticism replaces the static metaphysics of above and below, of the kingdom of God and the kingdom of the world.

4. Ibid.
5. On this point, see ibid., p. 361.

Within the paradigm of these paradoxes, it is clearly the case that Bonhoeffer in no way denied the transcendence of God. For him it was an unconditional truth that God really exists independent of the world. He denied only that the epistemological, Neo-Kantian notion of transcendence, which attempts to assign a place to God within its own outdated epistemological paradigm, has anything whatsoever to do with the biblical notion of a transcendent God who is at the same time far away and near. Bonhoeffer rejected natural theology's attempts to reserve "gaps" in its metaphysics for the deeds of God.

Already in his inaugural dissertation, *Akt und Sein,* Bonhoeffer made clear that the actually existing, biblically revealed God is a God who acts, and that in addition all being is shaped by the action, the act, of God. Furthermore, Bonhoeffer's thesis makes clear that the history of revelation is nevertheless not identical to the history of being, but rather that the revelation of God remains unapproachable for human beings. This is so because revelation is a matter of God's acting and his acting remains beyond all control that human paradigms might attempt to exercise.

The Christ-mysticism of Bonhoeffer is not a "prison theology." Rather, Christ-mysticism motivated Bonhoeffer's theology from the very beginning, including even his doctoral dissertation, and especially his inaugural treatise *Akt und Sein.* The actually existing, acting God, who created this world, always remains the unapproachable God who even when he reveals himself is out of reach and incomprehensible. This coming together of act and being characterizes the novel structure of Bonhoeffer's thought as it encounters the God of biblical revelation.

Thus the Christ-mysticism of Bonhoeffer is a participation in the life, struggle, and death of Christ. However, it never seeks to comprehend, and thereby limit, the being of Christ himself.

On June 18, 1939, Bonhoeffer had an experience of key importance in his development. In the Broadway Presbyterian Church in New York he heard a sermon by the extreme fundamentalist Dr. McComb. Bonhoeffer wrote the following about this encounter:

> The sermon was astonishing. It was about "our likeness with Christ" and was a very biblical sermon. The sections "we are blameless like Christ" and "we are tempted like Christ" were especially good. Later

on, after Riverside Church has long since become a temple of idolatry, this will be a center of resistance. I was very happy about this sermon. But how can a man who preaches like that be so oblivious to the miserable kind of music he allowed to be played? I will ask him about that. With this sermon a previously fully unknown America has opened up for me.[6]

The Christ-mystic Bonhoeffer experienced the otherworldliness of God exclusively in the this-worldliness of his life—and this is exactly what is genuinely Christian. He took the biblical truth of the incarnation seriously.

Bonhoeffer's Rejection of Religious Pietism

Already before his time in prison, Bonhoeffer rejected the psycho-sanctimonious pietistic cult of the soul, the psychological dissection involved in the inwardliness of experiential religiosity. He did not know any realm of the emotions that could be described as especially devout or reverent. This would have contradicted the distinguished and reserved manner of his "aristocratic Christianity," for starters. Bonhoeffer was an enemy of the psychologization of Christianity—in this regard also, he was, with his dynamic processual thought, an archenemy of any and all human attempts to fix or determine the encounter between Christ and the Christian.

Even in prison, he did not become what he had never been and never wanted to be—a pious hypocrite. He condemned religious pietism as the last attempt to preserve "Protestant Christianity as religion." For him, the pietistic "era of inwardliness and individual conscience" that represented an effort "to hold on (to God) at least in the personal, inwardly directed, private realm" was over once and for all. Bonhoeffer had an obvious deep aversion to the pietist or Methodist-oriented style of pastoral care that dwelt solely on the intimate private sphere or on the inwardly focused aspects of human existence.

6. Bethge, *Bonhoeffer*, p. 740. See also entries in Bonhoeffer's diary of the trip to America from June 18, 1939 (*GS*, 1:193ff.). Of course, Bonhoeffer was not converted to fundamentalism by this sermon. He remained formally too much in the captivity of so-called historical criticism. That the roots of all evil according to American fundamentalists were to be found in modernism and unionism seemed to the Bonhoeffer of 1939 too simplistic, because it did not sufficiently take Satan into account.

Bonhoeffer's convictions in this regard were not confounded by his time in prison. He did not become an opponent of the outside world, of God's creation. He had come across questionable types in the church (or generally speaking in the realm of Christendom) who as religious, pietistic people had surrendered before Hitlerism and let the world be the world. In the resistance, on the other hand, he came to know men of responsible political action who were estranged from institutional Christianity and who could and did not want to articulate themselves in a religious way, but who nevertheless acted rightly in their struggle for righteousness because they hungered and thirsted for it.

Bonhoeffer came to know a new distinction, a new "us" and "them," during the war years. The message of the Sermon on the Mount—that salvation belongs to those who hunger and thirst for righteousness—gained a new meaning for him. Bonhoeffer recognized that the Savior's healing word was not only directed to the sinners and to the poor, but also to those who hunger and thirst for righteousness and who are persecuted for righteousness' sake. It was precisely this truth of the gospel that Bonhoeffer fervently desired to see manifest in his last years. He endorsed the notion of humanity come of age because he had gotten to know existence in that mode and milieu at a gut level, above all in the German resistance that culminated in the coup attempt against the Nazi dictatorship on July 20, 1944. He had gotten to know it in men and women of conservative values who with mind and heart stood on the side of the rule of law.

On the opposite end of the spectrum, Bonhoeffer had again and again come up against quite different realities in the realm of a Christendom distinguished by hypocritical piety. He came to know that godlessness is often covered over with empty theological phrases; that religiosity is often nothing other than subjective self-actualization; that God then becomes a deus ex machina for the religious-subjective triumphs in the lives of dysfunctional persons; that those who find themselves on the losing end of life often spoil things for themselves and for those around them in order to build themselves up, and in their own way take revenge against everything that is true, beautiful, and strong. He came to know all of these things, and he condemned such religious subjectivism as alienation, albeit religious, from true Christianity. Behind this "religiosity" he saw the highest stage of subjectivity—the self-actualization of questionable, usually petty-bourgeois, human beings. As a prisoner, Bonhoeffer no longer could nor wanted to think about religious self-actualization.

Of course, this reaction against pietism run amok does not mean that Bonhoeffer ever considered anything like doing away with prayer, as much modern theology does due to its loss of belief in a transcendent God. Already in *The Cost of Discipleship*, Bonhoeffer discussed what "religionless" prayer is: "Genuine prayer is never 'good works,' an exercise or a pious attitude, but it is always the prayer of a child to a Father. Hence it is never given to self-display, whether before God, ourselves, or other people. If God were ignorant of our needs, we should have to think out beforehand *how* we should tell him about them, *what* we should tell him, and whether we should tell him or not. Thus faith, which is the mainspring of Christian prayer, excludes all reflection and premeditation."[7] These remarks of Bonhoeffer entail a condemnation of religious prayer, which subjectively and suggestively works its way up to God and attempts to earn, if not force, the realization of its desires from this religiously experienced God, this deus ex machina.

It is easy to learn what Bonhoeffer considers true prayer if we reflect upon the following lines of the last prayer he wrote in prison:

> Should it be ours to drain the cup of grieving
> even to the dregs of pain, at thy command,
> we will not falter, thankfully receiving
> all that is given by thy loving hand. . . .
>
> While all the powers of good aid and attend us,
> boldly we'll face the future, come what may.

7. *Cost of Discipleship*, p. 181. "When men pray, they have ceased to know themselves, and know only God whom they call upon" (ibid.). Bonhoeffer remarked critically: "The publicity which I am looking for is then provided by the fact that I am the one who at the same time prays and looks on. I am listening to my own prayer and thus I am answering my own prayer. Not being content to wait for God to answer our prayer and show us in his own time that he has heard us, we provide our own answer. We take note that we have prayed suitably well, and this substitutes the satisfaction of answered prayer. We have our reward. Since we have heard ourselves, God will not hear us" (p. 182). These sentences show not only what kind of pietism Bonhoeffer condemned, namely, the self-depicting, self-actualizing, psychologically observant pietism; they also show that Bonhoeffer's "critique of religion," the rejection of religion's infiltration of Christian faith, was fully developed before the letters from prison, already in the 1930s.

> At even and at morn God will befriend us,
> and oh, most surely on each newborn day![8]

Remember—Bonhoeffer wrote this at the end of his life. It is a clear expression of what Bonhoeffer understood by the presence, the this-worldliness—as well as the otherworldliness—of God.

God Is Not a Stopgap in the World for the World

By the time Bonhoeffer lay locked in his cell in Tegel, he had put something else behind him. It remained only in memories filled with suffering: the church as the "institution of salvation" that struggled for its own preservation; the religious and political ambition of a Protestant clergy that preached its gospel while at the same time adorning itself with the Iron Cross and an official limousine. Instead of the secularized church, which was precisely what the established institutional church had become, Bonhoeffer desired "Christ existing as the body of believers," in other words, the church that exists for others. In this point also, Bonhoeffer experienced the paradoxical nature of Christian witness: the body of believers is fully and completely in the world—and it is also fully and completely for the world. Yet it is also completely different from the world.

Modernist theologians of world revolution took up these first statements of Bonhoeffer with great rejoicing. For them, the church in the world and for the world became a church fomenting revolution in the world. For them, the political demonstration became the worship service, while their religionless Sunday services became Sunday morning happy hours. But in understanding their calling in such religious terms they misunderstood the other side of Bonhoeffer's paradoxical assertion. The church that is in the world and there for the world is different than the world, and stands face to face with the world separate from it. Bonhoeffer wanted this characteristic of the church, that it is different from the world, to be safeguarded through the discipline of the *arcanum,* which was to protect the church from the public at large. The body of believers was to live in an *arcanum,* a sphere of worship that is closed off to the outside. There was to be no Christianization of the world, and no secularization of Christianity. In the *arcanum*

---

8. *Letters and Papers from Prison,* pp. 400, 401.

Bonhoeffer believed the church would be kept from being infiltrated by religion or secularization. He did not think of this *arcanum* as an idyllic refuge for religious people but as a place where the tension between being a Christian and being completely and totally in the world could be lived through and prayed through.[9] Bonhoeffer's outlook here is very much affected by the totality of what he experienced and suffered. This led him to the following set of convictions:

The world cannot be overcome by attempting to flood it in cascades of pious words. The religious net can no longer simply be thrown over the world, unless one wants to attract no more than a few down-and-out frustrated types—the kind that already set the tone in many church congregations anyway. In the world—this was Bonhoeffer's opinion—Christianity is interpreted first of all based on the visible and active presence of its proponents. And only by means of observing Christian existence in its "being there for others," in its suffering and dying with Christ, can the word of "proclamation" go forth. One must live through the tension between being a Christian and being in the world if one is to avoid the mere spouting of empty religious phrases. It is senseless merely to say, "Jesus loves you." The mere word "Jesus" becomes some sort of idolatrous symbol to which one can gain access by simply learning the proper techniques and rituals. Behind this image of Jesus projected as it were, onto the wall lies only a product offered for religious consumption. Responsible and mature human beings have no choice but to reject such a product, and rightfully so.

Nevertheless, let it be said once more to modernism: Bonhoeffer did not advocate any type of identification of God with the world, nor any melting away of Christianity into the world. He advocated neither the Christianization of the world nor the secularization of Christianity. For Bonhoeffer the world was always the penultimate, and never the ultimate. Only the church that is really the church can be the church for others—that is what the true church is and will remain as it exists in a necessary state of tension with the world. Only in this tension, and not in an identification with the world, is the church's giving of itself for others both conceivable and possible. Modern theology has always interpreted Bonhoeffer monistically, one-dimensionally, and nondialectically—in other words, completely as could be

9. On this point, see Part 9.

expected given the outdated intellectual paradigm to which it is committed. But I repeat: Bonhoeffer's theology is a theology that can only be expressed in paradoxes, in the constant movement of a dialectic. The mysteries of Christian faith safeguard the body of believers against secularization, but they also safeguard the world against religion. Church without world is ghetto, world without church is the well-lighted emptiness of a pedestrian mall.

Bonhoeffer's "No!" to bogusly religious Christianity, to traditional understanding of the two spheres and the two realms, the religious and the secular, is unconditional. His rejection of the deus ex machina, of the stopgap God who exists to fill whatever gaps or deficits we may have discovered in our life aspirations, is unequivocal. With Bonhoeffer, religion is replaced by Christ-mysticism—the state of actually being in Christ, the Pauline dying and rising from the dead with Christ. Christ-mysticism is participation in Christ's death; in his life, his struggle, his suffering; in his overcoming; and finally in his resurrection as well. It is in this way that Christ is present in the midst of life. In this way, he is utterly this-worldly but yet utterly otherworldly. This life in Christ is actual incorporation into the Christ-event. This is not a matter of various tricks, means, acts, or religious techniques. Rather, it is the state of being included in the messianic birth pangs of the kingdom of God, which dawned in the incarnation of Christ and will reach its consummation at the second coming—but only then.

One does not experience this Christ by means of a special religious act. We do not include Christ in our life. Rather, Christ includes our life in his. Because we live the life that Christ has already lived for us, we can "proclaim" Christian faith through this life in the world. Because Christ is for us, he is there for others. That is why we can also be there for others. Thus, Christian existence is always in essence a lived-out interpretation of being-in-Christ.

How, then, can Protestant Christians, who live in the legacy of the Reformation, ever consider God a "stopgap"? God does not fill the gaps in our path to God. He does not intervene whenever we cannot progress any farther on our walk of faith. *Sola gratia* means that everything comes from grace. It does not mean that God fills in the gaps that we ourselves cannot manage as we climb the ladder to religious success. *Sola gratia* is valid not only for justification, but also for the whole of life. As Paul writes in Romans 8:31, "If God is for us, who can be against us?" Only a theology that has relegated Reformation Christian thinking to a forgotten oblivion could read something like a new theology of revolution into Bonhoeffer's thought. With a new dynamic-progressive paradigm Bonhoeffer issues a radical summons back to the Reformation heritage, because precisely this heritage has been lost in the old paradigm of religion and metaphysics.

God does not fill in the gaps. Rather, with total and unique sufficiency he brings about grace, reconciliation, redemption, and sanctification. In the biblical view, God as the Creator, Upholder, and Lord of this world can never be a mere "stopgap." No bird ever takes off from its perch without the will of our Father in heaven, and he knows what we need in our lives before we ask him for it—this is what Jesus proclaimed (Matt. 6:26–34; Luke 12:24–31).

In prison Bonhoeffer read C. F. von Weizsäcker's *Weltbild der Physik*.[10] The reading of this book confirmed for Bonhoeffer once again that the Neo-Kantian differentiation between judgments of being and value judgments is nonsense. It is not true that God is experienced only in the individual conscience and that we have to leave the visible, public world to those who seize reality with their irrefutable scientific worldviews. It is not the case that we cannot encounter God until we have reached the limits of worldly reality, as if God no longer had anything to say or do in the midst of the real world. In reading von Weizäcker's book, Bonhoeffer was confirmed in his conviction that absolutely everything is completely of this world, but as such also utterly through, from, and directed toward God. The will of God stands behind everything, although it is the will of God that revealed itself in Christ—in its powerlessness as well as its power. Thus the whole of this world is led, by way of struggle, suffering, powerlessness, dying, toward the resurrection. To see this involves recognizing how the ultimate structure of the world is rooted in the cross and resurrection. The power of God proceeds through powerlessness to glory. The whole creation, the whole of human life, is encompassed by the truth of Christ.

---

10. *Letters and Papers from Prison*, p. 311. In reading this book, it became clear to Bonhoeffer "how wrong it is to use God as a stop-gap for the incompleteness of our knowledge." Bonhoeffer was not saying that there is no God, but that "We are to find God in what we know, not in what we don't know."

Bonhoeffer is a Reformation figure through and through. Nevertheless, Lutheran critics of his theology were right when they accused
him of making a transition to a Reformed, Calvinistic type of Christianity. Perhaps Bonhoeffer could even be called a crypto-Calvinist.
Above all, Bonhoeffer was an enemy of liberal theology and thereby of
modernism. Both of these were so infiltrated by moralism and religious positivism that they necessarily misunderstood Bonhoeffer's
rediscovery of the socially revolutionary character of Reformation
thought.

7

Bonhoeffer as Reformational Christian

Christian Faith as the Contradiction of Religion

In the military prison at Tegel on July 12, 1944, Bonhoeffer wrote the following sentences, quite important to his reformational approach:

> I remember a conversation that I had in America thirteen years ago with a young French pastor. We were asking ourselves quite simply what we wanted to do with our lives. He said he would like to become a saint (and I think it's quite likely that he did become one). At the same time I was very impressed, but I disagreed with him, and said, in effect, that I should like to learn to have faith. For a long time I didn't realize the depth of the contrast. I thought I could acquire faith by trying to live a holy life, or something like it. I suppose I wrote *The Cost of Discipleship* as the end of that path. Today I can see the dangers of that book, though I still stand by what I wrote.[1]

We will discuss Bonhoeffer's criticism of his *The Cost of Discipleship* in another section of this book. His criticism of *The Cost of Discipleship* is, by the way, rooted in his critique of absolute pacifism, which

---

1. *Letters and Papers from Prison*, p. 369.

was advocated by the French pastor (Jean Lassere) of whom Bonhoeffer was speaking in the letter just quoted. For now let us take up a different matter.

Bonhoeffer's statements in this letter are completely in line with reformational theology as it was articulated by, for example, the Reformed theologian Hermann Friedrich Kohlbrügge,[2] who in the previous century upheld this type of theology through a bitter struggle with the pietism of his time. Kohlbrügge rejected religious Christianity with the same decisiveness as Bonhoeffer. In answer to the question of when and how he had been converted Kohlbrügge answered: "At Golgatha." Kohlbrügge was also a Christ-mystic: Christ fulfilled the law, he rose from the dead and has peace with God. Therefore we have fulfilled the law, have risen from the dead, and have peace with God. Kohlbrügge doggedly refused to describe sanctification "religiously." Also, he in no way wanted faith to be understood as a religious act that could be described in religious or psychological terms. Bonhoeffer was acquainted with Kohlbrügge's work,[3] and held his understanding of the Old Testament as a witness to Christ in especially high esteem. At any rate it is clear that Bonhoeffer stands completely in the tradition of the reformational rediscovery of Christianity that took place in the nineteenth century with, to name two examples, such men as Kohlbrügge and Abraham Kuyper, and which was then furthered by Barth.

Religion is Babel. It is how people build a tower in order to work themselves up to heaven and make a name for themselves. Religion is basically self-actualization, to which God, used as if he were a tool, is made to contribute. The deus ex machina is supposed to fill in the gaps that are still missing so that the religious individual can finally

2. Hermann Friedrich Kohlbrügge (1803–75) was rediscovered for the German-speaking world by Karl Barth and is still today one of the great Reformed figures in Holland. Kohlbrügge in his time pursued such a clear critique of the religious infiltration of Christianity that he can be seen as a forerunner of the Barthian and Bonhoefferian critique of religion. The idea of "self-sanctification" with its denial of *simul iustus et peccator* was the challenge that Kohlbrügge took up as a Reformed Christ-mystic, especially in *Das 7. Kap. des Briefes Pauli an die Römer in ausführlicher Umschreibung*, 1839, and in *Das Wort ward Fleisch, Betrachtungen über das 1. Kap. des Evangeliums nach Matthäus*, 1844. The latter book helped Bonhoeffer a great deal in his understanding of the prophecy of Christ in the Old Testament.

3. On this point, see Bethge, *Bonhoeffer*, p. 487. The Rhenish pastor Wilhelm Rott, a member of the Karl Barth school, drew Bonhoeffer's attention to Kohlbrügge in 1935: "Now he acquired whatever was available of the Reformed fathers, and used it," according to Bethge.

come out on top and reach his sought-after "high." Religion is a power trip for *Homo religiosus* to elevate himself heavenward. Bonhoeffer saw religion not only as a historical, passing form of expression of Christianity (which he knew it was). His harsh remarks against the religious infiltration of Christianity show that he went further than that. Above all, Bonhoeffer fought against the religious facade of godlessness just as Kohlbrügge had done before him. Subjective religiosity cast all biblical propositions about God and Jesus in an alien light. It perverted them into subjective experiential motifs for the act of self-redemption performed in the process of hypocritical self-actualization. This form of religious escapism, which then wanted and today still wants to save Christianity with its affected behavior, is not only a passing and historical fault but also a fundamental challenge to the essence of Christian faith—regardless of how pious it may present itself.

God is not an unskilled apprentice, not a gap-filler in humankind's process of self-sanctification. There is no such thing as a series of religious actions that can complete the process of sanctification. Sanctification is, in the true sense of the word, being in Christ, which in turn can be reduced to explicable and understandable proportions by neither rational nor psychological means. The Christian is completely flesh and completely of the world, yet completely incorporated into Christ's life through trust in him. Bonhoeffer, in embracing such views, stood completely in the tradition of the rediscovery of reformational Christianity that had its modern beginning in Kohlbrügge.

Tension in the World with the World

Just what is the "world come of age" and what does it mean according to Bonhoeffer? With the collapse of common decency in the 1930s, Bonhoeffer had gotten to know well enough the showiness and self-centeredness that characterized the coming of age of the rich, the *nouveau riche* and the petty bourgeois gone wild. He judged precisely this aspect of the spirit of the time very harshly. In view of the "disorderly and undisciplined" manner of this so-called society come of age, Bonhoeffer was a lonely outsider in *nouveau riche* Berlin in his rejection of modern lifestyles. His assessment of the "modern times" in the German capitol city of Berlin was very similar to the sobering observations of Jochen Klepper, another pastor who was a martyr to nazism, and who lived in Berlin at the same time as Bonhoeffer. True coming of age and irreligiosity, which may never be confused with the Philistinism of Bonhoeffer's contemporaries, will also be considered later on in this book. At this point I would like to make just one remark about Bonhoeffer's life history.

Already in 1932, Bonhoeffer had condemned the religious escapism that is so often and so readily confused with Christianity. This form of dependent religiosity, which makes human beings into slaves of a slavemaster God, brings about a mentality of subjugation without any of the freedom and mature autonomy to which Christ has called us.

But how can not only the religionless, but also the completely "unchristian" person, be a person come of age? Would that not be a kind of "unconscious Christianity"? Bonhoeffer himself asked this question, but did not answer it. In the next chapter we will pose the question of whether there was not a category or theological structure that was missing in Bonhoeffer's thought that would have made it easier for him to formulate more clearly what he sensed. At any rate, this "unconscious Christianity" cannot rightfully be usurped by modernist theology and interpreted to mean that the world as such—even without revelation—is becoming Christian by way of its revolutionary progressive development. This modernist occupation of the Bonhoefferian "unconscious Christianity" starts with the intolerable premise that God does not really exist. He is not above but rather in an evolutionary sense before the world, and thus is only a goal of a process inherent to the world.

Unfortunately Bonhoeffer was not acquainted with the theology of Abraham Kuyper. This Reformed theologian of the nineteenth-century Netherlands developed the doctrine of common grace.[4] According to Kuyper, common grace is the means by which God upholds, protects, and develops creation and culture, nations and states. Com-

4. Abraham Kuyper (1837–1920), a pastor who became prime minister of the Netherlands, brought about an ecclesiastical schism, and founded the Free University of Amsterdam in 1880, took as his starting point the assumption that there is not even the smallest part of life about which Christ does not say, "That is mine." The "one reality" was as much Kuyper's concern as it was Bonhoeffer's. For Kuyper, properly understood reforming (for him, "Calvinist") Christianity encompassed all spheres, including those of politics, science, economy, and culture. The doctrine of common grace made its appearance in his De gemeente gratie, 1931, in the third edition. The structural similarity between Kuyperian and Bonhoefferian theology is astonishing and illustrates how Bonhoeffer came to Reformed theology. (He always saw himself as a Lutheran, but others suspected him of being Reformed.)

mon grace is not the grace of salvation in Christ. It is the grace by which creation and the life of nations and society are upheld and kept from falling into chaos. Out of and within the grace of God, which according to Kuyper was promised in the covenant with Noah, the mature autonomy of humankind come of age can develop. Being a person come of age does not mean being a Christian. Nevertheless, the grace of God makes this coming of age possible. It is this grace that Bonhoeffer came to recognize among the people who, as Bonhoeffer himself did, fought for justice against National Socialism.

Common grace does not run along its own track completely unrelated to the grace of salvation—as if there existed two realities separated from each other. Rather, Christ's gift of salvation causes this grace that preserves creation to unfold to a greater degree. Common grace is the grace of the Triune God. It lies like a circle around the center, which is the revelation of Christ. This grace is not light, but it receives light. For Abraham Kuyper, Christ is at the same time the root of both the common preserving and protecting grace as well as the special saving grace of salvation. For Bonhoeffer, Christ is the one simultaneously protecting, preserving, and redeeming power that has its effects on the whole cosmos, even taking hold of people who stand outside of the realm of what we today would like to call Christian.

The state of having come of age is always a threatened condition. In the summer of 1944 Bonhoeffer wrote the following in attempting to summarize his thoughts:

> The coming of age of mankind (as already indicated). The safeguarding of life against "accidents" and "blows of fate"; . . . The aim: to be independent of nature. Nature was formerly conquered by spiritual means, with us by technical organization of all kinds. Our immediate environment is not nature, as formerly, but organization. But with this protection from nature's menace there arises a new one—through organization itself.
>
> But the spiritual force is lacking. The question is: What protects us against the menace of organization? Man is again thrown back on himself. He has managed to deal with everything, only not with himself. He can insure against everything, only not against man. In the last resort it all turns on man.[5]

5. *Letters and Papers from Prison*, p. 380.

Thus Bonhoeffer saw coming of age in connection with the technical revolution as well. But this coming of age is an endangered coming
of age. Consequently one must correctly understand Bonhoeffer's paradoxical theological thought in this area as well.

The coming of age of modern man should not be put down, or
unnerved by the borderline situations of life. In other words, it
should not be concealed by an outer layer of religion. That which
has come of age in the world come of age must be consistently lived
out. If the world come of age would present itself as religious, it
would be lying. The Christian "must really live in the godless world
and may not attempt to cover over or transfigure its godlessness in
some religious way. He must live in a worldly way, and in doing so
he participates in God's suffering. He is allowed to live in a worldly
way, that is, he is liberated from false religious ties and inhibitions.
To be a Christian does not mean to be religious in a certain way, or
to make something of oneself (sinner, or penitent, or saint) by
means of a certain methodology. Rather, to be a Christian means to
be a human being. Christ creates in us not a type of human being,
but a human being as such. The religious act does not make the
Christian, but rather the participation in the suffering of God, in the
secular life."

Bonhoeffer is not striking up a song of rejoicing here for the coming of age of the world. He is not falling captive to any triumphal
mood. In a certain sense he is suffering under the coming of age of
the world. After all, coming of age means participation in the suffering of God, being aware of limits and of resurrection. Coming of age
stands in tension with the powerlessness of God, which is experienced with suffering. It is extremely crucial to understand that Bonhoeffer interprets "living after having come of age" Christ-
mystically. The responsible person come of age is charged with the
task of resolutely bearing the God-forsakenness of this God-forsaken modern world, so that he—to formulate it paradoxically—is
initiated unknowingly into knowledge of the mystery of the cross.
Then, however, even the powerlessness of God as it is experienced
in this God-forsaken world becomes in the deepest sense a revelation of God's omnipotence. For the Christ-mystic Bonhoeffer, coming of age in the God-forsaken world stands under the reality of the
cross.

A Multidimensional Understanding of the World

In order to make the dialectical structure of his theological statements clear, Bonhoeffer often used the musical example of *cantus firmus* and counterpoint. In this regard he writes:

> God wants us to love him eternally with our whole hearts—not in such a way as to injure or weaken our earthly love, but to provide a kind of *cantus firmus* to which the other melodies of life provide the counterpoint. One of these counterpuntal themes (which have their own complete independence but are yet related to the *cantus firmus*) is earthly affection. Even in the Bible we have the Song of Songs; and really one can imagine no more ardent, passionate, sensual love than is portrayed there. . . . Where the *cantus firmus* is clear and plain, the counterpoint can be developed to its limits. The two are "undivided and yet distinct" in the words of the Chalcedonian Definition, like Christ in his divine and human natures. May not the attraction and importance of polyphony in music consist in its being a reflection of this Christological fact and therefore of our *vita christiana?*[6]

These sentences remind us again of the unique multidimensional thought of Bonhoeffer, a theologian in a time of irrevocable change. Bonhoeffer's theology is multidimensional and processual. The processual aspect of his theology is especially characteristic of his statements about the ultimate and the penultimate. The enjoyment of creation (creation is never the ultimate; rather, it is always the penultimate) may never be reduced by comparison to the ultimate, the eternal, or redemption.

> But, to put it plainly, for a man in his wife's arms to be hankering after the other world is, in mild terms, a piece of bad taste, and not God's will. We ought to find and love God in what he actually gives us; if it pleases him to allow us to enjoy some overwhelming earthly happiness, we mustn't try to be more pious than God himself and allow our happiness to be corrupted by presumption and arrogance, and by unbridled religious fantasy which is never satisfied with what God gives. God will see to it that the man who finds him in his earthly happiness and thanks

6. Ibid., p. 303.

him for it does not lack reminder that earthly things are transient, that it is good for him to attune his heart to what is eternal.[7]

Thus the Christian does not live in two separate realms, the "world" and the "world beyond." Fleeing to the world beyond and idolization of this world are both excluded by this Bonhoefferian succession of the ultimate and the penultimate. The one is related to the other. Bonhoeffer resisted any type of "radicalism" that, renouncing earthly life because of its fixation on the ultimate, despises creation. However, he also resisted the theology of compromise that sees the ultimate in the world and in so doing forgets that nothing in the world can ever be more than the penultimate:

> Radicalism hates time, and compromise hates eternity. Radicalism hates patience, and compromise hates decision. Radicalism hates wisdom, and compromise hates simplicity. Radicalism hates moderation and measure, and compromise hates the immeasurable. Radicalism hates the real, and compromise hates the word. . . . A Christian ethic constructed solely on the basis of the incarnation would lead directly to the compromise solution. An ethic which was based solely on the cross or the resurrection of Jesus would fall victim to radicalism and enthusiasm. Only in the unity is the conflict resolved.[8]

These lines from Bonhoeffer's pen, which reveal once again his multidimensional and processual thought, would be useful correctives to all those of our day who have fallen prey to political or religio-political radicalism. Bonhoeffer's theology resists occupation by the reactionaries, but also by the progressives. In either extreme, one distorts Bonhoeffer's dynamic theology until it fits the static either-or paradigm of the analytical rationalism of yesteryear. The result is a linear ideology of progress, a secularization of all biblical perspectives.

Present-Day Christian-ness and the "Representation of Christ"

Bonhoeffer's dialectical Christ-mysticism stood and stands in contrast to the churchliness of the established church in his time as well

7. Ibid., pp. 168–69.
8. *Ethics*, pp. 130–31.

as today. At that time Bonhoeffer was certain that the church would be completely different after the war. He foresaw a church of the minority, of the *arcanum*, which would be safeguarded from secularization and give its possessions up, which would not hold on to anything for the sake of self-preservation, but instead would be there for others. Whoever affirms the present-day established ecclesiastical system in Germany thereby rejects everything that Bonhoeffer wanted for the church. Whoever does not attempt at least to change this system radically may not properly appeal to Bonhoeffer. Bonhoeffer's life and thought were a testimony against the institutional church that we still have to live with today in the "state churches" of Germany.

However, that is no reason for the "progressives" (those seeking major reform in the German church) to rejoice. Bonhoeffer would surely have condemned their conception of church and of being a Christian sharply, the same way he fought against his contemporaries the "German Christians," who had fallen victim to the ideology of Hitlerism. Humankind is not the representative of or the earthly replacement for God. Such a view is an outrageously arrogant presumption that brings biblical revelation into question. Only one who allows himself to be motivated by God's questions, hears his Word, and responds to it can be God's deputy or representative.

> Who stands fast? Only the man whose final standard is not his reason, his principles, his conscience, his freedom, or his virtue, but who is ready to sacrifice all this when he is called to obedient and responsible action in faith and in exclusive allegiance to God—the responsible man, who tries to make his whole life an answer to the question and call of God. Where are these responsible people?[9]

The Christ-mysticism of Bonhoeffer is inevitably hostile to the man-as-replacement-of-God notion of a God-is-dead theology:

> We are not lords, but instruments in the hand of the Lord of history; and we can share in other people's sufferings only to a very limited degree. We are not Christ, but if we want to be Christians, we must have some share in Christ's large-heartedness by acting with responsibility and in freedom when the hour of danger comes, and by showing

9. *Letters and Papers from Prison*, p. 5.

a real sympathy that springs, not from fear, but from the liberating and redeeming love of Christ for all who suffer.[10]

How much the notion of substitutional representation is grounded in Christ's substitution for mankind in Bonhoeffer's Christ-mystical interpretation is clear from the following passage of his *Ethics:* "Jesus was not the individual, desiring to achieve a perfection of his own, but He lived only as the one who has taken up into Himself and bears within Himself the selves of all men. All His living, His action and His dying was deputyship. In Him there is fulfilled what the living, the action and the suffering of men ought to be. In this real deputyship which constitutes His human existence He is the responsible person *par excellence.*"[11]

Bonhoeffer's verdict against guilt on the church of his day could also be a verdict of guilt against the church of our day. It is absolutely clear that Bonhoeffer was an ethicist of order and that he logically expected the church also to declare its belief in law and order:

The Church confesses herself guilty of the collapse of parental authority. She offered no resistance to contempt for age and idolization of youth, for she was afraid of losing youth, and with it the future. As though her future belonged to youth! She has not dared to proclaim the divine authority and dignity of parenthood in the face of the revolution of youth, and in a very earthly way she has tried "to keep up with the young." She has thus rendered herself guilty of the breaking up of countless families, the betrayal of fathers by their children, the self-deification of youth, and the abandonment of youth to the apostasy from Christ. . . . She is guilty of the deaths of the weakest and most defenceless brothers of Jesus Christ.

The Church confesses that she has found no word of advice and assistance in the face of the dissolution of all order in the relation between the sexes. She has found no strong and effective answer to the contempt for chastity and to the proclamation of sexual libertinism. . . . The Church confesses herself guilty of breaking all ten commandments, and in this she confesses her defection from Christ. She has not borne witness to the truth of God in such a manner that all pursuit of truth, all science, can perceive that it has its origin in this truth. She has

10. Ibid., p. 14.
11. *Ethics*, p. 225.

not proclaimed the justice of God in such a manner that all true justice must see in it the origin of its own essential nature. . . . She bears the guilt of the defection of the governing authority from Christ.[12]

What theologian of liberation wishes to associate himself with this law-and-order ethic of Bonhoeffer? Bonhoeffer fought against the accommodation of the church to the uprising of the masses. He fought against this destruction of law and order. He saw the collapse of law in Germany lurking in the shadow of Nazi ideology. Today theologians of emancipation (and not only in Germany) laugh about the conservative theologians who teach a "repressive" ethics of law and order. Many theologians of emancipation even denigrate this type of ethics as fascist. If one does that, however, one must also remember that one thereby also denigrates Bonhoeffer as fascist—Bonhoeffer, the hero of the resistance against the Nazi regime. Here the failure to recognize Nazi ideology as an "uprising from below" is not the only shocking thing. Just as shocking is the way Bonhoeffer is martyred a second time—this time by making him into a church father of the theology of emancipation.

Today the task of theology, if it were to follow Bonhoeffer's intention, would be to oppose decisively the cultural and moral revolution of our time. It would be a downright maniacal misunderstanding of that which Bonhoeffer meant by "coming of age" if one were to misuse this concept in order to give one's theological blessing to the cultural and moral revolution and its "emancipation" from the created order and commandments of God. Whoever as a theologian fights for the preservation of family and marriage today, whoever calls for discipline and order, whoever reminds children of the authority of the parents, sets himself up for ridicule. The emancipatory equality-mania in the matriarchal and feminist thought of our present-day ecclesiastical structure thus shows itself to be an archenemy of the Bonhoefferian theology of order. No, Bonhoeffer is not a church father of the progressives, the feminists, or the emancipators. He should not be left to the left wing.

---

12. Ibid., pp. 114–15.

PART 3

The Decline of Christianity and Religionless Christ-Mysticism

8

World Come of Age

The Irrevocable State of Having Come of Age

In the spring of 1944 Bonhoeffer struck other themes in his letters. Secularization, worldliness, autonomous man, world come of age stepped into the foreground of attention. On June 6, 1944, he wrote: "Man has learnt to deal with himself in all questions of importance without recourse to the 'working hypothesis' called 'God.'" This is not an expression of Bonhoeffer's wishes or hopes, but rather a very clear diagnosis of our time. It is a fact that modern man in the wake of technological revolution is alienated from God, and that "everything gets along without 'God.'" It is a fact that in the modern world God is being "pushed more and more out of life," and that he is "losing more and more ground." That the Second World War did not change any of this, that no revival or wave of conversions came about through the experience of the devastations of the war, only substantiates the observation that "God as a working hypothesis in morals, politics, or science, has been surmounted and abolished."[1]

Here Bonhoeffer expresses more clearly and uncompromisingly than any other theologian a fact of modern life: modernity's techno-

1. *Letters and Papers from Prison*, pp. 325–26, 130.

logical revolution brings the ruin of the traditional, religious kind of faith in God.

Bonhoeffer does not see any "method" of breaking this state of having come of age, of converting it or of somehow undoing it:

> They ["Christian" apologists] set themselves to drive people to inward despair, and then the game is in their hands. That is secularized methodism. And whom does it touch? A small number of intellectuals, of degenerates, of people who regard themselves as the most important thing in the world, and who therefore like to busy themselves with themselves. The ordinary man, who spends his everyday life at work and with his family, and of course with all kinds of diversions, is not affected. He has neither the time nor the inclination to concern himself with his existential despair, or to regard his perhaps modest share of happiness as a trial, a trouble, or a calamity.[2]

Bonhoeffer considered a Christian apologetic of this kind to be pointless in the face of what it means to be human in the industrial revolution. He had three main reasons for this view. First, it is senseless. Experience shows that the process of technocratization of our existence is irreversible. Second, it is ignoble. Christianity is not meant to traffic in precipitating depression. Third, it is unchristian. "Religiosity" as formerly understood in Germany was only a passing mode of expression of Christianity.

Bonhoeffer depicted the state of having come of age as a phenomenon of modern life. But in this context he went beyond the diagnosis and reached an evaluation that was also unique to his theology.

Godlessness Full of Promise

Bonhoeffer distinguished between the secularization of Christianity and the worldliness of Christianity.[3] Secularization or secularized Christianity is the "Occidental godlessness" that pretends to be religious but in reality merely sells a "facade Christianity." This kind of godlessness only covers up the true nature of the godlessness behind it.

2. Ibid., pp. 326–27.
3. See R. Mayer, *Christuswirklichkeit. Grundlagen und Konsequenzen der Theologie Dietrich Bonhoeffers,* 1980, 212ff.

This is to be distinguished from the "promising godlessness" of the world come of age, which arose as a protest against the religiously disguised godlessness of facade Christianity. Undoubtedly, Bonhoeffer was influenced in this area by Kurt Leese,[4] whom Bonhoeffer read in prison. Leese understood atheism that opposed Western facade Christianity as a promising godlessness, because it is not really directed against God, but against the misuse of God. This promising, consistent godlessness exposes every mode of expression of a corrupted, ritual- and consumption-oriented Santa Claus Christianity. Mankind in the world come of age experiences the godlessness of his existence and faces it squarely without making the attempt to cover it over pseudoreligiously. Man come of age does not seek the protection of religion or ideology or a metaphysical system. Rather, in Bonhoeffer's understanding he squarely faces his God-forsakenness. The "man come of age" is the human being thrown back upon himself, freed from the falsely, suggestively, and convulsively assumed but artificial compulsive behavior of religious practice.

However, Bonhoeffer understood this godlessness of the world come of age as a dialectical process. It is real godlessness, but a godlessness in which man discovers his loss of God. One suffers under this godlessness because God's absence from things is palpable. Because man come of age has stepped outside of the false solutions of religion, it is precisely he who faces up to his godlessness who is somehow nearer to the reality of God. Godlessness come of age takes part in the messianic reality of suffering under being forsaken by God, because godlessness come of age does not allow itself to be falsely comforted by a facade of Christianity. Where religion is no longer the opium of the people, the possibility prevails of turning to the revealed and true God, who makes the light to shine in the darkness. Bonhoeffer interprets this state of having come of age, as it were, from the standpoint of his Christ-mysticism: Through *mortificatio* one goes on to *vivificatio*. That is to say, through the death of religion's

---

4. Kurt Leese, *Die Religionskrise des Abendlandes und die religiöse Lage der Gegenwart.* This book was not published until 1948. Nevertheless, it conveys an overall impression of that which had moved Bonhoeffer in Leese's earlier works. For example, on p. 243 Leese writes: "Thus one would like to say to Rilke: 'You are so pious and yet so godless.' That not only sounds contradictory, it is contradictory. This ruptured state of being pious and godless at the same time is what modern man carries within himself. It marks his character as practically demonic."

false transfiguration of existence, by wandering through the desert of God-forsakenness, one finds oneself on the path to a genuine encounter with God.

Alongside this evaluation of the state of having come of age, Bonhoeffer saw yet another aspect. Coming of age is also a positive result of the liberation that comes about through Christian faith. Man come of age is one who has been freed from being told what to do by religion—even if this freedom has been achieved by way of painful experiences. As Bonhoeffer made clear in his essay of 1933, "Der Führer und der einzelne in der jungen Generation" ["'Der Führer' and the Individual in the Young Generation"], man come of age is also one who is liberated from being told what to do politically or ideologically. He lives out of his inner resources in responsibility to the commandments of God. Man come of age is an expression of self-determination against hostile ideological, totalitarian, and religious domination. It is precisely the worldliness of the world that has given man the possibility to be free over against the world. Religion obscures access to the world. Rites, demons, myths, and gods throw a net of entanglement over the true relation between humankind and world. Christ liberated the world from these "powers," so that the possibility now exists of exercising dominion over the world in a genuine relationship to God as his children. This aspect—which of course cannot be separated from the God-forsakenness of the state of having come of age—also played a major role in Bonhoeffer's observations on the coming of age of the world. Therefore coming of age should be acknowledged and not suppressed: "God shouldn't be smuggled into some last secret place. . . . We shouldn't run man down in his worldliness, but confront him with God at his strongest point, . . . we should give up all our clerical tricks, and not regard psychotherapy and existentialist philosophy as God's pioneers."[5] Thus: through the pain of the experience of being a human alienated from God, through the pain of being in the desert of godless things, and in the apparent powerlessness of God—through all of this one experiences the nearness of God.

Christ is not only Lord of believers, but also as Pantocrator Lord of the whole world, including unbelievers. In a letter of July 27, 1944, Bonhoeffer asked in this context the question concerning "uncon-

---

5. *Letters and Papers from Prison*, p. 346.

scious Christianity."[6] He did this with regard to the positive characteristics of the coming of age of modern humanity. Together with Lutheran theologians he wanted to distinguish between *fides directa* and *fides reflexa*. Bonhoeffer knew figures in the church who shocked him with their salvation egocentrism and their running away from all social and political realities. And in the midst of the world Bonhoeffer encountered men who had lost touch with God and were estranged from the church, but who nevertheless were prepared completely to face their responsibility in the struggle for righteousness and truth. Do these people not stand within the messianic reality of Christ— these people who are persecuted, who hunger and thirst for righteousness, who face up to their responsibility, who experience the limits of their power and the power of guilt, who do righteousness?

Coming of Age Between Loss of God and the Coming of God

In order to exclude any misunderstanding, we observe once more: the aristocratic Bonhoeffer, the man of *contenance* with his understanding of discipline, order, and self-discipline, despised mass culture. He despised the crass lifestyle of the *nouveau riche* and the self-confident arrogance that could be observed on the streets of Berlin in the 1930s. He was a wide-awake critic of these upwardly mobile types, these shameless and unruly indicators of the decline of an entire culture. On July 21, 1944, Bonhoeffer wrote the following about coming of age: "I don't mean the shallow and banal this-worldliness of the enlightened, the busy, the comfortable, or the lascivious, but the profound this-worldliness, characterized by discipline and the constant knowledge of death and resurrection."[7] Thus it is a very particular type of coming of age that Bonhoeffer had in mind. It is a coming of age upon which the light of Christian reality falls. This coming of age is not convinced by mere talk of the limit set by death. Rather, it experiences this limit in the reality of life through responsible action in the world. And this coming of age also knows about the resurrection. It has quite simply and directly experienced an overcoming strength at the limits of its own powerlessness. This is not a conversion provoked through Methodistic technique, but a conversion that

6. Ibid., p. 373.
7. Ibid., p. 369.

arises naturally out of life. It is a kind of election to coming of age by means of passage through the shadows of death and fear to the horizon of the resurrection.

A human being can believe without knowing. And he can theologically know without believing. Bonhoeffer articulates a kind of coming of age of mankind by faith. The coming of age of the modern, Occidental person still stands within the reality in which Christ "took shape." This dialectically understood coming of age is not a triumphal, cheering, egocentric self-confidence, but a "Christian coming of age" that is aware of its limits, its cross, its powerlessness, and precisely because of its powerlessness also of its authority. Bonhoeffer formulated this paradox of modern Christian life as follows: "The world that has come of age is more godless, and perhaps for that very reason nearer to God, than the world before its coming of age."[8]

Bonhoeffer's dialectical understanding of "coming of age" is in the final analysis a mystical, Christ-mystical, interpretation of coming of age.[9] Coming of age is connected to the loss of God. On this theme, Bonhoeffer writes: "The God who lets us live in the world without the working hypothesis of God is the God before whom we stand continually. Before God and with God we live without God. God lets himself be pushed out of the world on to the cross. He is weak and powerless in the world, and that is precisely the way, the only way, in which he is with us and helps us."[10]

God is not pushed out of the world; God *allows himself* to be pushed out of the world—just as he allowed himself to be thrust onto the cross in Christ. And it is God who lets us live without the working hypothesis of God. Even when modern humankind come of age lives without the "working hypothesis of God," it is nevertheless the

---

8. Ibid., p. 363. This statement from Bonhoeffer's letter of July 18 is a key statement for the Christ-mystical understanding of "coming of age." Having come of age is more related to the suffering of the "time in the desert," of the loss of God, than to the triumph of self-assertion. But in that inner dying because of godlessness is prepared the nearness of the true coming or second coming of God—*post tenebras lux*, after the darkness light. But here as well—in the multidimensionality of Bonhoeffer's statements—we must remember that alongside this aspect of having come of age there is also the other aspect of existing in liberated responsibility.

9. Like "powerlessness" of God, "coming of age" in Bonhoeffer must be understood processually and Christ-mystically. "Coming of age" and "powerlessness" are related to each other dialectically in the structure of Bonhoeffer's theology—not in special theology, but in anthropology.

10. *Letters and Papers from Prison*, p. 360.

Almighty God who wills to allow it. Only within this dialectic do we speak authentically of "coming of age" and powerlessness as Bonhoeffer understood them.

Thus godlessness itself stands under the power of God. Religionless godlessness and genuine this-worldliness lead to the experience of powerlessness in this world come of age, and thereby to encounter with the God who reveals himself in Christ.

The antitheses of a Christ-mystical coming of age can never be systematized. Bonhoeffer conceives of "come of age" processually, in yes and in no, in no and in yes.

Coming of Age in Salvation History

Abraham Kuyper was the church father of the "Gereformeerde Kerken van Nederland" ["Reformed Churches of the Netherlands"], founded in 1886. Kuyper fought passionately against every compartmentalization of the spheres of reality that distanced them from Christ's reign: "A God for the church and for the heart, but outside of life, is something incomprehensible to a Calvinist."[11] God's Word is valid not only for the individual soul, but also for the entirety of a people, for all social communities. Christ is the gospel for state and society as well as for the church. Christ increases, Caesar decreases. Kuyper's slogan was: "Everything is yours, but you are Christ's." In this connection he came to the decisive recognition "that grace is at work also outside of the church in the world. Not eternal, saving grace but still temporal grace to thwart the ruin which sin inevitably brings about."[12] In Kuyper's opinion the Holy Spirit not only illumines church-going people, but also gives "the authorities of a nation the light to understand God's Word. . . . In both areas God, and not man, reigns. But it is also the case that the sovereign God gave each area its own institutions and personalities with their respective responsibilities, and then joined everything together in such a way . . . that the church is accorded honor."[13] Sin can destroy the state, culture, and science, but the church can be saved by spiritual rebirth through Christ.

11. On this point, see Kolfhaus, *Dr. Abraham Kuyper: Ein Lebensbericht*, 1925, p. 124.
12. Ibid., p. 191.
13. Ibid., p. 181.

The faith held by Bonhoeffer and Kuyper confesses that everything is subject to Christ. According to Kuyper, the upholding and preserving power of Christ, although of course not consciously discerned in the modern world, is at work in the struggle against "the fata morgana of modernism." Preserving grace is also at work in the secularized world of mankind come of age—Bonhoeffer saw it exactly the same way. Thus, starting from Kuyper's understanding of common grace, one can view Bonhoeffer's concept of coming of age as supported by common grace and at the same time standing under the light of special grace with regard to Occidental historicity. To this way of thinking there is, then, unconscious participation in the lordship of Christ. Does that mean that all of those spoken of in the Beatitudes of Christ in the Sermon on the Mount are already born again? The poor, the poor in spirit, the peacemakers, those who hunger and thirst for righteousness, those who are persecuted for righteousness' sake—are they already included in the saving reality of special grace? Or does that saving reality extend to people who live in spiritual poverty (in other words, those who are religionless), who fight for righteousness and are persecuted for righteousness' sake, just exactly as they are, without being born again or converted? Any kind of systematization of the path to salvation can only be fatal. Christ is the way of salvation and not the condition of being saved. This way of salvation—and that is the issue here—is incorporation into the messianic reality of the kingdom of God, which God himself, not a methodology from the theological sidelines, brings to pass in the midst of the world.

9

The Religious Perversion of Christianity

Already in the 1920s Barth viewed biblical revelation as the repudiation of religion. He argued that religion was man's way to God based on the *analogia entis* (analogy, though not identity, between God and created things). *Homo religiosus* infers God from the world. Thus, God becomes a projection of man. In connection with this, Barth considered Ludwig Feuerbach, who had understood God to be man's superman-illusion, or man's projection of his desire to be a superman, to be a farsighted discerner of error disguised as Christianity.

As no one else in his time, Bonhoeffer took Barth's theology seriously and allowed himself to be greatly influenced by it. Barth was the first theologian—and this remains his great accomplishment—to take up the critique of religion.[1] For Bonhoeffer, "religion" in Barth's negative sense was the individualistic concern for the salvation of one's personal soul. He held "that there are more important questions" than the religious one: "Does the question about saving one's soul appear in the Old Testament at all? Aren't righteousness and the Kingdom of God on earth the focus of everything, and isn't it true that Rom. 3.24ff. is not an individualistic doctrine of salvation, but the culmination of

1. *Letters and Papers from Prison*, p. 280.

the view that God alone is righteous?"[2] The issue should not be the other world, but this world. The issue is a world under God's law and its reconciliation and renewal through redemption.

By this Bonhoeffer did not mean a Christianized world, because Christianization of the world means secularization of Christianity. Rather, Bonhoeffer wanted the world really to be the world as God intends, and that it be free from ongoing ideological and religious perversion.

Religious Christianity is the self-justification of the individual in his need for personal protection and personal help. In religion, God becomes a deus ex machina whose function is to provide for the satisfaction of the needs of the moment. Thus, God is summoned in each individual case from the other world to this world. God gets brought in to serve inwardly directed individuality, and he is experienced by means of a particular type of heightened feeling. In this way everyone has his private god for his private self-actualization and for the fulfillment of wishes and notions that are purely his own. The private god represents the private life. He becomes a dear, nice god who accompanies, protects, and makes the wishes of his darling come true.

Bonhoeffer saw in pietism, as he believed he encountered it, the last attempt "to preserve Protestant Christianity as religion." There God became an instrument for the self-actualization of those who did not think they had gotten their fair share in the world. But this pietism as Bonhoeffer viewed it is basically only a cover for underlying godlessness, because its God has long since been pushed out of the world and is now worshiped in a little niche on the sidelines of its worldliness. Thus God is no longer in the world, but outside of the world. He becomes a God who has lost his world. The more this God is pushed out of the world, the more he becomes a guarantor of illusions. And they are not illusions about the real world but the kind of illusions that a person erects about himself.

Bonhoeffer opposed the shameless exposure of the intimate sphere. He opposed the unlocking of inwardliness, the religious striptease to reveal intimate experiences of an immediate kind with God himself. This type of personal, individualistic, salvation-egoistic interaction with God was repulsive to Bonhoeffer. In his opinion, this type of reli-

2. Ibid., p. 286.

gion was a means to the end of generating medicine for spiritual suffering and power to fulfill egoistic wishes. This is where the retreat to inwardliness begins, while one leaves the world in which one is, after all, still living, to the other powers. This type of needs-religiosity retools Christianity into an institution of needs-satisfaction.

Such overwrought rejoicing at being emotionally elevated to God, such claims to "possess" God, amount to discretionary power over God among the circle of the blessed and a perversion of the biblical revelation of salvation in Bonhoeffer's view. A community of such salvation-egotists is no longer a congregation that is the salt of the earth or the light of the world. It is rather a group in which the members merely exchange their personal experiences of salvation for the purpose of being better equipped to handle their problems with their own saving individualistic resources. In this way the salvation individualism of each member becomes salvation-egoism of the group, which then consciously and decidedly closes itself off from the world and leaves the world to itself.

A church that allows itself to be caught up in these practices of religious pietism must face Bonhoeffer's bitter criticism: "An escapist church can be certain that it will immediately win over all the weaklings, all those who are only too glad to be lied to and deceived, all the starry-eyed dreamers, all the unborn sons of the earth."[3] But this religious Christianity, in Bonhoeffer's opinion, opposes the saving will of Christ: "Christ does not want this weakness. Rather, he makes men and women strong. He does not lead people to fantasy worlds of religious refuge. He gives believers back to the world as its true offspring. Do not be escapist, but be strong."[4] Thus, according to Bonhoeffer, Christian life should consist not in flight from reality, but in preservation and perseverance within reality.

This does not at all mean that Bonhoeffer thought that the earth is a paradise or that it can be made into a paradise through "Christianization." He was very conscious of the contradictory nature of the world: "All of our longing to make, or win back, the field of blessings from the field of curses comes to nought because God himself cursed

---

3. *GS*, 3:270. From the lecture "Thy Kingdom Come," which was held in Potsdam on November 19, 1932. Here we see how early this protest against pious escapism was strongly developed in Bonhoeffer.

4. Ibid.

the field and he alone can take his work back and bless the earth again."[5] Once again Bonhoeffer's conception of the interpenetration of Christian existence and the world reveals itself dialectically! The Christian lives in the world and from the world but in tension with the world. But this tension must be borne, because the kingdom of Christ is "the kingdom of the other world that has entered completely into the inner conflict, into the contradictoriness of this world."[6] Bonhoeffer wanted to make clear that God may never be made into an "area" among other areas. All of the reality of this world is subordinate to God—even if dialectically, in its contradictory nature. One cannot find the way to God by attempting to pass over the realities of this world. "Religion always gives man the impression of having God, of knowing what there is to know about him, even if this occurs in all humility and modesty. Then religion becomes an area among other areas."[7] That is how Bonhoeffer expressed it as early as his winter semester lectures of 1931–32 on the history of twentieth-century systematic theology. Thus this critique of religion, which later came out in all its sharpness in his letters from prison, was a deep personal concern of Bonhoeffer's from the very beginning.

How "Pious" Was Bonhoeffer?

In his letters from prison, it is obvious that Bonhoeffer did not consider himself a *Homo religiosus*. On the contrary, he maintained that he had always harbored a mistrust, even a fear, of that which is called "piety" in Christian circles. Overly familiar and easy talk of God—as if God were at the speaker's disposal—and talk of "personal dealings" with God were always repulsive to Bonhoeffer. He abhorred the shamelessness of the well-turned religious phrase. He never tired of calling attention to the fact that the Israelites never uttered the name of God. Thus for Bonhoeffer religiosity was often to be equated with shamelessness. The quick and easy manner, the readiness to pray, to use religious phrases, to reveal oneself in communal prayers or reports of conversion experiences, was deeply repugnant to Bonhoeffer. What he so often said about "covering" as with a veil applied precisely to

5. Ibid., p. 274.
6. Ibid., p. 283.
7. *GS*, 5:218.

one's walk with God. That is why Bonhoeffer always left his conversion, his "personal salvation history," veiled in the inexpressible.

At the same time it would be completely wrong to view Bonhoeffer as an ice-cold intellectual. Christianity was not only a matter of rationality or of moral engagement to Bonhoeffer. And contrary to what is sometimes heard in pious circles, he did love Jesus. In his time in prison he began every morning with the sign of the cross. He wrote prayers and songs. In the evenings he learned hymns by Paul Gerhardt, which he could then recite by heart when he woke up the next morning. In Bonhoeffer's own song "By Good Powers," which is familiar to many Christians the world over, he wrote that human beings are surrounded by angelic powers, are protected and comforted and safe and secure in God.

Religionless Christianity is in no way an emotionless Christianity that has nothing to do with experience. Love for God, devotion, trust, overcoming of fear—as a Christian Bonhoeffer experienced and lived all of these things. But he allowed the mystery of the inexpressible to encompass the entirety of his life and faith. He did not talk his faith to death. His piety was not a calculating (mis)use of God. He did not ply his trust in God's providence so as to force God into egotistical plans for salvation or life. Thus we see Bonhoeffer's dialectic at work here again, or perhaps rather the multidimensionality of his piety: "To talk of God means at the same time to keep silent about him. To trust him means at the same time to allow him to lead us along other paths. To witness to God's revelation means at the same time to preserve his mystery."[8]

There is a religious and also a secularizing falsification of Christianity. As much as he criticized the religious falsification, Bonhoeffer became a victim of the secularizing falsification also, when he was made into a "martyr of the religionless."[9] Bonhoeffer's religionless Christianity was subverted by modernists into a kind of moral-political superweapon for themselves. His view of Christianity as "being there for others" became a program for a form of religious social democracy. It goes without saying that the attempt was also made to

8. On this point, see his sermons from the period in London in 1934 (*GS*, 5:516–17).
9. Mayer, *Christuswirklichkeit*, p. 268: "Bonhoeffer is the first martyr in this 'religion of the religionless.'"

transpose Bonhoeffer's nonreligious Christianity into the existentialist philosophical categories of Rudolf Bultmann. Who could have resisted this temptation? In this case, biblical words had to be replaced by existentialist-ontological categories. In all such cases, Bonhoeffer fell victim to a reductionist program. Bonhoefferian theology was reduced to sociological or existentialist-ontological paradigms.[10]

In all of this lies a misconception of what Bonhoeffer understood by nonreligious Christianity. He never called for replacing biblical words with other words. Bonhoeffer's worldliness did not mean secularization of Christianity or of biblical language, but solidarity with the world. He called for bearing up, for suffering under worldliness, but also for affirming its joys. Only someone who lives completely in the world and shows solidarity with it can suffer in its midst and overcome it through the cross and the resurrection. Only someone who has trekked through the godlessness and God-forsakenness of this world can experience the reality of God. Out of this participation in worldliness, out of this solidarity with the world grows the language that is understood in the world as the proclamation of God's word. The need, then, is not for an intellectual program but for entering sensitively into the life in this world. In this way the strength arises to proclaim the same words of biblical revelation using fresh and different words.

Bonhoeffer's views here are explicitly rooted in Christ's taking on flesh and becoming man. Just as Christ entered into the lowliness of this world in order to witness to God's truth, so also should the Christian enter into the worldliness of this world in order to be a witness to Christ. It was precisely this solidarity with the world through emulating Christ that Bonhoeffer saw as missing in the tendency of "religious" Christianity to flee from the world and distance itself from it.

Religionless Christianity

Bonhoeffer believed that Christian revelation had been lived, experienced, and witnessed to for 1,900 years in the garb of religiosity.

---

10. Ibid., pp. 20f., 254f., and 270, discusses the problems and possibilities of an existential-ontological interpretation, especially in regard to G. Ebeling. Fortunately, Mayer does this critically. Moreover, he does it so thoroughly and comprehensively that we do not have to repeat the discussion of this theme here. The existential-ontological interpretation was not part of Bonhoeffer's paradigm.

"Our whole nineteen-hundred-year-old Christian preaching and theology rest on the 'religious *a priori*' of mankind."[11] It was clear to Bonhoeffer, however, that this religiosity was a historically conditioned and passing form of human expression. He was certain that religionless Christianity must be judged as "only a preliminary stage to a complete absence of religion" but that Christ would become the "Lord of the religionless."[12]

In this 1,900-year history of Christianity, its religious clothing had been naive [innocent] and immediate and thereby genuine. It was a natural result of the preindustrial understanding of reality. But through the rationalist-technological-industrial revolution this understanding of reality changed, so that religiosity is no longer genuinely naive, but rather artificially produced. It is no longer woven into the reality of this world, but detached from it. "But we don't worship anything now, not even idols. In that respect we're truly nihilists."[13] Thus, according to Bonhoeffer, one must distinguish clearly between a premodern, genuinely naive religiosity and a postmodern, partial, and more or less artificial religiosity. Religionlessness is not an adventurous, joyful phenomenon of modernity that should be greeted with rejoicing. Rather, it is a bitter challenge to Christianity. Religionlessness is not something that one decides for. Rather, it is a prescribed necessity. In our rationalist-technocratic approach to being, we no longer have the option of interpreting the world religiously. As a theologian, Bonhoeffer took the modernity of contemporary man absolutely seriously.

What is, then, a religionless Christianity? How do we now speak of God without religion? What does it mean that Christ is no longer the object of religion?

In contemporary, we might say separatist-subjectively experienced Christianity, biblical revelation is filled with religious contents that

11. *Letters and Papers from Prison*, p. 280—as we find it in a very important "turning point" letter of April 30, 1944.

12. Ibid., p. 279.

13. In this letter of June 27, 1944 (*Letters and Papers from Prison*, pp. 335–37), Bonhoeffer wrote that idolatry "implies that people still worship something." He saw the end of religion so radically that the technological human being would be incapable of any religiosity, including idol worship. This letter especially shows how radically Bonhoeffer saw religonlessness as the destiny of modern man. Contemporary religious practices in the realm of the New Age and the so-called renaissance of the occult do not contradict this diagnosis of Bonhoeffer. Rather, these are surrogate solutions that cannot seriously qualify as "religious" in the traditional sense.

bar access to the revelation of salvation. Modern man looking for meaning thinks that, in order to experience God, he has to feel a special feeling, be it a "feeling like Christmas," or a certain degree of fervor in prayer, or a psychologically measurable kind of deeply felt joyfulness, or a proud ascetic aloofness from worldly concerns. But such emotional elements always exist alongside other elements of existence. The ostensibly believing person at some point reaches a schizophrenic split. More and more he squeezes himself into a role that contradicts the realities of his existence. In other words: such religious contrivances do not comport with the actual dimensions of daily existence. The consequence is religious role playing—pharisaism and hypocrisy. Grasping this permits understanding of such sharply challenging utterances as this passage from a significant letter Bonhoeffer wrote on April 30, 1944:

> I often ask myself why a "Christian instinct" often draws me more to the religionless people than to the religious, by which I don't in the least mean with any evangelizing intention, but, I might almost say, "in brotherhood." While I'm often reluctant to mention God by name to religious people—because that name somehow seems to me here not to ring true, and I feel myself to be slightly dishonest (it's particularly bad when others start to talk in religious jargon; I then dry up almost completely and feel awkward and uncomfortable)—to people with no religion I can on occasion mention him by name quite calmly and as a matter of course. Religious people speak of God when human knowledge (perhaps simply because they are too lazy to think) has come to an end, or when human resources fail—in fact it is always the *deus ex machina* that they bring on to the scene, either for the apparent solution of insoluble problems, or as strength in human failure—always, that is to say, exploiting human weakness or human boundaries.[14]

If these roles are not played perfectly, then the need grows all the more for a kind of religious *Führer* who can make real what one can no longer realize oneself. Thus the religious charismatic leader

14. *Letters and Papers from Prison*, pp. 281–82. Bonhoeffer viewed himself as religionless in the sense he had expounded it and could no longer accept the genuineness of such statements of modern Christianity's contemporary religiosity. In religionless people, however, he saw the possibility of finding a way back to the original intent of biblical statements. This had to happen in total contrast to the subjective-instrumental deviancy of affected pious jargon.

becomes an integral feature of religious Christianity, be it an evangelist or pastor or some other religious visionary. Religious Christianity is always a transferred and imposed Christianity. It derives its life from pseudopersonal ties to others, who are supposed to represent the Christianity that one can no longer live out oneself. Thus the pastor finds himself under the enormous pressure of a congregation that forces a role upon him and expects him to play it. In this way, the problem of the religious Christian is transferred and imposed on the religious leader. He in turn is forced to suffer through the contradiction between the constraints of his role and reality. He then becomes a kind of ever-present Santa Claus. He becomes a St. Nick, an ongoing representation of our dear Father Who Art in Heaven. The consequence of this role play under the pressure of the expectations of a religious community is "ecclesiogenic neurosis." Anyone who has even once in his lifetime experienced a meeting at which several pastors were present has certainly witnessed this type of ecclesiogenic neurosis as it erupts in frustration and aggression. The neurosis typical of so many of today's German Protestant pastors is a result of the pressure of role expectation that issues from religious Christianity in a time that is unfortunately but consummately religionless.

In the discussion of Bonhoeffer today, one very often hears that Bonhoeffer was quite mistaken in his assessment of the future of religion. After all, mankind come of age has not replaced "religion" at all. On the contrary, right after the war there was a great deal of religious revival.

However, Bonhoeffer was not in the least mistaken about the future of religiosity. On the contrary. One must simply make a fine distinction between naive and original ancient religiosity and artificially stimulated modern religiosity. The old, genuine religiosity was tied to a premodern approach to reality. It is dead—once and for all. We may see admirable examples of it here and there where technological life structures have not yet fully established themselves. However, those are only rare exceptional situations that no longer play a role in modern reality.

The "religious wave" that we observe today is a religiosity that differs from naive religiosity in that it is not naturally present but is rather artificially induced. What would today's modern evangelists be without their marketing and their planned emotional stimulation, which is often accompanied by a veritable electronics factory? What does this modern religiosity have to do with traditional religiosity as described by Rudolf Otto in his book *The Holy*?[15] Neoreligiosity that claims to be Christian is completely tailored to the intensification of religious highs. It is dedicated to purely subjective, consumptive self-actualization. It is total and complete salvation-egoism. It was exactly this type of neoreligiosity that Bonhoeffer perceptively analyzed. This religiosity is a religiosity of promises for the "powerful life." These promises sometimes even go so far as to promise the "convert" not only health but also luxury and wealth. In these types of evangelization people experience a "high." Instead of true "rebirth" we have here nothing more than stimulated mountaintop experiences, a product that is consumed in a moment and has no significance for the general living of life in the modern world.

Religionless Christianity begins with the critique of the religious falsification of reality. The gods of illusion must be broken and their altars burned. Religionless Christianity presupposes a radical critique of religion such as that which Barth had already begun and which for the sake of Christian truth must be applied to the emotionally stimulated neoreligiosity that is shooting up all over.

Religionless Christianity does not in any way mean secularized Christianity. Neither is religionless Christianity the "publicized" Christianity that we find more or less portrayed in our mass media today. The way that this type of proclamation accommodates itself to modern sociological and humanistic paradigms is precisely the kind of secularization of Christianity that Bonhoeffer rejected and fought against. The message of salvation may not be mass-marketed. According to Bonhoeffer the event of Christian salvation should take place in the *arcanum*, not on the naked public stage. In the *arcanum* (secret place) the event of Christian salvation can be shielded from secularization. Bonhoeffer consciously reestablished the link with arcane discipline.

15. Rudolf Otto, *Das Heilige* (*The Holy*) has appeared in many editions since 1917. It is a classic phenomenology of traditional and premodern but genuine and natural religiosity. In Bonhoeffer it is crucial to distinguish between genuine, premodern, and naturally developed religiosity on the one hand and distorted, postmodern religiosity on the other. The one is a possible form of Christianity, but the other is a perversion of Christianity because it denies Christianity its normative relevance to all of reality and restricts it to the subjective ghetto of salvation-egoism. The one form of religiosity is genuine, the other only a facade for atheism and an aesthetic, consumer-oriented charade.

Arcane discipline, as it existed in the mystery cults of the ancient world, meant the obligation to keep messages of salvation secret. In these cults, strict commandments forbade the passing on of rites or cultic texts. The early Christian community also practiced arcane discipline, which remained in force until well into the fifth century. The sacraments, baptism and the Lord's Supper, the Lord's Prayer, and the Apostles' Creed were only passed on to the inner circle of the Christian community. The church order of Hippolytus expressly ordered that baptism and the Lord's Supper must remain concealed to unbelievers. The issue was always to protect that which is holy from being profaned! Holy things were to be for the holy people. They were not to be thrown before the dogs (Matt. 7:6). In the fifth century, arcane discipline was given up. The justification for this was that there was nothing more to conceal from unbelievers because the people had all become believers. Ever since then, the established church and arcane discipline have been mutually exclusive. Typically, Bonhoeffer had a dialectical relationship to arcane discipline. On the one hand, the Christian should go into the world and interpret Christianity in the midst of the world, in this-worldliness, through his life and his being there for others. On the other hand the Christian should experience the revelation of the true meaning of his life in the *arcanum,* under the Word of God, in prayer and through the sacraments. Bonhoeffer's dialectical view excluded the monastic and sectarian mentality. Words and sacraments should not be hawked as cheap grace. The Word of God should be safeguarded from dwindling to a mere empty phrase in a meaningless linguistic shell. The ancient word—now free from religious and secular domination—should hit home in its original and unadulterated power and significance for the benefit of those who hear it and live it in the *arcanum.*

This view of Bonhoeffer opposes the notion that Christianity can be presented to the world simply by broadcasting a mundane "devotional moment" or by televising Sunday worship services. The price for this is the secularization of Christianity and therefore the trivialization of the Christian message. Such a secularized and trivialized Christianity has no missionary power. This needs to be taken to heart by those who labor tirelessly in publicity work and public information capacities in the hope of spreading Christianity at bargain prices. The testimony of Bonhoeffer speaks against such managers of Christianity, Inc.:

In the traditional words and acts we suspect that there may be something quite new and revolutionary, though we cannot as yet grasp or
express it. That is our own fault. Our church, which has been fighting
in these years only for its self-preservation, as though that were an end
in itself, is incapable of taking the word of reconciliation and redemption to mankind and the world. Our earlier words are therefore bound
to lose their force and cease, and our being Christian today will be limited to two things: prayer and righteous action among men. All Christian thinking, speaking, and organizing must be born anew out of this
prayer and action.[16]

Naturally, Bonhoeffer never intended to replace religionless Christianity with a kind of concept-mysticism: "it is not abstract argument,
but example, that gives its word emphasis and power."[17] Religionless
Christianity gains significance through the Christian life. The significance of the Christian life is conveyed through this life in this world.
This does not entail merely an ethical example, an ethical program
with the goal of moral education. The example Bonhoeffer has in mind
means much more: the Christian in his life is the physical illustration
of incarnation, cross, and resurrection. A new language comes out of
a new life and not vice versa. "I'm thinking about how we can reinterpret in a 'worldly' sense—in the sense of the Old Testament and of
John 1.14—the concepts of repentance, faith, justification, rebirth,
and sanctification."[18] John 1:14 is: "The Word became flesh." When
Bonhoeffer thought about the Word's becoming flesh, he really meant
becoming flesh. He meant the concretization of Christian life through
the Christian's being a Christian for others. In his ability to suffer, in
the strength that makes it possible to bear the cross, in his walking
through the valley of powerlessness, and in his receiving the power of
the resurrection in the midst of his life—in all of these things, the
Christian shows what Christianity is. That happens first and foremost
not through words, but through deeds.

Thus the religious act in its partial restriction to the religious
sphere is augmented as the act is made real in life.

16. *Letters and Papers from Prison,* p. 300.
17. Ibid. p. 383.
18. Ibid., pp. 286–87.

In this sense Bonhoeffer stood with the Reformers. Luther liberated the act of confession from its religious domination and brought confession into real life, because the entire life of a Christian is a *mortificatio* (dying) and *vivificatio* (being made alive). Here we are reminded of the first of Luther's 95 theses of October 31, 1517: "Since our Lord and Master Jesus says: Repent . . . he desired that the entire life of believers should be a life of repentance." And in the last two theses (94 and 95) Luther proclaimed: "One should admonish Christians to strive to imitate their head Jesus Christ through punishment, death and hell and thus set their hopes more on entering the Kingdom of Heaven through much affliction rather than through the false security of peace [Acts 14:22]." Through these statements Luther clearly brought into real life the content of that which had been "imprisoned" by a religious act. That is precisely what Bonhoeffer meant by religionless Christianity. For Luther, confession was not the religious act, the performance of the sacrament, the mere confession of sin, nor the prescribed feeling of remorse followed by the absolution—although that could be part of it. The key to confession is the radical turnaround through life, the catharsis brought about through the challenges of the world, through death, struggle, and resurrection with Christ. After that, faith is no longer a case of holding these truths to be self-evident, but a real trust that comes to fruition in real life. Asceticism does not take place outside of the world in a monastery, but in the world as discipline and order—as "inner-worldly asceticism" (Max Weber).

Bonhoeffer did not yet see the realization of the new words of a religionless Christianity, an impulse first set in motion with the Reformation. Even today, these words still await realization. Simply to replace biblical words with new words, as for example sometimes happens in ultramodern Bible translations or topically relevant "preaching," would be a secularization of Christianity. To describe life under the biblical Word in a new way would indeed be the language of a religionless Christianity. However, authentic Christian life precedes the description of this life. Since we do not yet have the words to describe it, we know we have not yet achieved the religionless Christian life.

Religionless Christianity is not an intellectual program. It is the new paradigm of an altered Christian existence. At issue is the life of the Christian who must in a new way bear, suffer, and overcome the loss of God in the era of a technocratic world come of age. None of this is a "new invention" but a return to the origins of Christian belief. For according to Bonhoeffer's conviction, the original lived-out faith of Old and also New Testament was emphatically not religious.

10

Bonhoeffer's Real Christ-Mysticism

It should be stated again that for Bonhoeffer "religionless" by no means entails encountering God or Christ without, say, love, reverence, or any feelings whatsoever. Right up to the end it is clear how Bonhoeffer was impacted by the seminal experience of love, trust, supplication, and reverence. His concern is always centered on encounter with the "living" God. Only the person who is likewise "living" in the entirety of his thinking, understanding, willing, and feeling will experience this encounter. It would be pointless to show in individual passages what is actually palpable on every page of Bonhoeffer's works—namely, that he experienced this encounter with the living God, the God who is entirely other, and that he did not view human existence as a substitute for God.

"To exist for others" does not mean meeting social needs or stirring up revolution. Flattening Bonhoeffer's thought to the point of reading it as advocacy for socialism produces the opposite of what he actually wished to assert. To exist for others in Bonhoeffer's view means to do precisely that which Christ also did: bear the cross of this world, wage the battle for righteousness in this world, experience the resurrecting power of God, and know, even in one's deepest helplessness, that God is there.

In this connection it is important to recall that Bonhoeffer's concern from the start is the concrete manifestation of what is distinctly and authentically Christian. This is to take place in the world, not be somehow primarily other-worldly. At the onset of the 1930s this hankering for such concrete manifestation grows especially strong. For a time he believes that what he seeks can simply no longer be found in Western Christianity. Bonhoeffer experienced this concrete manifestation, however, but in an entirely different fashion than he had originally imagined. He had supposed he would find it in India in an ashram (religious retreat) with Mahatma Gandhi. He would most certainly have not found it there. His life became concretely incorporated into the reality who is Christ through his incorporation into the messianic suffering of Christ amidst the harsh reality of the 1930s and 1940s. This led him, of course, to the experience of utter impotence in prison and beyond that to martydom by execution. The concrete manifestation that he himself sought was then placed upon him by God.

What Is Christ-Mysticism?

The term "mysticism" was discredited in the theology of Karl Barth and Emil Brunner. They took mysticism to denote submersion into, being swallowed up by introspection in order to discover and experience the reality of God in the depths of one's own existence. But that is precisely what the "word theology" of Barth and Brunner did not wish to promote. They sought encounter with God through proclamation, the call, the revelation of the word. Their criticism of mysticism is doubtless justified.

Yet Christ-mysticism in Bonhoeffer's sense is somewhat different.[1] Albert Schweitzer actually expressed quite clearly in his *The Mysticism of Paul the Apostle* (first ed. 1929) what Christ-mysticism is. It is in no way comparable to some kind of secular or even Hindu mystical God-experience. Christ-mysticism means that the Christian takes part in the life and death and resurrection of Christ. And he gains this access to the reality of Christ through encounter with Christ in the word of proclamation. Christ-mysticism does not, therefore, mean to discover

---

1. "Christ-mysticism" as used here is not a matter of inner inspiration or experience, but of union with Christ through the encounter with Christ in the Word of Christ.

a Christ in the depth of one's soul. It means participation in the reality of the Christ who encounters me and takes me in tow, incorporating me into his reality. Albert Schweitzer also expresses the view that Luther was a Christ-mystic in the sense that the doctrine of justification was only secondary alongside his understanding of dying and rising in Christ.

Now Bonhoeffer wanted to live out this Christ-mysticism right in the middle of the world. He did not understand redemption as something obtained by passing into the world to come or first received after dying and then arriving there. Rather here, in the midst of life, he wanted a share in the messianic reality of Christ. The Christian "like Christ himself ('My God, why hast thou forsaken me?'), . . . must drink the earthly cup to the dregs, and only in his doing so is the crucified and risen Lord with him, and he crucified and risen with Christ. This world must not be prematurely written off. . . But Christ takes hold of a man at the centre of his life."[2] Christ-mysticism in light of this means that Christ as the one raised from the dead, existing as a person, incorporates people into his reality. Other words are important too: "Life in this world must not be given up prematurely." Here note especially "prematurely." For life in the here and now always remained for Bonhoeffer only the second-last, never the ultimate and final. Bonhoeffer was an enemy of reducing existence merely to its this-worldly dimensions, just as he opposed reducing existence to merely other-worldly dimensions. He centered on the dialectical interrelationship between this world and the next. This shows up in his ethics in the dynamic-progressive category of "penultimate and ultimate." The Christ of the world to come is the Christ who is with us in the present world. When the Christian lives in a totally worldly fashion, that is, struggles, works, loves, and thinks responsibly in this world, then he participates in God's suffering in the world. Bonhoeffer presents us, then, with a dialectical Christ-mysticism that by no means can or should be systematized.

Suffering

It has been said several times that religionless Christianity is not secularized Christianity. The dialectic is essential: The more the

2. *Letters and Papers from Prison*, p. 337.

Christian involves himself in the world, the more he participates in the suffering of God. To live in the world without this suffering is cheap worldliness. To suffer without involvement in the world is religious masochism. On July 18, 1944, Bonhoeffer wrote that the Christian "must live a 'secular' life, and thereby share in God's sufferings. . . . It is not the religious act that makes the Christian, but participation in the sufferings of God in the secular life."[3] With this statement Bonhoeffer excluded banal this-worldliness just as strongly as the religious instrumentalization of God through religious acts for the purpose of self-actualization. For if the Christian does not get involved in the world, then he can only live for himself and thus misuse Christianity for his religious self-actualization. The Christian allows himself "to be caught up into the way of Jesus Christ, into the messianic event, thus fulfilling Isa. 53."[4] The Christian participates in the messianic suffering because the kingdom of God has already dawned. Of course, the kingdom has not reached completion. That will not happen until Christ's return. But the kingdom of God is already present among mankind, and whoever lives in this kingdom of God or participates in it also participates in the messianic suffering of Christ as is stated in Isaiah 53. "This being caught up into the messianic sufferings of God in Jesus Christ"[5] is what constitutes the special aspect of the Christian existence in engagement for the sake of this world. And the suffering of God is always the suffering of God in Christ. Through Christ, God participates in Christ's suffering and thereby also in the suffering of the Christian.

This participation in the suffering of Christ does not mean that suffering as such has value in and of itself, nor that it is a religious means of "having God." Once again, that would be a religious misunderstanding of suffering. By no means was Bonhoeffer of the opinion that one first had to have become debilitated through suffering before one could find the way to redemption in Christ: "The centurion of Capernaum (who makes no confession of sin)" is named as an example of faith. The Ethiopian eunuch (Acts 8) and Cornelius (Acts 10) were for Bonhoeffer likewise "not standing at the edge of an abyss." Bonhoeffer

3. Ibid., p. 361.
4. Ibid., pp. 361–62.
5. Ibid., p. 362.

points to Nathanael, "'an Israelite indeed, in whom there is no guile,'" and to Joseph of Arimathea—all of them suffer not because of themselves or for the sake of their own sins. They are all shaped by the "their sharing in the suffering of God in Christ. That is their 'faith.'"[6]

Thus whoever wants to find the way to God does not have to make himself out to be a bad person or seek out sins. Rather, through involvement in life, in the midst of life, in the acceptance of responsibility, one will soon enough be wounded by the world and recognize that everyone who struggles for righteousness will have to suffer from his own unrighteousness.

Suffering is the essence of the world. But a human being cannot elevate himself to God simply by suffering. The meaning of suffering is found not in suffering but in liberation from suffering. Suffering is penultimate to the resurrection. Thus Bonhoeffer wrote on July 28, 1944: "In suffering, the deliverance consists in our being allowed to put the matter out of our own hands into God's hands. In this sense death is the crowning of human freedom."[7] Thus it is none other than the "other," the transcendent God who encounters us, who frees us from suffering. And the pathway into the "other" reality (through the gate of death) brings us our final liberation. To act without suffering is impossible. Bonhoeffer's turning toward the world is not some ebullient activism: "Whether the human deed is a matter of faith or not depends on whether we understand our suffering as an extension of our action and a completion of freedom. I think that is very important and very comforting."[8]

Of course, for Bonhoeffer the way to God is not the way of speculation or of gratifying religious needs or of some kind of wishful thinking. "The God of Jesus Christ has nothing to do with what God, as we imagine him, could do and ought to do," wrote Bonhoeffer on August 18, 1944. The religious god is the painted god. The god of our wishes is the religious god, the god of needs gratification. This is the way of cheap religiosity, the way of deception. The true way to God follows a different route: "If we are to learn what God promises, and what he fulfils, we must persevere in quiet meditation on the life, say-

6. Ibid.
7. Ibid., p. 375.
8. Ibid.

ings, deeds, sufferings, and death of Jesus."[9] That is not resignation. Renouncing or rejecting the "god of our wishes" does not mean clinging to our suffering or languishing in resignation. In Christ, God is simultaneously the powerless and the powerful God. In Christ-mysticism, the way extends from the suffering of powerlessness into the power of freedom. Bonhoeffer held that nothing is then impossible for us, because all things are possible with God; that no earthly power can touch us without his will, and that danger and distress can only drive us closer to him, for in suffering is our joy concealed, in dying we find our life.[10] In this context it is appropriate to quote the following verse once again:

> In me there is darkness,
> But with you there is light;
> I am lonely, but you do not leave me.[11]

Bonhoeffer is not describing a safe, straight path. Rather, it is the way of death and resurrection in Christ. But this Christ-mystical way is emphatically not the way of religion, which always desires the straight path. Rather, it is the way of overcoming in the light of the revelation of God.

H. F. Kohlbrügge's Christ-Mysticism

In his Christ-mysticism as in other aspects of his views, Bonhoeffer stands entirely in the Reformation tradition. Luther's Christ-mysticism has already been discussed. Bonhoeffer was also familiar with H. F. Kohlbrügge's works and thought very highly of his Christ-typological interpretation of the Old Testament. Unfortunately, it is impossible to say how much Bonhoeffer's Christ-mysticism was influenced by Kohlbrügge.

Kohlbrügge was a Reformed theologian who lived from 1803 until 1875. He founded the Dutch congregation of Elberfeld. Originally he belonged to the Lutheran Free Church in Amsterdam but came into conflict with the pastors there because he publicly criticized their

9. Ibid., p. 391.
10. Ibid.
11. Ibid., p. 139.

"negative theology." He then turned to Calvinism, but was not accepted into the Reformed Church (Hervormde Kerk) because it was feared he would be a trouble-maker. That was a unique event in Dutch church history. So he finally founded a free Reformed congregation in Elberfeld. The great discovery of his life was Romans 7:14: the Christian is justified and yet carnal and sold under sin. Because of this, Kohlbrügge was an arch-enemy of all religious notions that the Christian is perfectly holy. *Simul iustus et peccator* was for Kohlbrügge the shibboleth of existence in the Reformation heritage. The Christian is carnal, yet God has sanctified him.

This dialectic caused Kohlbrügge to reject any psychological description of faith or sanctification. For Kohlbrügge there was no such thing as description of the religious condition. And yet for Kohlbrügge there was participation in Christ—not by means of a religious act, but in the type of Christ-mysticism that Bonhoeffer lived out: "Thus a certain moment . . . arrives in our life, at which we are transplanted in the spirit of faith into this salvation and cross over from death into life. That is the complete reshaping of a human being, a reshaping that is also called being born again."[12] "Whoever is seized by grace is thus seized in a way that all good works from the same grace follow after him and go before him; and yet he feels nothing but melancholy over the fact that he is not even capable of untying the Lord's shoelaces."[13]

Thus there is no religious possession, no demonstrable religious bearing, that the Christian can take out of his pocket and show people. The Christian lives in grace like "the dog lives with his master."[14] In other words, the Christian is included in the life, suffering, and death of Christ—but not because of himself, not through a decision, deed, or religious act, but through Christ himself in a way that is indescribable and inconceivable—"in Christ, but still in the flesh; different, but still the same"—an unresolvable dialectic.

Against the "religious" notion of Christian existence being perfectly incorporated by and into Christ, Kohlbrügge wrote: "Whatever a person does out of himself as a good work, he does not do for God,

---

12. H. F. Kohlbrügge, *Die Lehre des Heils*, 1903, p. 67.
13. See J. van Lookhuyzen, *Hermann Friedrich Kohlbrügge en zijn prediking*, 1905, p. 442.
14. *Die Lehre*, p. 443.

but for himself."[15] Kohlbrügge recognized the religious depiction of
self in salvation-egoism. Real existence in Christ was always "unconscious" for Kohlbrügge. That is reminiscent of passages from Bonhoeffer's *The Cost of Discipleship*. "What God wants to have done to his
honor he brings out in his own through the grace of his Holy Spirit.
Mankind cannot account for the how, the what and the purpose of
this. He cannot even really value these deeds, because he does them
without knowing it himself."[16] Kohlbrügge was of this opinion
because "it is by God's doing that we are competent."[17] In a Christ-
mystical sense, Kohlbrügge expressed himself this way: "Now I can do
nothing other than his will. But if I were outside of his blessed limits,
oh, I know too well what would happen then." If Bonhoeffer denied
all prerequisites, rules, and statutes that might prescribe in advance in
appearance of the "holy life" (which he did, by the way, in his own critique of *The Cost of Discipleship*, to be dealt with later), then Kohlbrügge certainly did also. His opinion: "There are no regulations, no
rules or methods for sanctification."[18] And about the mystery of election to salvation Kohlbrügge wrote: "Those who are, are not; and
those who are not, are."[19]

The Bonhoefferian "veiling" and the Bonhoefferian "mystery" are
reminiscent of Kohlbrügge's statements about election, being born
again, faith, and sanctification. It is the genuine, clear, and reformational line. Along this line Bonhoeffer lived out and pondered his
Christ-mysticism, his being in Christ.

15. Ibid., p. 29.
16. Ibid., p. 449.
17. Ibid., p. 469.
18. Ibid., p. 477.
19. Ibid., p. 152.

PART 4

Biblical Revelation in Babylonian Captivity

11

Bonhoeffer and Historical-Critical Methodology

Historical-Critical Theology

Disappointment and shock are the rule when Bible-believing Christians hear how Bonhoeffer was indebted to the historical-critical method of Bible criticism, and what Bonhoeffer said about Bultmann. At a June 1987 convention of the Conference of Confessing Congregations, at which an ethical theme in Bonhoeffer's theology was under discussion, a "leading personality" of the Confessing movement dismissed all arguments on the grounds that Bonhoeffer read the Bible just as historical-critically as Bultmann.

Undoubtedly, Bonhoeffer's theological development took place completely within the rationalist paradigm of early twentieth-century Protestant theology, a paradigm that imprisoned the Bible in the one-dimensionality of an analytical way of thinking and an underlying worldview dictated by modern conceptuality.

Bonhoeffer was a prominent member of the seminar held by Adolf von Harnack, the classic proponent of modern liberal theology in Germany. At the turn of the century, von Harnack stirred up controversy

with his view of the Apostles' Creed.[1] He thought that the creed's
assertions distorted Christianity. He wanted to get back behind the
metaphysical or hellenistic distortion of Christianity "to the simple
and straightforward gospel of Jesus of Nazareth." It should not be the
Son of God who stands at the center of the gospel message, but the
loving Father, in keeping with the Son's own testimony. As a result, all
statements in the Bible about salvation that were connected to so-
called saving acts were rendered invalid. The virgin birth, the reconciling death on the cross, the resurrection from the dead, and Christ's
return at the end of time were all to have no more significance for the
simple essence of Christianity. The question arises whether Bonhoeffer was ever liberated from this way of thinking, or whether von Harnack was later replaced in Bonhoeffer's thought by the other radical
Bible critic Rudolf Bultmann. Did Bonhoeffer ever declare his agreement with Bultmann?

On June 1, 1941, Bultmann gave his exciting lecture on the New
Testament and mythology. This lecture was published in volume 7 of
Beiträge zur evangelischen Theologie and entitled "Offenbarung und
Heilsgeschehen."[2] It caused quite a stir within the Confessing
Church, of which Bultmann was a member. After the war the lecture
was passionately discussed and debated until well into the 1960s. In
it Bultmann attempted to disqualify the "mythological" framework of
the Bible as not acceptable for modern thought. The worldview of the
New Testament was depicted as a mythological worldview that is not
compatible with modern thought. The beginning and end of the
world, the saving acts of Jesus, his unfulfilled expectation that the
kingdom of God was coming soon, his redeeming death, the resurrec-

---

1. Bonhoeffer also considered a revision in the confessional issue in regard to the Apostles'
Creed, to be precise, in connection with a revision in conflict theology, in the preparation for
office and in the discharge of office (*Letters and Papers from Prison*, p. 382). In Bonhoeffer's
judgment, the confession belongs in the *arcanum*, as in early Christianity. Whether the Apostles' Creed can be an adequate expression of Christian faith for modern man is not so much a
"historical-critical" question as it was during the Apostles' Creed controversy of 1891–1912 in
which von Harnack intervened as a liberal. In contrast, Bonhoeffer was concerned with the
question of understanding and of "publicization"—with the use of the Apostles' Creed outside
of the *arcanum*.

2. This essay became the basis of a theological discussion in the 1950s and 1960s whose dimensions may be described as vast. As *Kerygma und Mythos—ein theologisches Gespräch*, many
volumes and editions have appeared since 1949 on the debate about Bultmann's program of demythologization.

tion of the dead, and of course also the virgin birth—all of that was mythology. At best, Bultmann acknowledged this mythology as an outer sign of an inner existential event. It was never made clear, however, how something like that could even be possible.

At any rate, Bonhoeffer took a stand for Bultmann in the controversy surrounding this essay. "I take great delight in the new Bultmann issue. Again and again, I am impressed by the intellectual honesty of his works."[3] It made Bonhoeffer angry that many people in the Confessing Church wanted to dismiss Bultmann's position as heretical and thereby cut off discussion about it. Bonhoeffer sent this essay as well as Bultmann's commentary on the Gospel of John to his students, who by this time had been drafted or were already at the front. In a letter to the theologian Ernst Wolff, Bonhoeffer wrote: "He dared to say what many people repress within themselves (and I include myself here) without having overcome it. In doing so, he performed a service to intellectual uprightness and honesty."[4] Thus Bonhoeffer took a stand for Bultmann because he desired an open discussion of repressed problems within the theology of the Confessing Church. But there is confusion surrounding an essential point here. Bonhoeffer advocated open discussion, but he did not agree with Bultmann himself: "I am one of those who welcomed his essay—not because I agree with it."[5]

Before we can make a judgment as to Bonhoeffer's real stand on the issue of so-called scientific historical criticism it must be noted that it is other theologians who forced Bonhoeffer's theology completely into the paradigm of the modern-analytical understanding of time and space. Bonhoeffer's statements about mankind come of age, about the "working hypothesis of God," about encountering God not in transcendence, but in our neighbor—theologians took all such statements as a sign that Bonhoeffer felt completely indebted to modern thought and not only accepted but championed the cause of demythologization in the Bultmannian sense. East German theologian Hanfried Müller went so far as to depict Bonhoeffer as the theologian who drew the farthest-reaching conclusions from Bultmann's theology.[6]

3. Letter of March 24, 1942 (*GS*, 3:45–46).
4. Ibid.
5. Ibid.
6. H. Müller, *Von der Kirche zur Welt. Ein Beitrag zu der Beziehung des Wortes Gottes auf die societas in Dietrich Bonhoeffers theologischer Entwicklung,* 2d ed., 1966.

And John A. T. Robinson, the man who popularized Bonhoeffer's theology more than anyone else, put forward the theme in his book *Honest to God* that there was not only no room for God in the inn in Bethlehem, but that there is also no room for God in the universe or in any other world outside of this universe. The Bonhoeffer who was against all metaphysics in theology was also, according to Robinson, the Bonhoeffer who rejected any notion of "above" and "below," or of heavenly reality above earthly reality. Robinson maintained that Bonhoeffer was the great denier of all "supernaturalism," and thereby the theologian who allowed God to be completely absorbed in and contained by this one physical world.

When weighing such assessments of Bonhoeffer's position, however, one must keep in mind that then as now, especially in Germany, official academic theology was completely committed to historical criticism. That was the case from Adolf Schlatter to Rudolf Bultmann. In principle it made no difference. The question was not *whether* historical criticism was applied, but *how* and *how much*. The only question that arose was which theory or hypothesis one should go by in analyzing or attempting to understand biblical passages. To a greater or lesser degree, historical criticism was accepted by all professional theologians in the Protestant Church. That was the case in the Third Reich even in the Confessing Church.

In this more or less radical critique of the Bible, biblical passages were analytically questioned according to a "scientific method." The historian approached biblical texts just as a chemist would analyze the material in his laboratory, with the goal of analyzing how the respective texts were put together from any number of hypothetically assumed original sources. Once the sources had been adequately "analyzed," they were put back together with a hypothesis or comprehensive theory according to a current view of history. In this new context of meaning, one came to an understanding of each biblical text that was completely different from the original understanding.[7]

Well-known examples of this are the so-called documentary hypothesis of the Pentateuch, the five books of Moses,[8] and the anal-

---

7. On this point, see my examination of the analytical-critical method in the chapter "Technik und Wahrheit" in *Provozierte Theologie in technischer Welt*, pp. 59ff.

8. On the dubiousness of Pentateuch criticism, see Samuel Külling, *Zur Datierung der "Genesis-P-Stücke,"* 1964, particularly the chapter on Genesis 17.

ysis of the Synoptic Gospels (Mark, Matthew, and Luke). In each case, the texts were analytically broken up in order to arrive at the sources supposedly lying behind them. Then the Bible was reexplained and reinterpreted according to a new synthesis. As for the scientific rigor of these procedures, one is bound to say that they remained theories and hypotheses whose application never resulted in soundly verified results. Thus, in the narrow sense, these theories and hypotheses cannot be judged as scientific according to the modern understanding of science. Apart from that the question arises whether the presuppositions of historical criticism of the Bible, namely, the paradigm of the analytic-synthetic view of science, is a generally valid paradigm or a temporally conditioned one leading to an intellectual dead-end. Modern scientific theory assumes the temporal conditionality of such scientific systems, though present-day theology holds tight to the old view.

One wonders whether or to what extent the Bible is still God's Word when it is held as a virtual prisoner to such a paradigm, especially when this paradigm consists of a web of scientific-analytic methods that are themselves temporally conditioned. Bonhoeffer once expressed his view of the matter as follows:

> Of course, one can also read the Bible just like one reads every other book, applying textual criticism, etc. There is nothing at all to be said against this. Yet that is not the way to open up the essence of the Bible, but only its surface characteristics. Just as we do not grasp the word of a person whom we love by dissecting it; just as we simply accept such a word, just as that word may stay with us for days simply because it is the word of that person whom we love; just as the person who said the word becomes more and more accessible to us the more we "ponder [this word] in our heart" like Mary [Lk 2:19]; that is how we should deal with the Word of the Bible. We will find delight in the Bible only if we dare to be drawn into the Bible as if in it, the God who loves us and does not want to leave us alone with our questions were really talking to us.[9]

By this Bonhoeffer means that we should read the Bible as if historical criticism did not exist—*si criticus non daretur.* Bonhoeffer thereby

9. *GS*, 3:27.

admits that historical criticism has a crippling effect on biblical interpretation, making correct understanding of the Bible difficult if not
impossible. For Bonhoeffer, historical criticism became a more or less
necessary evil. Rainer Mayer interprets Bonhoeffer's position correctly: "Critical exegesis stands outside of 'being in Christ.' It can be
practiced by unbelievers as well as believers and does not yield anything decisive in the search for the truth of the Scriptures."[10] Mayer
reminds us that for Bonhoeffer as well as for Karl Barth human understanding may never be allowed to bring us into dependence on human
beings. Thus on the one hand we observe in Bonhoeffer a turning
away from historical criticism. On the other hand, however, we see
that he came to terms with it: "At every step along the way we have to
deal with the problematic state of affairs in which sermons must
explore the Word, when philological and historical work conclude
that Jesus never spoke the Word in the way that Scripture records."[11]
Here we must interrupt with some questions: How does one really
know that Jesus did not say this or that word? Is not the amount of
verifiable knowledge that has been attained through historical criticism grossly overestimated? Bonhoeffer, completely within the trend
of the theology of his time, rejected the notion of verbal inspiration.
He did not believe that every word of holy Scripture as it appears in
the original text was inspired by God. The doctrine of verbal inspiration was for Bonhoeffer a "bad surrogate for the resurrection."[12]
According to Bonhoeffer, the Resurrected One speaks even through
the words of the Bible that he himself did not speak when he was on
earth in human form. Thus Bonhoeffer did participate in the schizo-
phrenia of modern theology, which on the one hand analyzes the Bible
critically but on the other hand wants that which has been critically
analyzed to remain the Word of God: "The Bible remains a book
among other books. One has to be prepared to accept the disguising
effect of history and therefore the path of historical criticism."[13]

In line with this "acceptance," Bonhoeffer called the virgin birth a
hypothesis: "It is both historical and dogmatic. The biblical witness

10. Mayer, *Christuswirklichkeit*, p. 136.
11. Thus in the lecture course on Christology in the summer semester of 1933 Bonhoeffer
saw the relativity of historical investigation: "from history there is no way to absoluteness" (*GS*,
3:204ff.).
12. Ibid.
13. Ibid.

about it is uncertain. . . . The doctrine of the virgin birth is meant to express the incarnation of God, and not merely the fact of him who was incarnated. But does not this doctrine miss precisely the crucial point of incarnation, namely, by not corresponding completely to how all human beings come into existence?"[14]

Thus Bonhoeffer is also an example of how one can very well go from historical criticism of the Bible to criticism of biblical content—in this case of the virgin birth. Many theologians at that time argued that the biblical testimony to the virgin birth was an attempt to explain mythologically the real incarnation of God. This was Bonhoeffer's opinion in his Christology seminar of the summer semester of 1933. Here we must remember that even conservative theologians such as Paul Althaus and Karl Heim shared the same opinion. This contrasted with Barth's view. In his lectures at Utrecht in 1934,[15] he fully affirmed the theological meaning and significance of the virgin birth.

Bonhoeffer also counted the "empty grave" as one of the historical uncertainties. His comment in the Christology seminar of 1933 ran: "Empty or not empty; it remains an annoyance that we will never be certain of the historicity of the empty grave."[16] However, Bonhoeffer formulated it differently in 1940 in a "Theologischer Brief über die Auferstehung."[17] Here he asserted that the empty grave may be historically uncertain to the world, but for faith it is the necessary and historically certified sign of God in the history of mankind.

It is totally clear that Bonhoeffer did not escape the captivity of so-called historical criticism. He himself asserted, "None of us can go

14. *GS*, 3:234.

15. Published in *Credo*, 1938. Later, Barth expressed it similarly in *Dogmatik im Grundriß*, 1947. Feminists will certainly find it difficult to follow Barth's interpretation of the virgin birth when he writes (p. 114): "God did not choose man in his pride and in his intrepidity, but in his weakness and humility; not in his historical role, but in the weakness of his nature as it is represented in the woman." For Barth it was very clear "that when one wanted to flee from this miracle there was always a theology at work that in fact no longer understood and appreciated the mystery, but that tried to conjure away the mystery of the unity of God and man in Jesus Christ, the mystery of the free grace of God. And on the other hand: wherever this mystery has been understood and every attempt of natural theology has been avoided because it was not needed, that is where the miracle was acknowledged thankfully and joyfully. It became so to speak inwardly necessary at that point."

16. *GS*, 3:241.

17. On this point, see the more precise references in Rothuizen, *Aristocratisch Christendom*, p. 236.

back again to the precritical period."[18] Bonhoeffer's biographer
Bethge sums it up as follows: "Bonhoeffer identifies with all of the
results of the research of the time, as he heard them from Harnack and
read of them in Bultmann."[19]

Was Bonhoeffer in the final analysis a modernist theologian after
all? Or can we find in Bonhoeffer the beginning, the very substantial
initial stages, toward the breaking up of this modernist system?
Could Bonhoeffer be comparable to Moses, who led God's people to
the Jordan but never crossed over into the promised land himself—
the land of freedom from the Egyptian darkness of so-called historical
criticism?

Bonhoeffer and Modern Biblical Criticism

Bonhoeffer did rattle the prison bars of historical-critical exegesis,
with weighty consequences. The relativity of the paradigm in which
historical-critical theology is housed became clear to Bonhoeffer.
Many of his statements substantiate this. Two statements are especially
significant in this regard: "But wherever the question of present application becomes a theme of theology, that is where we can be certain
that the matter has already been betrayed and sold down the river."[20]
And the other statement: "The differentiation between eternal and
temporal, chance and necessity in the Bible is fundamentally false."[21]

The logical consequence of historical-critical theology is the
resolve to differentiate between past and present elements in the Bible;
between what is once and for all out-dated (because it no longer fits a
modern view of the world) and what has eternal significance. Theology thus possesses virtual papal authority to judge what in the Bible
is significant for our time and what is not. The theologian places his
judgment above the Word of God. Bonhoeffer rejected precisely this
possibility as fundamentally false, as both of the statements quoted
above show unequivocally. The theologian is not allowed to take upon
himself the authority to decide about the Bible—that was and
remained Bonhoeffer's opinion.

18. Bethge, *Bonhoeffer*, p. 109.
19. Ibid., p. 150.
20. *GS*, 3:305.
21. *GS*, 3:311. See also Mayer, *Christuswirklichkeit*, p. 139.

In 1936 a paper written by Bonhoeffer became the target of a barrage of criticism from the historical-critical school. The paper was about the rebuilding of Jerusalem according to Ezra and Nehemiah.[22] These books of the Old Testament maintain that believers are not allowed to rebuild Jerusalem with the help of those who have fallen away from the faith of the fathers and become apostate. Bonhoeffer took this statement of the Old Testament as valid for his time: the Confessing Church was forbidden to work together with the German-Christian heretics in any way, shape, or form. The Confessing believers had to go their way without any compromise whatsoever with the teachers of heresy. Bonhoeffer viewed these Old Testament passages as having immediate significance for his time.

His theological colleagues saw it differently. The protest of the historical-critical school went so far as to accuse Bonhoeffer of being unscholarly. The statements about Ezra and Nehemiah, they insisted, had to be understood in the context of their own historical situation and could not be applied to the present. That means: historical criticism viewed statements that Bonhoeffer wanted to make relevant to his time as relative statements. They had their own significance only in their original historical context and were not applicable as God's Word to the present day.

But this way of dealing with the Old Testament was not the only thing that reaped criticism for Bonhoeffer. He was also criticized for the way he presented the Gospel of Matthew in his book *The Cost of Discipleship*. In the postscript to the original German edition, Bethge writes: "Critical exegetes found fault with Bonhoeffer's naive biblicism. Bonhoeffer actually did not worry about differentiating between the Words of Christ and the words of Matthew."[23] So Bonhoeffer was accused of accepting the Sermon on the Mount as the Word of Jesus and of not concerning himself with any "Jewish-Christian redactions" that may have been postulated by "historical criticism." He was reproached for not applying any kind of dissections or relativizations

---

22. *GS*, 4:321ff. On this point, T. R. Peters writes in *Die Präsenz des Politischen in der Theologie Dietrich Bonhoeffers*, 1976, p. 54: "Almost every one of the statements of his biblical interpretation that are in this sense central can be unhinged merely through historical textual criticism." Thus Bonhoeffer now stands in the same line of fire with the much reviled "fundamentalists" or "evangelicals."

23. See the postscript to the original German edition of *Cost of Discipleship*, pp. 299ff.

or any sort of source criticism. Bonhoeffer very "naively," it was charged, accepted the Sermon on the Mount recorded in Matthew as the word of Jesus. Thus Bonhoeffer had ignored historical criticism to a culpable extent. According to the judgment of "historical criticism" Bonhoeffer's handling of the Old Testament was even worse. For Bonhoeffer the Old Testament was a testimony to Christ. Therefore Bonhoeffer could pray the Psalter as a Christian. He could even pray the deprecatory psalms, because in those psalms he heard Christ as the judge of the world. And he could also pray the psalms of innocence that every historical-critical Old Testament scholar had relativized and disqualified as expressions of late Jewish pharisaical piety. For Bonhoeffer, these psalms of innocence represented the prayers of the congregations who had experienced forgiveness in Christ. In all of this Bonhoeffer affirmed what historical-critical investigation had declared impossible. Thus one reads in the *Theologische Realenzyklopädie* that Bonhoeffer affirmed to the end an "almost antimodern biblical foundation."[24]

But it is not the case that Bonhoeffer only dealt with the Bible that way on a practical level, so to speak. He saw the dangers of a relativizing, selective biblical criticism: "We prefer our thoughts to the thoughts of the Bible. We no longer take the Bible seriously. We no longer read the Bible against ourselves, but only for ourselves."

Bonhoeffer did not create historical criticism. He accepted it unwillingly as a necessity he thought was unavoidable. Nevertheless, he never drew the conclusions that should have arisen inescapably from the application of the historical-critical method. He should have dismissed the deprecatory psalms as historically conditioned expressions of Jewish piety (as even the evangelical evangelist Gerhard Bergmann advocated).[25] By the same token, Bonhoeffer should have relativized the Sermon on the Mount as an eschatological ethics shaped by Jesus' mistaken belief that the end of the world was imminent. Bonhoeffer accepted the historical-critical paradigm, but he did

---

24. See *Theologische Realenzyklopädie*, 1981, 7:59—the article on Bonhoeffer by Gerhard Krause.

25. G. Bergmann, *Alarm um die Bibel*, 1963, p. 100. While according to an evangelical theologian the deprecatory psalms are in the Bible only "to show the sinful nature of man," the historical-critical Bonhoeffer saw in these psalms the judging word of the risen Christ. On this point, see Mayer, *Christuswirklichkeit*, p. 134.

not unreservedly endorse it. That is a beginning. It is certainly not the beginning of the end of the historical-critical paradigm, but it does set a process in motion which ultimately questions the absolute validity of the historical-critical paradigm of biblical criticism.

Bonhoeffer's Rejection of Theological Modernism

From prison Bonhoeffer wrote the following about the problem of Bultmann: "My view of it today would be, not that he went 'too far,' as most people thought, but that he didn't go far enough. . . . The New Testament is not a mythological clothing of a universal truth; this mythology (resurrection etc.) is the thing itself."[26]

Mayer interprets this statement as follows:

> On the one hand, Bultmann went too far, because the mythology of the New Testament cannot be separated from the thing itself. On the other hand he was not radical enough, because he consciously refrained from placing all of world reality under God's Lordship. One can "not separate God and miracles from each other [in Bultmann's opinion], but one must interpret and proclaim both nonreligiously." In its partiality, the program of demythologization is religious.[27]

What Mayer means is that it is impossible, according to Bonhoeffer, to restrict the message of the New Testament to particular existential experiences—especially to experiences at the limits of existence. Bultmann is still religious in that he attempts this reduction to particular spheres of experience. He assigns a place to biblical revelation. But for Bonhoeffer the basic issue is that Christ is the Lord of the whole world, and that the whole creation is included in his suffering and death, in his powerlessness and resurrection. Bultmann did not grasp this expanse of biblical witness. He did not recognize that to encounter God in existential experiences of one's limits was different from being completely included in the salvation event of Christ, a cosmic event that is not experienced through a religious act but in the totality of being human and of being a part of the cosmos.

26. *Letters and Papers from Prison*, pp. 285, 329.
27. Mayer, *Christuswirklichkeit*, p. 254.

But Bonhoeffer did not criticize only Bultmann's modernism. In a letter of June 8, 1944, Bonhoeffer condemned liberalism as such: "The weakness of liberal theology was that it conceded to the world the right to determine Christ's place in the world."[28] We encounter here again the central point of Bonhoeffer's critique of theology: Christ must not be limited to a role, a religious role, an ethical or moral realm of conscience. In this Bonhoeffer was in complete agreement with the second thesis of the Barmen Declaration (1934): "We reject the false doctrine that there are spheres of our life in which we belong not to Jesus Christ, but to other lords; spheres in which we do not need justification and sanctification through Him." By assigning a role to Christ, liberal theology assured the church a place in the world, but at the price of a "comparatively easy terms of peace."[29]

Bonhoeffer's critique of modernism is also a critique of Paul Tillich's theology. Tillich's theology is, as it were, the other face of liberal theology. While liberal theology strives for a place in the world in order to survive, Tillichian theology attempts a religious transfiguration of the whole world. To this Bonhoeffer replied: "Tillich set out to interpret the evolution of the world (against its will) in a religious sense— to give it its shape through religion. That was very brave of him, but the world unseated him and went on by itself."[30] Thus: it is not a matter of assuring "Christianity" a place in the world so that it survives. Neither is it a matter of interpreting the world as such in a Christian religious way. Both cases deny the Bonhoefferian dialectic of Christ as Lord of the world in tension with the world.

Bonhoeffer did not desire to understand the world one-dimensionally as "comprehensible." He saw creation as of God, against God, but yet then again responsive to God. He saw it as creation under the cross, under powerlessness, but then in the future as creation in the resurrection. For Bonhoeffer, the world was integrated in the drama of Christ. He understood this world Christ-mystically.

In early 1986 a university student in Münster, Germany, Mario Depka von Prondzinski, polled ten West German university theology faculties. A student of both theology and medicine, Prondzinski asked

28. *Letters and Papers from Prison*, p. 327.
29. Ibid.
30. Ibid.

whether he would be allowed to pursue theological studies outside the paradigm of the historical-critical method. The answer was uniformly negative. We see, then, that it remains impossible in the Federal Republic of Germany to study theology "without obligatory application of historical-critical research."[31]

Historical-critical research is the sacred cow of official church policy in German-speaking Protestantism. Gerhard von Rath once described an encounter with Bonhoeffer in the 1930s: "Much later—at that time I was a professor in Jena—he suddenly appeared in one of my lecture classes. In this class period I was explaining Psalm 51, and discussed the conclusion of the psalm that had been added to it later. On the way home we talked about the right and the duty of historical-critical scholarship, which I was passionately defending at the time against a countercurrent arising in the struggle between the church and the state. I did not understand him at all, and we argued. Today I would probably understand better what he was concerned about, without giving up what I was concerned about at the time."[32] The trends calling historical criticism into question that von Rath mentions never took hold in the Confessing Church. The selective, reductionistic, and relativistic critique of biblical revelation continued to be accepted within the Confessing Church. However, von Rath's recollections show that Bonhoeffer challenged this position all alone, so alone that von Rath could not even understand him at all at the time. Although it is well known today that the history of historical-critical scholarship (see, for example, Albert Schweitzer's *The Quest of the Historical Jesus*) actually refutes historical criticism, because one can easily uncover its alternating motivations, theologians act as if historical criticism were the most problem-free scholarly method in the whole world. At the same time it is well known that Kantian or Hegelian philosophy provides the presuppositions for historical criticism; that, for example, Hegel's scheme of evolution was applied to the origin of the Old Testament, especially the Pentateuch, and that precisely this scheme of evolution has been rendered extremely questionable by archaeological discoveries, as Samuel Külling has shown in one of his seminal works.[33]

31. Informationdienst der Evangelischen Allianz (*idea*) 28 (1986).
32. In *Begegnung mit Dietrich Bonhoeffer*, 1964, p. 141.
33. Samuel Külling, rector of the FETA (Freie Evangelisch-Theologische Akademie) of Basel, *Zur Datierung*.

When Bonhoeffer, in his own way, disregarded the relativization of Old Testament passages that had been undertaken by "historical criticism," he met resistance from within his own ranks. Helmut Gollwitzer recalls:

> Without a doubt, we were in danger of falling into a fundamentalism that would simply sweep away the work of historical-critical scholarship. . . . The critical work of both Schlatter and Baumgärtel as well as of Gerhard von Rath engaged us forcefully, but we in our youthful arrogance considered it to be an affair of the older generation, which was unable to overcome its liberal and rationalist premises. Our fundamentalism seemed to us to be the wave of the future. Because of that, Dietrich Bonhoeffer found a message that spoke to our situation in his interpretations of Old Testament passages, but in my opinion he was undoubtedly incorrect in the theological grounds by which he thought he could take the Christian significance of, say, the books of Ezra and Nehemiah directly out of the text while ignoring their historicity.[34]

This recollection of Gollwitzer makes it clear that Bonhoeffer argued "fundamentalistically" to his contemporaries at the time, and that he was strongly determined to overcome the outdated rationalist premises of liberal theology. In that sense, Bonhoeffer was a stranger within the historical-critical school. He still is today, as his concepts "coming of age," "religionless," and "unmetaphysical" are misunderstood as affirmations of the historical-critical method with its one-dimensional view of reality. But at no time did Bonhoeffer give up his protest against historical-critical scholarship. He appealed to such theologians as Kohlbrügge and F. A. Vilmar. At the time, he did not have the archaeological findings that we now have to expose purely scientifically the dubiousness of historical criticism.

In regard to Kohlbrügge's "fundamentalist" view of the Old Testament Bonhoeffer said: "Yes, that is how we should be able to adhere to the Word!" Wilhelm Rott remembers:

> Kohlbrügge's typological interpretation of the Old Testament attracts [Bonhoeffer]. He accepts historical-critical scholarship as a given, but for him it is an incursion, even an impediment. He says, "The profes-

---

34. Albrecht Schönherr et al., *Begegnungen*, p. 112.

sors who accuse me of not being scientific because of my papers on Old Testament passages [which were related to the struggle between the church and the state] forget that there was genuine biblical interpretation going on before the still very young historical-critical and history of religion research.'" . . . Bonhoeffer wanted by any means to bring out what the texts had to say to our present-day situation (even the so-called deprecatory psalms), and to accomplish that he would use any help or interpretation necessary. Thus we held Vilmar's *Collegium biblicum* in honor and possibly used it more often than Lietzmann's *Handbücher zum Neuen Testament*.[35]

So historical-critical scholarship was simply an "incursion" for Bonhoeffer. The historical-critical method did not keep him from placing himself completely under the Word. He did this by simply disregarding this method. The task of theology today, if it were truly to follow in Bonhoeffer's footsteps, would be to take his attempt to escape the captivity to this method to its logical conclusion—and do away with the historical-critical method once and for all. Only in this way can the "reduction" of Christianity through the dismantling of God's Word be overcome.

35. Ibid.

12

Earth Without a Heaven?

Modern This-Worldly Theology and Bonhoeffer

Bonhoeffer's statements against a metaphysically misunderstood Christianity and his emphasis on the one worldly reality have been misconstrued in the sense that they have been taken to mean that no God exists outside of this physical world. Thus Robinson, the popularizer of Bonhoeffer's theology, said that the "metaphysical God" was slowly dying, that there was no above and below, but rather only the encounter with God in the depths, as Tillich expressed it: "you must forget everything traditional that you ever learned about God, perhaps even that word itself. For if you know that God means depth, you know much about him."[1] What does it mean to find God in the depths of existence? According to Tillich, a human being always encounters God where he is immediately affected, in the "ultimate concern." Thus God is no longer personal and actually existent. Rather, he is "the ground of our being," and that is the end of all supernaturalism. As Tillich once wrote: "The phrase *deus sive natura,* used by people like Scotus Erigena and Spinoza, does not say that God is identical with nature but that he is identical with the *natura naturans*—the creative nature, the creative ground of all natural objects."[2] And that

1. Robinson, *Honest to God*, p. 22.
2. Ibid., p. 31.

means, according to leftist interpreters of Bonhoeffer, the end of "theistic theology" once and for all.

But what stand did Bonhoeffer really take? Did he not say: "God is other-worldly in the middle of our life," or "the other-worldly is not infinite distance, it is our neighbor"?[3] If in Bonhoeffer's view being a Christian means being there for others, then does that not mean that God is only a symbol for encounter with other people and that belief in his existence as a person outside of this reality is illusory? Is God not then in the final analysis a symbol for interpersonal relationships, for social togetherness?

If the "religious act" is not the key, if "vaulting oneself up to God above" is not the key; if rather participating in the suffering of God in the world is the key, then does not Christian existence mean to participate in the suffering of the oppressed, in the social misery of the down-and-outers? Is not revolutionary engagement, in the Bonhoefferian sense of "being there for others," the essence of Christianity?

Without a doubt, there is an armada of theologians who understand Bonhoeffer in this way. For them, the Lord's Supper becomes enjoying a good meal with friends when the day's work is done. The worship service becomes a protest against social injustice or technocracy. Serving God for them is serving the world or society, or nowadays the environment. For them, things cannot become profane enough, because the sacred, the religious, the other-worldly is over and done with. For them, Bonhoeffer is the real church father of a real this-worldly theology. According to Robinson, for example, belief in a world beyond is an attempt to infuse infinity into the limited possibilities of human society. Because God is not a stopgap, because we encounter him in the midst of the world, therefore the principle of change must be the essence of God (as George Macleod writes in *Only One Way Left*).[4] Prayer becomes nothing more than trusting action toward a goal concerning this world. God himself becomes "hallowed worldliness" and "sacral secularity."

In this context we quote once again the decisive sentences from the letter of July 16, 1944, in which Bonhoeffer wrote:

3. For words to this effect see ibid., p. 76 (here the quotations of Bonhoeffer are in the context of Robinson's view of things). See also *Letters and Papers from Prison*, p. 381.

4. Ibid., p. 94.

God as a working hypothesis in morals, politics, or science, has been surmounted and abolished; and the same thing has happened in philosophy and religion (Feuerbach!) For the sake of intellectual honesty, that working hypothesis should be dropped, or as far as possible eliminated. A scientist or physician who sets out to edify is a hybrid.

Anxious souls will ask what room there is left for God now; and as they know of no answer to the question, they condemn the whole development that has brought them to such straits. I wrote to you before about the various emergency exits that have been contrived; and we ought to add to them the *salto mortale* [death-leap] back into the Middle Ages. But the principle of the Middle Ages is heteronomy in the form of clericalism; a return to that can be a counsel of despair, and it would be at the cost of intellectual honesty. It's a dream that reminds one of the song *O wüsst' ich doch den Weg zurück, den weiten Weg ins Kinderland* [Oh, if only I knew the way back, the broad path back to the world of childhood.] There is no such way—at any rate not if it means deliberately abandoning our mental integrity; the only way is that of Matt. 18.3, i.e. through repentance, through *ultimate* honesty.[5]

Bonhoeffer as a Theologian of Transcendence

When Bonhoeffer emphasizes that God is not a "working hypothesis," he does not at all mean that God himself is a hypothesis. God is not a working hypothesis because that would mean he is only needed as a hypothesis for the paradigm of an only relatively valid, modern way of understanding reality. When Bonhoeffer said that God can no longer serve as a "stopgap," he said it because premodern gaps in knowledge no longer exist as they did earlier. What is necessary now is that "we are to find God in what we know."[6] Bonhoeffer expressly emphasizes: "This world must not be prematurely written off."[7] After all, God is not a God who is separated from this world and exiled to the next. The rejection of "metaphysical faith in God" does not at all entail that God does not exist. On August 10 and 14, 1944, Bonhoeffer still wrote: "But all the time God still reigns in heaven. . . . God does not give us everything we want, but he does fulfil all his promises, i.e., he remains the Lord of the earth, he preserves his church, constantly

5. *Letters and Papers from Prison*, p. 360.
6. Ibid., p. 311.
7. Ibid., p. 337.

renewing our faith and not laying on us more than we can bear, gladdening us with his nearness and help, hearing our prayers, and leading us along the best and straightest paths to himself."[8] Clearly, the above passage flowed from immediate, personal encounter with the actually existing God who promises "that nothing is then impossible for us, because all things are possible with God; that no earthly power can touch us without his will."[9] That is testimony to a God who works in this world and whom we therefore can encounter in this world as the one who transcends this world.

It is always and only in his revelation, in the "self-witness of the living God," that we encounter this personal God directly. What was already thought through in *Akt und Sein* remains valid: "God is the superworldly reality that transcends consciousness. He is the Creator and Lord. This proposition is the unconditional requirement of Christian theology."[10] Here Mayer writes: "This proves that those who monistically dissolve Bonhoeffer's concept of transcendence and make it an innerworldly transcendence are wrong."[11] Bethge also acknowledges unequivocally that Bonhoeffer did not disregard transcendence. Bonhoeffer simply objected to metaphysics as an "elongation of the world." He was against metaphysics as a superstructure over this world and in the image of this world. He objected to the fact that God's otherness becomes boxed in by metaphysical notions and concepts. In this sense, he wanted to have nothing to do with supernaturalism. This metaphysically boxed-in God, who is called forth as a deus ex machina whenever needed, is the God of "pious godlessness." Atheism is correct in its opposition to this Christian-religiously dressed godlessness. Atheism in this role acts as "godlessness full of promise," exposing the idols of metaphysics as false gods.

Bonhoeffer's Theology of Tension

The proposition that "the transcendent is . . . the neighbor who is within reach"[12] means: precisely because Christ came into the world and because the kingdom of God has already begun in him, Christ

8. Ibid., pp. 384, 387.
9. Taken from one of Bonhoeffer's last letters, August 21, 1944, in ibid., p. 391.
10. *GS*, 3:107.
11. Mayer, *Christuswirklichkeit*, p. 95.
12. *Letters and Papers from Prison*, p. 381.

acts upon people and through people in the world for the world. In a meditation on Psalm 119, Bonhoeffer wrote: "Because I am nothing but a guest on earth, without rights, without a foothold, without certainty; because God has made me so weak and insignificant . . ."[13] These sentences say that that which is transcendent is not at our disposal in this world, that the transcendent is not realized on earth, that the Christian can only encounter it intermittently. Being in Christ is not a having, but a becoming. The neighbor who is within reach at any given time is transcendent only because Christ has brought the power of his kingdom into this world: "I do not have a firm foothold through people nor through things. As a guest I am subject to the laws of the inn."[14] Bonhoeffer wrote these sentences at the beginning of the war, at a time when his thought had fully matured.

The affirmation of the earth and being a stranger on earth—once again we note the dialectical thought present in Bonhoeffer's tension-filled life. In the lecture "Dein Reich" he said: "Become weak in the world and let God be Lord." But then he also said: "Whoever flees the world will not find God. . . . Whoever flees the world in order to find God finds only himself." Neither neurotic preoccupation with this world nor flight from this world, but rather life in tension—the kingdom of God as present yet future—this is the theme of Bonhoeffer's theology. He thereby excluded the utopian dream of a Christianization of the world. A statement about the endtimes makes this fully clear: "Because the kingdom of God is to be in eternity, God will create a new heaven and a new earth. But it will really be a new earth."[15] This reveals the eschatological dimension of Bonhoeffer's theology. To live in this world means to be challenged to live with the many tasks, questions, successes, failures, perplexities. "In so doing we throw ourselves completely into the arms of God, taking seriously not our own sufferings, but those of God in the world—watching with Christ in Gethsemane. That, I think is faith; that is *metanoia* [repentance]; and that is how one becomes a man and a Christian."[16] For we may not forget that to be a Christian means to take part in the suffering of Christ in this world and to take part in the world itself, in order to

---

13. *GS*, 4:539.
14. *GS*, 4:538.
15. Lecture in Potsdam, "Dein Reich komme," November 19, 1932, in *GS*, 3:284.
16. *Letters and Papers from Prison*, p. 370.

overcome the world. To live in the kingdom of God that has already begun means to be a part of the reality of Christ in this world. The God into whose arms one throws oneself is not the God "of the depths" as Tillich thought. Rather, he stands over against this world, and the Christian experiences his reality through personal encounter with this God through the Word. The question of transcendence is a who-question. As it is expressed in *Akt und Sein*, "The question of the who is the question of transcendence." Thus one can infer that the question of transcendence is the person-question.

An example may help clarify this chapter's thrust. When performing an operation on the heart, a surgeon will work within the tangle of instruments and apparatus "as if there were no God." After all, while operating and fully engaged in the task at hand he will not be holding a prayer meeting but rather fully exerting his human understanding in accordance with all of his knowledge and reason. Under the pressure of responsibility he is condemned to the free action of mankind come of age. The technological man does not invoke any ghosts or demons in his technological actions, and he should not long to return to magic instead of medicine, chemistry, or physics, or to have the medicine man instead of the doctor. Wherever we have knowlege, God is in one sense out of the picture for us(!) But the paradoxical truth for Bonhoeffer is that the more we are thrown back upon our having come of age and the less we "use" God as a magical, religious working hypothesis, the more "he is with us and helps us." The painful experience of being forsaken by God brings us the joyful experience of being near to God so "that no earthly power can touch us without his will."[17] Christian existence does not get beyond this paradox posed by Bonhoeffer.

17. Ibid., p. 391.

13

Bonhoeffer's Theology of Revelation

Revelation and Science

"Wisdom and folly are not ethically indifferent, as Neo-Protestant motive-ethics would have it."[1] In this sentence of Bonhoeffer lies a critique of the Neo-Kantian, liberal Protestant division of science and ethos. The inner, moral distinction between good and evil belonged to the sphere of ethos. The knowledge of the world through the laws of nature was purely secular according to Neo-Kantian liberal theology. It was impartial and was accepted as absolute—but at the same time also outside of the sphere of biblical revelation.

In 1935 Bonhoeffer wrote in his essay "Die bekennende Kirche und die Ökumene" that the church "cannot accept any confessionally neutral sphere."[2] Here the view of the Barmen Declaration that "[there are no] spheres of our life in which we belong not to Jesus Christ but to other Lords" is expressed again. All knowledge stands between good and evil. All knowledge, even the so-called profane knowledge of the natural sciences, has to do in the final analysis with God's reality. And that is precisely why God is not a stopgap. From the biblical point of view it is impossible to assign God a place outside of the limits of knowledge, a place that he leaves now and then in order to work his

1. *Letters and Papers from Prison*, p. 10.
2. *GS*, 1:243.

miracles by breaking natural laws. On this point, Hans Küng's views echo those of Bonhoeffer: "In the Old Testament as well, there is no distinction between miracles that correspond to the laws of nature and miracles that break the laws of nature; every event through which Yahweh reveals his power is considered a miracle, a sign, a great and mighty deed of Yahweh. God, the source and creator, is at work everywhere. Human beings can experience miracles anywhere. . . . In the language of the Bible, a miracle (sign) does not mean a breaching of natural laws through immediate divine intervention, but rather a miracle means everything that brings forth awe in human beings, including creation and preservation of the world and humankind itself."[3]

And because the object of human knowledge is always God's reality, mistaken knowledge is not only a mistake, but also something for which human beings are culpable.

Already at the end of the 1920s and then of course at the beginning of the 1930s, it became clear to Bonhoeffer that the modern view of the world, the classical mechanical understanding of nature, was out of date. He was very familiar with the findings of relativity theory, and above all of quantum theory. In 1932, in a lecture at Union Theological Seminary in New York entitled "The Theology of Crisis and Its Attitude Toward Philosophy and Science,"[4] Bonhoeffer described Barth's position that our "knowledge" of reality is always only "news" about reality. Our knowledge never grasps being itself. Bonhoeffer maintained energetically that our categories are never identical with reality. For this reason, he ruled out all naive views of science. Thus, for Bonhoeffer there is no autonomous, profane science and no ultimate knowledge of reality through science. His view of science was always affirming and critical at the same time. As Mayer summarizes: "Bonhoeffer characterizes the subjection of theology to the monistic-empirical concept of science as theology's grossest aberration. Relativity theory and quantum theory have long since shown that the identity of the categorical system and reality may no longer naively be assumed. Therefore, theology may not appeal to this view of science as system or as doctrine."[5]

3. Hans Küng, *Existiert Gott?* 1978, p. 711.
4. GS, 3:124.
5. Mayer, *Christuswirklichkeit*, p. 88. See also idem, "Theologie und Glaube. Recht und Grenze des Theol. Systems nach D. Bonhoeffer," *Evangelische Theologie* 31 (1971): 51–58.

In succession to Barth's theology, Bonhoeffer understood himself as a theologian of revelation. In his inaugural thesis *Akt und Sein*, which was completed in 1930, he wrote: "The direction of theological thought goes from God to reality, not from reality to God."[6] Because it is God's way to move toward human beings, because we encounter God only in obedience to his Word, and because ultimately all human thought is darkened by sin, there can be no all-encompassing scientific system that could act as the final and conclusive interpretation of all being: "This means however that every system devised by man, who does not reside eternally in truth, is an invalid system and must be broken."[7]

Of course, for Bonhoeffer there was no way from nature to the knowledge of God. Precisely because of that he had to rule out God's being a "stopgap" for human knowledge. God as a stopgap would mean that there are still some gaps in natural man's path to knowledge within which God would be allowed a right for his activity. Naturally, a theology of revelation has to say a clear "No!" to this. For only through revelation by the Word, only through encounter with Christ, is there encounter with God. "Theology may be practiced only where the living person of Christ himself is present. . . . Theology is positive science, because it possesses a given object, namely, the spoken Word of Christ in the church." The theologian contributes only "the pre-serving, ordering memory of these words."[8] Thus theology is nothing other than the explication of God's Word. And there are no standards that could be asserted in this reflection on the Word of God: "There is simply no reflection involved in the knowledge characteristic to faith. The question of the possibility of faith can be answered only through the reality of faith."[9]

Thus faith is the entirely unmediated turning to God. It cannot be derived from reflective thought nor based upon or explained by way of reflective thought. That is why, as Mayer correctly claims, "a natural ability to receive revelation [remains] totally impossible."[10]

Did Bonhoeffer hold to this position until the end? In a letter post-marked April 27, 1944, he wrote: "The question how there can be a

6. On this point, see the third main section of *Akt und Sein*, in *GS*, 3:81ff.
7. Ibid.
8. Ibid., p. 111.
9. Ibid., p. 112.
10. Mayer, *Christuswirklichkeit*, p. 279.

'natural piety' is at the same time the question of 'unconscious Christianity,' with which I'm more and more concerned. Lutheran dogmatists distinguished between a *fides directa* ['unmediated faith'] and a *fides reflexa* ['faith arrived at through conscious process']."[11]

But these thoughts are actually not at all new. Already in *Akt und Sein* Bonhoeffer quoted the Danish theologian Pontoppedan: "But there are many who have taken up Christ although they do not feel that they have taken him up. Nevertheless, these people are justified."[12] In other words, one can be seized by the reality of Christ without being aware of it, and without being able to verbalize this unconscious faith. After all, the light of Christ shines from out of the church to the outside world. This unconscious Christianity is not a natural Christianity in the sense that there might be a way to the truth other than through the reality of Christ. Rather, unconscious Christianity stands in the light of Christ and is hit by his light, even if the one who receives this light does not live within the confines of the church. Unconscious Christianity is above all possible as a phenomenon of human existence in the West, where Christ had taken form for centuries, in Bonhoeffer's view.

Moreover, the number of the elect is greater than the number of those who have the opportunity to hear God's Word. There is a Christianity that is not a Christianity *in reapse* (already realized), but a Christianity *in voto* (on the way) which will not be fulfilled until the end of time, just as Israel was chosen *in voto* although redemption will not be experienced *in reapse* until the end of time. Of course, Bonhoeffer's cosmic Christology plays a role in this line of thought. Because the entire reality of the world is already seized by the strength of Christ and ruled by it in spite of demonic resistance, this unconscious turning to Christ is possible.

The Logos of the Bible and the Logos of Science

God is free to reveal himself as he chooses. It was pleasing to God to reveal himself not in a stone, not in a color, not in an emotion, but in the Word: "For humankind's sake, Christ is present as the Word," said Bonhoeffer in his lecture course on Christology in the summer of

11. *Letters and Papers from Prison*, p. 373.
12. Mayer, *Christuswirklichkeit*, p. 280.

1933. "Since mankind has a logos, God encounters him in the Logos that speaks and is the Word itself."[13] The world came into being through the Word. Because the world came into being through the Logos, the world has a logical structure.

But the logos of the fallen, unredeemed world can no longer be the logos of the knowledge of God. For this logos of a world that is closing itself up within itself, Christ is the "Antilogos," which cannot be accepted by the old logos: "The old logos is judged by the transcendence of the person of Christ, and learns to comprehend its new relative standing—its limits and its necessity." Science must therefore be conscious of its limits. There can be science only because there is the Logos of God. But because the logos of this world is the imprisoned logos, the science of the world cannot recognize God. Thus, any highhandedness of science, any scientism, and above all any scientistic ideology is ruled out. However, in the light of the Antilogos, science becomes free: "As logology [human exercise of logos constantly corrected by Antilogos], Christology is that which makes any science possible at all."[14] Because the world is created in the Logos, the logic of science exists. That is why the cosmos is ordered. On the other hand, because the world is a fallen world, the logos of the world must find its redemption and liberation in the logos of Christ. Thus, the logos of the world is not to question theology. Rather, theology questions the logos of the world. Theology is not guided by the standards of secular science. Rather, secular science finds its limits and its meaning through theology.

So to state it once again: science does not call theology into question but vice versa. That means that theology brings even the so-called historical-critical method into question. How can revelation be the standard for science, if revelation is brought into question by the scientific discipline of historical-criticism? Can the biblical Word in its axiomatic infallibility be questioned by some hypothesis or theory that has the purpose of determining which part of the biblical revelation is myth (to be understood only relative to its historical context) and which part is kerygma (valid for all time)?

Thus science is always only the penultimate. The revelation of Christ is the ultimate. The penultimate of science must be seen and

13. *GS*, 3:172.
14. Ibid.

understood in the ultimate of revelation. On the other hand it is also true that revelation as the ultimate does not cancel out science as the penultimate; it rather liberates and redeems it. For its part, the penultimate in the light of the ultimate is significant for the ultimate. Any view other than this would be sectarianism and would lead to a splitting up of reality, which is exactly what Bonhoeffer unequivocally rejected. Bonhoeffer upholds *fides quarens intellectum* ["faith seeking understanding"], and not *credo, quia absurdum est* ["believe, because it is absurd"]. Grace does not cancel out nature, and theology does not cancel out science. Rather, nature and science are liberated and redeemed by grace and theology. However, this relation between the ultimate and the penultimate is not a peaceful coexistence. Science as the penultimate rebels against revelation as the ultimate, and revelation can be understood by theologians in such a way that its responsibility to science as penultimate is evaded. This is another case typical of Bonhoeffer's thought of a relation characterized by tension. It remains under the cross and the experience of powerlessness but also contains the promise of purification and thus the liberation of science.

Are Theology Students Theologians?

As a private tutor at the Friedrich-Wilhelm University in Berlin, and then especially as the leader of the seminary in Finkenwalde, Bonhoeffer gained much experience in dealing with students and pastors in training. In addition, he was a prominent spokesman in Adolf von Harnack's seminar for a time. He had insider's knowledge of the system of academic training at German theological schools. He knew the process of lecture classes, seminars, papers, theological examinations, and the like. However, he could not tolerate this type of training in the form he encountered it. He saw an abstraction from spiritual life in this way of training theology students. Here one must also keep in mind that in Germany every baptized person, every intellectually qualified nominal church member, can be admitted to the study of theology. No endorsement by a congregation is needed; at most there might be an official permission slip to study theology from a pastor. There were professors (like Adolf von Harnack) who had never held church office and had never in their lives preached a sermon.

Already in his lectures in the winter semester of 1931–32, Bonhoeffer bemoaned the lack of concreteness in theological education. He was frustrated by its abstractness and its lack of connection with reality: "Because of this [type of training] our sermons are so weak that they stick in the middle between general principles and concrete situations. The crisis of the church is always a crisis for the theological school as well. Unfortunately, as a rule, the theological schools are blind to this!"[15] Thus, Bonhoeffer's critique of the system of theological training he observed was not so very decisively connected to the infiltration of Nazi ideology into the theological schools and universities.

This is how one must understand Bonhoeffer's letter to Erwin Sutz of September 1934. At that time, Bonhoeffer was undecided whether he should remain in London or visit Gandhi in India in order to experience the "concretization" of Christianity: "All of the training of the new generation of theologians should take place at ecclesiastical or monastery schools where pure doctrine, the Sermon on the Mount, and worship are taken seriously. Unfortunately, none of the three are taken seriously in the university."[16] Thus, the interconnectedness of doctrine, learning, community, discipleship, prayer, and worship was decisive for Bonhoeffer. He hated the dualism of learning and living, doctrine and spiritual life. He rejected the "dry" anonymity of overcrowded lecture halls and the intellectual gamesmanship of seminars. Undoubtedly, Bonhoeffer was influenced in this area by the training of Anglican theologians, especially by the Anglican monasteries. It is just as certain that Bonhoeffer later no longer desired this type of retreat of theologians from worldliness. It is bitter to observe that to this very day nothing of that which Bonhoeffer wanted to change has changed. Especially since the many who do not want to change are only too eager to appeal to Bonhoeffer's theology.

From Immanence to Transcendence and Back: Bonhoeffer at Prayer

If one subscribes to the general religious view of prayer, then one would think that Bonhoeffer's rejection of the notion of a stopgap God, or deus ex machina, would rule out the possibility of prayer. If

15. *GS*, 5:227.
16. *GS*, 1:41ff.

an omnipotent God cannot "intervene" in life, then what purpose does prayer serve? Can God help, direct, save, heal if he is, as Bonhoeffer said, the powerless God? Could one not appeal to Bonhoeffer in saying with Robinson that prayer is to be understood "as penetrating through the world to God" in that we involve ourselves unconditionally in the world? Then we could understand prayer as involvement in the world out of the "sense of basic trust" in God. In this view, deep personal commitment to the world involves "confiding to another person out of love and without reservation" what moves us inwardly. George Macleod sees prayer as follows: "The Christian says his morning prayers with his appointment calendar and daily newspaper spread before the face of God." And because prayer "simply cannot be planned out" there remains only the free and spontaneous prayer of man come of age, which is determined in each situation by the kairos in the "ultimate concern" of man come of age.

Whoever "secularizes" prayer in this way has no right to appeal to Bonhoeffer. Throughout his life, he knew prayer as a request directly to God, even as a request for help in the concrete situations of his existence. Bonhoeffer even approved of prayer in situations of dire need. In January 1944, toward the end of his life, he wrote: "The whole history of the children of Israel consists of such cries for help. . . . it needs trouble to shake us up and drive us to prayer."[17] Thus, we are to pray not only when involved in the world, but also precisely when we can no longer find the strength to be involved: "I believe that God will give us all the strength we need to help us to resist in all time of distress. But he never gives it in advance, lest we should rely on ourselves and not on him alone."[18] Here once again we see the qualitative distinction between ourselves and the wholly other God who is near to us through his Word. There is no trace of horizontalism or "secularization of trust." In his "account of the year" at the beginning of 1943 Bonhoeffer wrote: "I believe that God is no timeless fate, but that he waits for and answers sincere prayers and responsible actions."[19] Thus, God answers prayer.[20] In one of his last letters, written in August 1944, Bonhoeffer wrote: "God does not give us everything we

17. *Letters and Papers from Prison*, p. 199.
18. Ibid., p. 11.
19. Ibid.
20. That God answers prayer was for Bonhoeffer not "stopgappery."

want, but he does fulfil all his promises, i.e., he remains the Lord of the earth, he preserves his church, constantly renewing our faith and not laying on us more than we can bear, gladdening us with his nearness and help, hearing our prayers, and leading us along the best and straightest paths to himself. By his faithfulness in doing this, God creates in us praise for himself."[21]

But this prayer is not instrumental prayer. It is not a means to an end. Prayer does not mean bringing God in to plug the gaps in one's life. Only those who live responsibly in discipleship to Christ can pray. Whoever takes part in the suffering of Christ in this world, whoever is included in the messianic birth pangs of the Christ-event, can and may pray: "Not even prayer affords direct access to the Father. Only through Jesus Christ can we find the Father in prayer. . . . We pray at his command, and to that word Christian prayer is always bound."[22]

Thus, prayer is not a conjuring up or a blackmail of God. It is not a work, and may therefore not be ostentatious. It is "nonpublic in every way."[23] Above all, the Christian is not to make himself a spectator of his own praying. Neither may prayer be misused as testimony, nor suggestively as indoctrination in order to get a troublesome brother to "pray along." Bonhoeffer certainly does not rule out prayer groups, "however clearly we may be aware of its dangers."[24] But above all, prayer should really be petition: "The child asks of the Father whom he knows."[25] Prayer is not subject to testing of its quality or its religious identity. Then the Christian would be a spectator of his own prayer and would make the fulfillment of his request dependent on the intensity of his praying. That would be the religious way of praying—starting from below and striving upward. Prayer is always just a request to the Father through Jesus Christ.

It goes without saying by now that Bonhoeffer was not a proponent of a closed worldview that would rule out the possibility of prayer and

21. Of course, Bonhoeffer believed to the end in the meaning, power, and strength of intercessory prayer: "I've often found it a great help to think in the evening of all those who I know are praying for me" (from a letter of August 21, 1944). Bonhoeffer repeatedly spoke positively of intercessory prayer because that is just how Christian existence as existence for others is realized (*Letters and Papers from Prison*, pp. 391–92).

22. *Cost of Discipleship*, p. 181.

23. Ibid.

24. Ibid., p. 183.

25. Ibid.

God's answering prayer. God is above everything: "I believe that God can and will bring good out of evil, even out of the greatest evil."[26] If there is no direct prayer to God, but only prayer out of participation in the suffering of Christ in this world, if, in other words, prayer can only be "Christ-mystical," then the answer to prayer will also come to pass only through Christ. The fulfillment of our requests uttered in prayer does not serve the purpose of our self-affirmation. Rather, even the fulfillment of the prayer of the Christian passes through the cross and the resurrection. God always grants a request in such a way that he takes away the egotistical fleshliness of the request in his granting of it. That is precisely why God is not a "stopgap" for our fleshly thirst for miracles, but our helper, our "rod and staff," even in "the valley of the shadow of death." Prayer too passes through the cross, just as prayer's fulfillment must pass through the cross.

26. *Letters and Papers from Prison*, p. 11.

PART 5

The Power and Powerlessness of God

14

The Powerlessness of God

God the Father almighty, the Creator of heaven and earth—that is the belief professed in the first article of the Apostles' Creed. The biblically revealed God is the almighty God—otherwise he would not be God. A powerless, suffering God would be a self-contradiction. But it is precisely this belief in the omnipotence of God that becomes a temptation to unbelief. The why-question arises. Why does God allow evil to happen? How can the reality of this world, the dark inscrutability of the holocaust be harmonized with the omnipotence of God? Why does creation suffer? Why do human beings suffer? Why do all creatures suffer?

On July 16, 1944, Bonhoeffer wrote: "God lets himself be pushed out of the world on to the cross. He is weak and powerless in the world, and that is precisely the way, the only way, in which he is with us and helps us." In Bonhoeffer's view, "Christ helps us, not by virtue of his omnipotence, but by virtue of his weakness and suffering. . . . The Bible directs man to God's powerlessness and suffering; only the suffering God can help." Thus, for Bonhoeffer the God of the Bible is the God "who wins power and space in the world by his weakness. This will probably be the starting-point for our 'secular interpretation.'"[1]

1. *Letters and Papers from Prison*, pp. 360–61.

When Bonhoeffer wrote this, he was in prison and had to look on helplessly as political events moved in a direction that he wanted to prevent. As one who was completely powerless, he was at the mercy of the course of events. On January 23, 1944, he wrote: "This realization of one's own helplessness has two sides . . . it brings both anxiety and relief."[2] Bonhoeffer found this liberation in the fact that his life was "placed wholly in better and stronger hands."[3] He did not only see it this way in regard to his own life, but also in regard to the lives of the people he himself could no longer help. By experience of suffering Bonhoeffer grasped one of the basic New Testament principles, found in Matthew 10:38 ("anyone who does not take his cross"); and his frequent mention of the "powerlessness of God" is a reminder of Matthew 27:40, in which those who passed by at Christ's crucifixion called out to him to "come down from the cross, if you are the Son of God."

Bonhoeffer always saw the "powerlessness of God" exclusively in connection with the cross. And it was in regard to this cross, to the powerlessness of Christ and thereby in regard to the "powerlessness of God" who allowed his Son to suffer on the cross, that the difference between Christian faith and religion became clear to Bonhoeffer. Religion is the projection of one's own wishes, but the cross is the descent of God rather than the ascent of man. It is the incarnation, the Almighty become flesh. As a result the Christian must also go where he does not want to go (see John 21:18). Thus, this experience of powerlessness destroys religion as an instrument of human self-actualization. Powerlessness and cross mean crucifixion of the flesh. Here we come once more upon the basic feature of Bonhoefferian Christ-mysticism: *mortificatio* and *vivificatio*—the Pauline "as dying, yet behold, we live" (2 Cor. 6:9).

It is very important that the dialectical nature and structure of his many statements on the subject be recognized when Bonhoeffer speaks of the "powerlessness of God."

As Müller rightly saw, Bonhoeffer did not make the cross into a principle. There is no "positivism of powerlessness" in Bonhoeffer. As Müller correctly points out, it is undoubtedly therein that an essential

2. Ibid., p. 190.
3. Ibid.

difference lies between the Kierkegaardian and Bonhoefferian views of the cross:

> In Kierkegaard the negativity of the cross becomes the determining factor of his whole world-and-life view and to that extent really an absolute principle. His doctrine becomes a kind of "methodism." In contrast, the cross in Bonhoeffer's thought does not become the principle for a worldview, but rather a presupposition of faith and thus the exact opposite of all contemplatory notions. . . . When the cross becomes a principle, it becomes surreptitiously a positive standard; it is robbed of its "contingency" and becomes immanent in the wrong way. The hiddenness of God is again removed by the cross.[4]

Thus, the cross cannot become a method in the sense of "through humiliation to reawakening." Once again Müller: "That is: the Christian must, precisely in all godforsakenness and through participation in the godforsakenness of Jesus, live in the world. He must do this without denying this godforsakenness by creating a god for himself who is powerful in the world and whom he finds not in suffering but in visible omnipotence."[5]

These last sentences are significant insofar as they show that Müller's interpretation of Bonhoeffer begins to show signs of making powerlessness—if not the cross as well—into a principle. Here, powerlessness becomes a kind of theological principle of knowledge. But that is wrong: this breaks the whole tension of the Bonhoefferian dialectic. We can never devise a system to undo the dialectic of powerlessness on the cross on the one hand and triumph of grace on the other hand. On August 15, 1941, Bonhoeffer wrote in a letter to the approximately 100 students of his who were serving in the German Army: "But God does not make any mistakes. . . . In the face of death we cannot fatalistically say: 'God wills it.' We must immediately add: 'God does not will it.' Death shows that the world is still not as it should be and that it needs redemption. Christ alone is the overcoming of death. Here, 'God wills it' and 'God does not will it' reach their sharpest point of tension and their resolution."[6] In these lines we

---

4. Müller, *Von der Kirche zur Welt*, p. 386.
5. Ibid., p. 387.
6. *GS*, 2:573.

sense what Bonhoeffer's dialectic means, precisely in regards to the powerlessness of God. The mistake of many modern Bonhoeffer interpreters is precisely that they have made Bonhoeffer's view of powerlessness into a principle of powerlessness. The will of God is done unconditionally—and the will of God is not done, but should be done. That is why the third request of the Lord's Prayer is in the subjunctive: "Thy will be done."

That Bonhoeffer's dialectic was far removed from any dualism or tension between light and darkness or God and demonic powers, and that Bonhoeffer was certain of the triumph of God's grace, is shown clearly in a letter of the fourth Sunday of Advent of 1943: "nothing is lost, . . . everything is taken up in Christ, although it is transformed."[7] Thus all reality, even that which is hostile to God and in which God appears powerless, is brought under the triumph of Christ that will be revealed at the end of time. Nothing is in vain, nothing is lost, no eternal abyss of nothingness threatens—at the second coming every pain, every death, every tear will make sense. But whoever removes this eschatological thinking from Bonhoeffer's theology will have to make powerlessness into a principle of knowledge for Bonhoeffer's theology.

Finally, everything that Bonhoeffer said about the powerlessness of God was a part of his Christ-mysticism. As mentioned before, Bonhoeffer wrote on July 18, 1944, that we do not experience Christ in a "religious act," but through "participation in the sufferings of God." Bonhoeffer replaced salvation-egoism with another way: "allowing oneself to be caught up into the way of Jesus Christ, into the messianic event, thus fulfilling Isa. 53." Thus in and with the Suffering Servant of God, in and with the powerlessness of the Suffering Servant of God we go our way. But it is always the way to resurrection. Participation in the suffering of Christ always means participation in Christ's rising from the dead as well: "That God will approach where men turn away, that Christ was born in a stable because there was no room for him in the inn—these are things that a prisoner can understand better than other people; for him they are really glad tidings."[8] Why is it good news? Because the Christian recognizes that in his powerlessness he is not forsaken by God, but that it is precisely when he is pow-

7. *Letters and Papers from Prison*, pp. 170–71.
8. Ibid., p. 166.

erless that God carries and accompanies him. Suffering and powerlessness are not sought after. Rather, the world brings them inexorably to pass.

Bonhoeffer knew well that the biblically revealed God is not an apathetic God, not a power of fate, not an impersonal principle, not an "it." Hans Küng writes, "The biblical God is not an emotionless God who is incapable of suffering and remains apathetic to the immense suffering of the world and human beings. Rather, He is a sympathetic and compassionate God who, changing everything in the future, leads through liberation from guilt, suffering, and death to final justice, unbroken peace and eternal life—He is a God of conclusive redemption."[9] These lines describe well what Bonhoeffer understood by powerlessness, suffering, and the triumph of the grace of God. The tension between suffering in the world and the omnipotence of God can only be understood as Küng expresses it: "When one looks upon the unending suffering of the world, one cannot believe that there is a God. But on the other hand one can also say: Only if there is a God can one look upon this unending suffering of the world at all!"[10] In the Bonhoefferian sense: the reality of this world and the powerlessness of human beings in the face of the dreadfulness of this world can be borne only if there is a God who participates in the powerlessness of human beings and who suffers human powerlessness on the cross.

The meaning of suffering does not lie in allowing oneself to lick one's own wounds in a permanent state of self-pity. There is no methodical ladder of suffering into eternity. Suffering arises out of the world in the hunger and thirst for righteousness, peace, and mercy. Suffering arises because the *sensorium* of God has been brought into this world. It arises out of "participation" in the powerlessness of God and the world. Biblically, the powerlessness of God in the world means that there is a reality that stands against God: death, sickness, hate, war, fear, injustice, and the like. To experience and suffer this reality means to participate in the powerlessness of God in the world. Christ, suffering and overcoming, participated in this powerlessness. That is not salvation-egoistic suffering. Viewed in regard to human beings, it is exactly the kind of suffering that the responsibly active

9. Küng, *Existiert Gott?* p. 727.
10. Ibid., p. 758.

person come of age experiences in this godforsaken world: "The world that has come of age is more godless, and perhaps for that very reason nearer to God, than the world before its coming of age."[11] For the world come of age experiences more profoundly the tension between a godforsaken reality on the one hand and the righteousness of God on the other hand. The person come of age is thrown back upon himself because he discovers the godlessness of this world and because he is forced to recognize how much facade-Christianity is at work wherever the "Christianization" of the world has been pushed ahead the most. Therefore it is precisely the human being come of age who possesses the simultaneously painful and liberating possibility of experiencing the powerlessness of God in his own powerlessness. He experiences the godlessness of this world in and around himself and does not allow himself to be misled by empty phrases about the loss of God. Thus, he may discover the cross in and around himself and thereby encounter in his powerlessness the power of God that overcomes the world.

The "Disempowerment" of God

With great jubilation, feminist theology has perverted Bonhoeffer's statements about the powerlessness and suffering of God for its own ends. After all, the Almighty God the Father is a great stumbling stone for feminist theology. Thus, it had to happen that this *theologumenon* of the powerlessness of God should become a downright festive gate of entry for feminine divinity: the suffering and crying God who mourns over this world and for whom the world and human beings are necessary in order to avoid being destroyed by loneliness. This is the effeminate God in need. Bonhoeffer's powerless God is transformed into a needy and tender God. At the German National Church Convention in Frankfurt in 1987, the tender, femininely sensitive God was proclaimed. In an interpretation of the biblical creation story, God was portrayed as a "being in need" who created human beings out of loneliness and needs human beings. In this view, talk of an "all powerful" God would represent a "retreat" of God from his creation. This presentation referred to the "suffering form of God" as recognizable in sick, depressed, and broken people. Thus, the tendency is

11. *Letters and Papers from Prison*, p. 362.

increasing to see God as a passive, suffering, crying, and, in the final analysis, feminized God who is the victim of the powerful, the healthy, and the strong. Out of this suffering grows the longing for tenderness, tolerance, and a "flowery view" of this world. And those who hold to this new view of God are unanimous in their condemnation of the past, especially of the recent fascist, National Socialist past, which to the disaster of humankind allegedly believed in the authoritarian system, in being dominant, and thereby in a powerful, fatherly God.

However, it is completely incorrect to characterize the feminization of God as a theological product of the 1960s and 1970s. First of all, the prophets already struggled against the mother deities of the ancient world. God very clearly reveals himself in the Bible in masculine terms. That is not by chance, but in conscious repudiation of the mother deities of the ancient world. No doubt there were matriarchies in the dawning ages of human history.[12] This historical aspect is not our theme, however. We are discussing the process of the feminization of God in the twentieth century. And a high point of the feminization of God was reached precisely where modern theologians search for it least of all, namely, in the "faith of Adolf Hitler"—in the so-called Nationalist Socialist worldview that brought with it an either-or confrontation with Christianity. Like today's creeping infiltration of Christianity through new age feminism, this confrontation brought on by nazism was not an openly fought intellectual or spiritual battle, but a creeping infiltration.[13] Everything that today wants to suffocate Christianity with its feminist kisses, this "neomatriarchal uprising," lay very clearly within the trend of Nazi ideology and the "faith of Adolf Hitler." The belief in "salvation out of the maternal lap of the

---

12. See E. Borneman, *Das Patriarchat. Ursprung und Zukunft unserer Gesellschaft*, 1975. Borneman places the replacement of matriarchy with patriarchy, the happy communist consensus of antiquity with the rule of capitalism, in the neolithic period. According to Borneman, the future of society lies in the return to its origin, the matriarchal-communist community.

13. On this point, see H. Afflerbach, *Die sanfte Umdeutung des Evangeliums*, 1987. Afflerbach names the following example (p. 24) in addition to many others. The feminist Hanna Wolff identifies the return of the prodigal son in Luke 15 with the courage of self-encounter and of finding oneself. Instead of the return to God the Father she sees the redirection to the Mother Soul. The longing for the inspirational appearance of images of God in the depths of the soul replaces the encounter with the Father in heaven who speaks to us in his Word. Today, this utter contrast to the theology of revelation as represented by Bonhoeffer portrays itself as Christian.

great Mother Germany"[14] was something akin to a predecessor-ess of new age feminism.

In another part of this book we will cover the strategies and tactics of the Nazi regime in its fight against Christianity. Here we are discussing only the matriarchal aspect of this ideology that is being continued in present-day new age feminism. Lanz-Liebenfels, the man who inspired Hitler's worldview, was an obvious proponent of a mother cult, as W. Daim correctly interprets: "The racial cult is basically a kind of subspecies of the mother cult." Blood becomes the god of a nation. Retrogression is an integral part of this cult of the mother goddess "race and blood"—the secret and sinister longing for death, death-mysticism (practiced above all in the SS) as a return to the *uroboros*, the ancient lap of the mother deity that extinguishes all individuality. From the very beginning, death-eroticism, faith in war, and race-blood matriarchy have belonged together.

Hitler may have talked often of the "Lord God," especially until the mid-1930s when his actual ideological turning point took place. This Lord God, however, was only a facade for his artful manipulation of the archaic-atavistic ultimate ground of the soul of the people. Hitler could empathize with this soul of the people as no other person in the twentieth century. Furthermore, he could express it in language and activate it politically. As Bonhoeffer clearly brought out in his uniquely illuminating essay of 1933, the *Führer* was a function of the masses. He did not stand in an authoritative position over against the people. Rather, he only proclaimed to it the confirmation of what the people wanted in the primal ground of its archaic-atavistic soul.

In this context Hitler never pursued open dispute with Christianity, in contrast to many other prominent Nazis such as Hitler's secretary Martin Bormann or Alfred Rosenberg, the National Socialist leader of political education, or Kerrl, the Secretary of Ecclesiastical Affairs in the Third Reich. The worship and dogmas of the various Christian confessions were not to be infringed upon. They were to be slowly overcome by a creeping archaic uprising, seduced so to speak with the kisses of the matriarchally manipulated soul of the *Volk*. Hitler's goal was not the rejection, but the "gradual infiltration" of Christianity. It

---

14. In his *Der Glaube des Adolf Hitler*, 1968, Friedrich Heer offers the best interpretation of Hitler's view of Christianity and "religiosity." See p. 49.

was his firm conviction that the old Christian symbols of the Father God were worn out and used up and would soon die. Friedrich Heer described very well how Hitler's belief in a Lord God gradually melted into a religion of nature and fate: "Just as the old Christian 'Lord God' merges more and more with 'nature' and the merciless law of nature in Hitler's imagination, worldview, and speech, so the God of Christianity merges with the 'Master of the Worlds,' fate, and a sometimes graceless nature."[15] Precisely this idolization of nature, *Volk,* and race is however basically the awakening of a feminist view of God. In June 1937 Hitler said in Würzburg: "On this earth, next to believing in our Lord God we German National Socialists believe in our German *Volk.*"[16] Here again, we see the tie not only between nature and God, but also between *Volk* and God. Hitler's speech in Salzburg on April 6, 1938, shows how much the racial and nature-worshiping aspects had moved more and more into the foreground: "In the beginning the *Volk* came into being, the *Volk* was, and after that came the *Reich.*"[17] Later we will see how Bonhoeffer in his *Ethics* advocated just the opposite and placed the occidental view of the state above the ethnic nation— a typically Father-God oriented view of society that Bonhoeffer fought for against the "revolution from below," and thereby against feminism.

Feminism did not fall suddenly from the sky. Rather, it gradually developed to the point at which the belief in God the Father was pushed more and more out of the hearts and minds of people. That happened gradually, and the radical feminism we see today is not yet the end of a long process. For now it suffices to note how Bonhoeffer's theological thought was already challenged by this prehistory of feminism. National Socialism is not feminism and feminism is of course not National Socialism. Of course, Hitler was not the initiator or inventor of this feminization of the content of Christian faith. The influence of women, even if there were no female pastors or women in church consistories, was already enormous in German Protestantism toward the end of the nineteenth century. In their own circles and church pews women already were active in the religious mawkishness of late Protestantism because Christianity had already been pushed

15. On this point, see ibid., pp. 287ff.
16. Ibid., p. 318.
17. Ibid., p. 341.

out of the reality of the world and everyday life. And in regard to the Roman Catholic Church Heer writes:

> Every truly manly activity was suppressed. Any creative, liberating enthusiasm and masculinity in priests was viewed unfavorably. And if priests exhibited these traits they were diverted to nonspiritual activities. Thus a type of priest was bred who was weak, infantile, often obsessed by mother complexes, homoerotic, deeply unmasculine, effeminate, and monastic. These were defenseless victims of an abortive spiritual development who from time to time allowed their latent homoerotic tendencies to break out in open homosexuality. However, inwardly fragile priests and monks of this type, continually tortured by their sexual temptations, offered the curial and ecclesiastical bureaucracies and hierarchies an especially suitable material.[18]

A history of the feminization and thereby of the destruction of Christianity remains to be written. But on one point there is a surprisingly clear agreement between Hitler and his Nazi followers and today's radical feminists: they all shared the selfsame hatred of Paul and the selfsame contempt for the Old Testament that the radical feminists zealously proclaim in our time.

Whether nature, ecology, community, or society is the starting point, as these concepts are used today they are feminist concepts.

Lutz E. von Padberg reminds us, especially through his view of transformation, how feminist culture and religiosity, through gradual infiltration and the unjustified taking over of Christian concepts, intend to and are able to assert themselves against Christianity—and to do this all in the name of Christianity.[19]

As opposed to Bonhoeffer's view, the feminists do not suffer through God's disempowerment, but rather they desire it. The powerful God is to be replaced by the all-feeling godwoman.

The Power of God

Modern theology wants to free the world from the imposition of the Father God so that it can fix the world through social programs. Thus, Christ becomes at the most a principle for a new world order. Thus

18. Ibid., pp. 368, 590.
19. See Lutz E. von Padberg, *New Age und Feminismus*, 1987.

the quantity of the powerlessness of God is transformed into the quality of the power of society. The powerlessness of God is seen as the obligation to disempower all systems of authority. As we will see, Bonhoeffer advances the exact opposite opinion in his *Ethics*. One cannot appeal to Bonhoeffer nor to his view of the powerlessness of God if one wants to fight against "masculine values" such as power, law, order, and authority of God's commandments. He actively opposed the subversion of all values that took place in the Nazi revolution's rebellion from below.

Bonhoeffer set authority over against impudence: in the middle of "the levelling down of all ranks of society,"[20] he wanted to testify to the authority of God and his commandments. Wherever impudence is tolerated and approaches too near, "the flood-gates are opened, chaos bursts the dam that we were to defend; and we are responsible for it all. . . . [Christianity's] business today will be to defend passionately human dignity and reserve. The misinterpretation that we are acting for our own interests, and the cheap insinuation that our attitude is anti-social, we shall simply have to put up with; they are the invariable protests of the rabble against decency and order." That is how Bonhoeffer wrote at the end of 1942 about the relation between power and order.

It was in this struggle for power and order, and especially for law, in which the participation in the powerlessness of God grew in Bonhoeffer. He experienced the powerlessness of the Master of order and law in a time and in a society that rebelled against the commandments of the Master. In the struggle for the power of righteousness Bonhoeffer came to participate in the suffering of God in the world: "it is only when one submits to God's law that one may speak of grace."[21] The imprisoned and powerless Bonhoeffer, who fought for justice against a regime and became a victim of that regime, experienced the powerlessness of law and justice. The powerlessness of justice became for him the powerlessness of God.

20. *Letters and Papers from Prison*, pp. 12–13.
21. Ibid., p. 157.

15

God's Substitutionary
Presence on Earth

In the lecture course of the summer semester 1932, "Das Wesen
der Kirche" ["The Essence of the Church"], Bonhoeffer said: "Christ's
substitutionary work means that Christ puts himself in our place
where we would have had to stand before God. . . . In this act, Christ
offers up his person. In this substitutionary activity Christ functions
as the new humankind, and the church is established in him."[1] For
Bonhoeffer it was crucial that the substitutionary work of Christ is
experienced and believed in the body of believers. For the body is
grounded "in the reality of his substitutionary acts as the God-man."[2]
But Christ existing as the body of believers always means that Christ
stands over against the body. He identifies himself with it through his
substitutionary work. He upholds the body and incorporates it in his
fighting, suffering, dying, and resurrection. Christ's substitutionary
ministry is thus understood Christ-mystically.

That also brings about a Christ-mystical understanding of the body
of believers, because Christians are parts of the body of Christ. There
is, then, no equating of human existence and Christ; no lack of dis-

1. *GS*, 5:249.
2. Ibid.

tinction. "Humankind always remains of Adam. The cross retains its lasting validity."[3] The Christ-mystical view of Christ's substitutionary work means that "Jesus claims for himself and the Kingdom of God the whole of human life in its manifestations."[4] The substitutionary work of Christ is not for sin alone, for "Jesus did not make everyone a sinner first."[5] But Jesus also serves in a substitutionary capacity for the creation in the sense that God actually intended for it: "Never did he question a man's health, vigour, or happiness, regarded in themselves, or regard them as evil fruits; else why should he heal the sick and restore strength to the weak?"[6]

In this context it was important to Bonhoeffer that Christianity not be misunderstood as a "revolution of inferiority." He did not want people to doubt the goodness of creation. Christians should not be lovers of suffering and hold fast to what is sick and weak. Here it shows how much Nietzsche was read at that time. For Nietzsche Christians were losers, degenerates, and broken people who lived in resentment of everything that was strong, heroic, and healthy. The Christian ethic was a neurotic ethic of resentment. Especially in the 1930s, such arguments, which were of course popularizations of Nietzsche, were used often against Christianity.

At any rate Bonhoeffer made the following clear: what is sick, weak, destroyed, or injured is always only the penultimate over against the ultimate redemption in a new and whole creation. For Bonhoeffer, Christ is the substitutionary representative for the whole cosmos, the Pantocrator, who will create a new heaven and a new earth at his second coming. Bonhoeffer was concerned that "we shouldn't run man down in his worldliness, but confront him with God at his strongest point."[7] Christ is not a symbol of weakness for weakness' sake. He is not the No, but the Yes. After all, Christ made the sick healthy, opened the eyes of the blind, cleansed the lepers, and caused the lame to walk. Christ is the substitutionary representative of a new creation, and Christians are called to this new creation.

3. Ibid., p. 248.
4. *Letters and Papers from Prison*, p. 342.
5. Ibid., p. 341.
6. Ibid., pp. 341–42.
7. Ibid., p. 346.

Man as a Stand-in for God

As many concluded from Bonhoeffer's theology, if God is powerless or even dead then man would himself have to be the substitute or stand-in for God. For this type of modern theology, the man Jesus became the stand-in for God in a godless and godforsaken world. Man steps into the vacancy left by the now disempowered God. Christ becomes the anticipation of man come of age who acts for the absent God. That is Christianity without God. Dorothee Sölle appealed to Bonhoeffer in her book *Atheistisch an Gott glauben*. For Sölle, representation becomes protest against this world that has been forsaken by God: "Whoever would accept the world as it is would be dead."[8] This world is unacceptable. The powerless God has not been able to change it. In the attitude of protest against this world lies also the protest against the Father God who created it. In this view, the substitutionary work of Christ was not that he bore our punishment on the cross. Rather, Christ died because God did not erase his obligation to the world to change the world. Thus, substitution becomes a program for changing the world through man come of age *etsi deus non daretur.*

Can this atheism really lay claim to God? How could it happen that this cause appropriated Bonhoeffer and continues to traffic in his memory?

Godforsakenness and Christ-Mysticism

Modernist theology made a god-woman out of the powerlessness of God. In its substance, the moderns' anti-father theology is an act of "revenge against that which is" (Nietzsche). This theology desires no suffering for the world, but rather confrontation with creation and thereby with the Creator God the Father as well. In this paradigm of modern theology, little "theologizing" is done on human sin and guilt, and even less on the wrath and reconciling work of God. This leaves all the more room in this theology for the rejection of God and his creation. For modern theology, man come of age is the starting-point. Man come of age lives not only without God, but finally against God—and that in the name of Christianity. For some who reject the creation of God, the great "Mother" becomes the utopian dream of a

---

8. Dorothee Sölle, *Die Wahrheit ist Konkret*, 1967, p. 43.

world in bloom. Sin, guilt, and reconciliation are attributed to the Oedipal nature of the masculine way of encountering God. Wherever the male ruling structure is no longer in control, there is no longer need for reconciliation. The omni-motherliness and omni-safe-and-sound-ness of the god-woman suffocate everything "hostile to women" with the kisses of her value-extinguishing elemental force. The powerlessness of God becomes the death of God and the resurrection of the woman-god. Anti-father god is in principle anti-Old Testament, anti-Paulinism, anti-Judaism. Modern feminism is in its essence anti-Semitic and anti-Christian at the same time.

Taken by itself, Bonhoeffer's *theologumenon* [theological principle] of the "powerlessness of God" is a bad *theologumenon*. Also, one should not speak of the "self-limitation of God." At least terminologically, this is speculation that goes beyond God's revelation. But what Bonhoeffer meant to say by "powerlessness of God" hits upon the essence of the revelation of Christ. This creation as fallen creation, as creation hostile to God, rules God out and brings to naught his intention for creation regarding this world and the human race. In this regard it is crucial that precisely the God who has been betrayed in this way participates in Christ, out of grace, in the powerlessness of the godlessness for which man is to blame. Therefore, the "powerlessness of God" is good news for those who are powerless, because God shares the burden of powerlessness. In the Bonhoefferian view it is absolutely necessary that the "powerlessness of God" be understood Christ-mystically. It is the God who in Christ bears the cross of the lost. If the "powerlessness of God" is understood Christ-mystically, then this powerlessness is not the ultimate, but always only the penultimate, just as death is the penultimate and not the ultimate. The ultimate is the triumph of grace in the resurrection.

16

On the End of Time

The End of the World
and the Second Coming of Christ

Modern, horizontally oriented theology rejects the "dualism" between heaven and earth. Included in this rejection is the fact that the second coming of Christ at the end of time can no longer be part of the content of Christian faith. If there is no end to the world, then there can be no second coming of Christ. The penultimate of the end of this world is the precondition for the ultimate of the second coming of Christ and the creation of a new heaven and a new earth. Furthermore, the second coming of Christ will not display the powerlessness, but the power of God. But this belief in the second coming of Christ at the end of time and at the end of this world is ruled out by modern theology as "apocalyptic." At best a resurrection of Christ "into this world" is confessed—that the coming of a new society is "anticipated," or a coming socialist society promised, in the myth of the resurrection.

Did Bonhoeffer live and think apocalyptically—in anticipation of the second coming of Christ? In a lecture in Potstam on November 19, 1932 on the theme of "Thy kingdom come," Bonhoeffer said: "Because God's kingdom shall be in eternity, God will create a new heaven and a new earth. But really a new earth."[1] Thus Bonhoeffer professed a belief in a new creation at the second coming of Christ. But Bonhoeffer did not want the ultimate of the second coming to render people indifferent to the penultimate of the already present kingdom. After all, the kingdom of God is already in our midst: "Not as the one visible, powerful empire, as the new kingdom of the world; but the kingdom of the other world that has completely entered into the conflict of the world: as the powerless, defenseless gospel of the resurrection, of miracle; and at the same time as the state that possesses authority and power and preserves order. Only in the genuine relationship and limitation of both is the kingdom of Christ reality."[2]

Bonhoeffer saw—and he also held to this in his *Ethics*—the present working of Christ not only in his church, but also in political reality, in that Christ is the power that binds chaos and preserves justice and order. The present working of Christ, the kingdom of God, has its effect not only in the church but also in the political realm. Bonhoeffer emphasizes that "he is always among us in double form: as the ultimate kingdom of resurrection and of miracle; a kingdom that breaks through, repudiates, overcomes, and destroys all kingdoms of the earth and all human kingdom-making, which is subject to the curse of death; and at the same time he is among us as the preserving kingdom of order that affirms the earth and its laws, communities, and history."[3]

In 1932, when Bonhoeffer gave his lecture "Dein Reich komme" ["Thy Kingdom Come"], the significance of which should not be underestimated, all was not well in the world. Germany's Weimar Republic teetered on the edge of chaos. It is amazing how Bonhoeffer professed the political obligation of the Christian, even the political presence of Christ as ordering power, in the face of this developing chaos. And this was before Barth had written *Evangelium und Gesetz* [*Gospel and Law*] and *Rechtfertigung und Recht* [*Justification and Justice*] in the mid- to late 1930s, works that effectively brought out the *usus politicus* as the hidden reality of God's kingdom in Christ.

1. *GS*, 2:284.
2. Ibid.
3. Ibid., p. 80.

In the year 1932, 400,000 SA-men and 100,000 SS-men were running about on the streets of Germany and brawling, sometimes under circumstances similar to civil war, with the communist organizations of the time. The economic distress in Germany was also so great that unemployment support, emergency support, and welfare rates all had to be cut, by 23 percent, 10 percent, and 15 percent, respectively. The government was without the parliamentary backing of the Social Democratic party and the Communist party. Even the Catholic-bourgeois center, on which Bonhoeffer at that time pinned his political hopes, no longer supported the government. In 1932 all of the ministers of the Prussian State Government were removed from office. A state of emergency was declared in Berlin and the province of Brandenburg. After the *Reichstag* elections on November 6, 1932, 50.7 percent of the members of parliament were radical communists or National Socialists (although the National Socialists lost seats) who did not desire a parliamentary solution to the governmental crisis, which now could be withstood only by means of emergency decrees. Order and justice were directly threatened. Undoubtedly, Bonhoeffer saw through this chaotic situation. He fought to the end to defend the values of law and order against the revolution from below.

Bonhoeffer's dismissal of all revolutionary utopias was clear: "All of our longing to win back the cursed field and make it blessed again must fail, because God himself has cursed the field and he alone can take back his Word and bless the earth again."[4] In *The Cost of Discipleship* as well, Bonhoeffer did not lose sight of this call to order. In regard to the meek who will inherit the earth he wrote: "We must not interpret this as a reference to God's exercise of juridicial punishment within the world, as Calvin did: what it means is that when the kingdom of heaven descends, the face of the earth will be renewed."[5] Bonhoeffer replaced utopia with the "apocalyptic" second coming of Christ: "The older the world grows, the more heated becomes the conflict between Christ and Antichrist, and the more thorough the efforts of the world to get rid of the Christians. Until now the world had always granted them a lodging-place by allowing them to work for their own food and clothing. But a world that has become one hun-

---

4. Ibid.
5. *Cost of Discipleship*, p. 123.

dred per cent anti-Christian cannot allow them even this private sphere of work for their daily bread."[6]

With these words, which were put in final form in 1937, a time in which 800 employees of the Confessing Church were behind bars for short or long terms of imprisonment, Bonhoeffer recognized where the utopia of a political heaven on earth leads. For Bonhoeffer, utopia is the enemy of justice: "It is true that, according to the Holy Scripture (Luke 21.16), one of the portents of the approaching end of the world is the destruction of the natural in every respect; here a limit is set to the immanent optimism. Indeed the biblical prophecy extrudes this optimism once and for all from its role as a historical principle and as a quietive."[7]

In *The Cost of Discipleship* there is an "eschatological concentration," as Mayer puts it,[8] because the world in which Bonhoeffer lived seemed to him ripe for the end.[9] Bonhoeffer wrote at a time in which, with eyes gleaming, people were singing: "The brittle bones of the world are trembling before the great storm," and, "with us marches a new era." Bonhoeffer formulated his apocalyptic thought at a time of heady political awakening in which the new shores of a paradise for a happy Nordic race were believed to be coming ever more clearly into view.

In his last letters as well, Bonhoeffer thought apocalyptically: "It may be that the day of judgment will dawn tomorrow; in that case we shall gladly stop working for a better future. But not before."[10] In these last years it became important to Bonhoeffer that the immediate political problems of the day that were challenging Christians and society not be brushed aside because of the expectation that Christ would come soon. It was also clear to him that Christ would bring redemption to creation as well: "I will restore all things"—"that is, we cannot and should not take it back ourselves, but allow Christ to give it back to us."[11] The "restoration" of all things through the second coming of Christ did not mean to Bonhoeffer "sublimation," "spiritu-

6. Ibid., p. 299.
7. *Ethics*, pp. 148–49.
8. Mayer, *Christuswirklichkeit*, p. 281.
9. *Cost of Discipleship*, p. 225.
10. *Letters and Papers from Prison*, pp. 15–16.
11. Ibid., p. 171.

alization," or "infusing things with a soul"—in the Platonic sense. Rather, Bonhoeffer believed to the end of his life that a really new creation would be "restored."

The Ultimate and the Penultimate:
The Coming and Already Present Kingdom of Christ

The New Testament anticipation of the kingdom of God is dialectical: on the one hand the kingdom of God has already arrived; on the other hand it will not arrive until the second coming of Christ. After the war had begun, Bonhoeffer as an ethicist was concerned above all with the immediate significance of the Christian faith amidst the dangers and uncertainties of the time in which he lived.

Moreover, the "social gospel" did not fail to make an impression on Bonhoeffer during his first stay in America as a student before the Nazi rise to power in 1933. He was always very concerned with "practical Christianity." Speaking of the kingdom of God on earth was for Bonhoeffer "entirely biblical and correct in contrast to an escapist view of the Kingdom."[12] Against the challenge of National Socialism, which wanted to make Christianity into an "affair of the age to come," Bonhoeffer consciously made the social and political, present-day significance of the Christian faith into the centerpiece of his theological thought.

According to M. Honecker, "It is striking how the eschatological dimension fades into the background in all of Bonhoeffer's writings; the body of Christ exists in the world and is not on the way to its future."[13] However, this opinion as Honecker formulates it is incorrect. Bonhoeffer very much believed in the second coming of Christ and the restoration of all things. The emphases simply lay for him in

---

12. *GS*, 1:110. In *Ethics* almost ten years later, Bonhoeffer spoke of the failure of "practical Christianity": "The issue is not the shaping of the word through planning and programs" (p. 85). At this point, Bonhoeffer used the word "shaping" or "forming" (*Gestaltung*) mainly for the relation of Christianity to reality: "Rather, forming (*Gestaltung*) exists solely as the event of being pulled into the figure (*Gestalt*) of Jesus Christ, as being formed in the same way (*Gleichgestaltung*) as the only figure (*Gestalt*) of Him who has become human, been crucified and resurrected." Thus the integral relation of Christ and natural, historical, and political reality is understood Christ-mystically.

13. M. Honecker, *Kirche als Gestalt und Ereignis. Die sichtbare Gestalt der Kirche als dogmatisches Problem*, 1963, p. 156. See also Bethge, *Bonhoeffer*, p. 118.

the present-day significance of Christianity. Bonhoeffer did not want to see the significance of the penultimate overlooked because of the greater significance of the ultimate.

The presence of the kingdom since the first coming of Christ always remains merely the penultimate to the eternal kingdom at his second coming. This presence of the kingdom now is the penultimate of the ultimate. And for its part, this present-day kingdom is an ultimate to the penultimate of social-practical and ethical actions: "To give bread to the hungry man is not the same as to proclaim the grace of God and justification to him, and to have received bread is not the same as to have faith."[14] The "social engagement of the Christian" is always merely the penultimate of the ultimate. From the point of view of the ultimate it is all-important "everything depends on this activity being a spiritual reality precisely because ultimately it is not indeed a question of the reform of earthly conditions, but it is a question of the coming of Christ. Only a spiritual preparation of the way will be followed by the merciful coming of the Lord."[15] That is a clear rejection of the notion of a societal realization of the kingdom of God as proclaimed by much modern theology in its one-dimensionality. Now it is obvious that whoever has nothing to eat and cannot sustain physical life cannot hear the gospel either. But it is nevertheless the decisive and ultimate concern that the gospel be heard. On the other hand, of course, this ultimate concern does not exclude the penultimate of "food for the poor," but rather unconditionally includes it. This dialectical relation safeguards Christian faith from both this-worldliness and other-worldliness. Christ is in the world, but he is not of the world.

In Bonhoeffer's view, the kingdom of Christ in the world is not identical to the church, nor of course to the state. The kingdom of Christ is real not just "here and there" but "within you" (Luke 17:21). Thus the kingdom of God is on the one hand narrower than the body of believers, but on the other hand wider than the body of believers; the light of God's kingdom, the light of common grace, also falls upon those who live outside of the body. Bonhoeffer himself did not view his time as the endtime, but at best as the preparation for the endtime.

14. *Ethics*, p. 137.
15. Ibid., p. 138.

He did not see the Antichrist in Hitler (Hitler had too little class for that in Bonhoeffer's opinion), but rather something akin to the penultimate of the ultimate Antichrist. Bonhoeffer knew that the figure of the Antichrist is building itself up successively as the apocalypse nears and will not reveal itself in its full power until the very end.

Living in the Shadow of Death—"Religionless Pietism"

In Bonhoeffer's case one may never overlook that his this-worldliness, which he affirmed on the one hand, was always accompanied by shadows of death on the other hand. Bonhoeffer always knew he was in close proximity to death. He preached, talked, and wrote often of death. However, this was not the death-mysticism, the downright erotic view of dying, that presented itself in National Socialist and especially SS ideology. On the contrary, Bonhoeffer consciously traversed the zone of tension between life and death. For him, death was not natural. Death was the enemy of humankind. Nevertheless, Bonhoeffer recognized that the world of National Socialist ideology showed that man can die without the consolation of religion. Therefore death was not a "starting point" for Bonhoeffer in his proclaiming of the Good News: "Christ overcame death as 'the last enemy' (1 Cor. 15.26). There is a real difference between the two things; the one [coping with dying] is within the scope of human possibilities, the other [overcoming death] means resurrection. It's not from *ars morendi*, the art of dying, but from the resurrection of Christ, that a new and purifying wind can blow through our present world."[16]

16. *Letters and Papers from Prison*, p. 240. "Freedom, how long we have sought thee in discipline, action, and suffering; dying, we now may behold thee revealed in the Lord" (p. 371). Bonhoeffer correctly assessed the idolization of death in National Socialist ideology as well as its strange, neurotic tension between a mysticism of death and a passionate greed for life. In *Ethics* (pp. 78–79), Bonhoeffer wrote: "The miracle of Christ's resurrection makes nonsense of that [idolization of] death which is prevalent among us today. Where death is the last thing, fear of death is combined with defiance. Where death is the last thing, earthly life is all or nothing. Boastful reliance on earthly eternity goes side by side with a frivolous playing with life. A convulsive acceptance and seizing hold of life stands cheek by jowl with indifference and contempt for life. There is no clearer indication of the idolization of death than when a period claims to be building for eternity and yet life has no value in this period, or when big words are spoken of a new man, of a new world and of a new society which is to be ushered in, and yet all that is new is the destruction of life as we have it. That drastic acceptance or rejection of earthly life reveals that only death has any value here. To clutch at everything or to cast away everything is the reaction of one who believes fanatically in death."

Basically Bonhoeffer is a theologian of rebirth (being born again). That becomes clear in his reflections on inward and outward death:

> But the other thing [i.e. inward death] is the death that takes place in us. It is our own death. It also [like outward death, the physical death of the body] is part of human existence since Adam's fall. But it belongs exclusively to us. We either die this death in Jesus Christ daily or we refuse this death. This death in us has something to do with the love for Christ and man. We die this death when we love Christ and our brothers with all our heart; for to love means to sacrifice oneself totally to the person whom one loves. This death is grace and is the culmination of life. It should be our prayer that we die this death, that it is given to us, and that outward death does not strike us until we have been prepared for it through this, our own inward death; then our outward death will really only be a passage to the perfected love of God.[17]

Thus the ultimate of grace can only occur in the penultimate of the dying of the old man. It is expressed very clearly in *The Cost of Discipleship*: "The first Christ-suffering which every man must experience is the call to abandon the attachments of this world. . . . every command of Jesus is a call to die."[18] Thus being a Christian means the dying off of earthly ties. When Bonhoeffer later said in his letters from prison that we encounter God in the midst of life and do not have to die to encounter him, Bonhoeffer was by no means taking back the above statement from *The Cost of Discipleship*. All of what is entailed by dying in this world lies precisely in all of what is entailed by living a full life in this world. The key here is always the relation between the penultimate and the ultimate. After all, Bonhoeffer meant a this-worldliness "characterized by discipline and the constant knowledge of death and resurrection."[19] Whoever forgets this, even for a moment, makes a primitive positivism of this-worldliness out of Bonhoeffer's theology. Bonhoeffer's attention to this world, to the present order must be understood in light of his Christ-mysticism: the more we engage the world, the more we are obligated, and the more we are obligated, the more we must die to these obligations.

17. *GS*, 2:558.
18. *Cost of Discipleship*, p. 99.
19. *Letters and Papers from Prison*, p. 369.

Bonhoeffer lived what he taught. He was a man living in the dialectical tension of life. He was completely devoted to this life and the world—this athletic, physically rugged-looking intellectual. On the other hand, he was the sensitive and emotional theologian who suffered again and again because of the world, often blamed himself, and was often overcome by *acedia* and *tristitia*. Especially during his time in prison, he was no doubt harried by the valley of the shadow of death to a greater extent than he ever indicated to his friends and students.

Bonhoeffer himself expected an early death. Moreover, his dangerous life from 1939 on made him subject to death on short notice at all times. Therefore he viewed himself—and this is clear by what he wrote at the beginning of the war—as a guest in this world: "I may not evade my lot of having to be a guest and stranger, nor God's call to this situation of being a stranger, by dreaming my earthly life away in thoughts of heaven. There is an extremely godless type of homesickness for the other world that will certainly not be granted a homecoming."[20] Bonhoeffer did not want to shirk his responsibility in this world in favor of the world to come. Nevertheless, his last words were a profession of eternity that lies in another reality: "This is the end, for me, the beginning of life."[21]

Thus Bonhoeffer lived in the tension between this world and the other world, earth and heaven, death and life. In a letter of November 27, 1944, he formulated this tension with Christ-mystical overtones:

> The difference between the Christian hope of resurrection and a mythological hope is that the former sends a man back to his life on earth in a wholly new way which is even more sharply defined than it is in the Old Testament. The Christian, unlike the devotees of the redemption myths, has no last line of escape available from earthly tasks and difficulties into the eternal, but, like Christ himself ("My God, why hast thou forsaken me?"), he must drink the earthly cup to the dregs, and only in his doing so is the crucified and risen Lord with him, and he crucified and risen with Christ. This world must not be prematurely written off; in this the Old and New Testaments are at one. Redemption

20. That is how Bonhoeffer preached at the beginning of the war. See *GS*, 2:431f.
21. Bethge, *Bonhoeffer*, p. 1037.

myths arise from human boundary-experiences, but Christ takes hold of a man at the center of his life.[22]

Thus one can view Bonhoeffer, with his understanding of conversion and being born again, as a "religionless pietist" who truly endured the tension between death and resurrection, heaven and earth. That is what the process of being born again in Christ entails.

22. *Letters and Papers from Prison*, pp. 336–37.

PART 6

Christian Existence as Concrete Truth

17

Discipleship

Cheap Grace

According to secular Protestantism's conception of itself, the way of mankind leads to salvation through morality. A good person goes to heaven because he is good. Grace as such is not the concern of the nominal Protestant. The Protestant who is unfamiliar with Christianity and is nothing more than officially a member of a Protestant church is typically a self-redeemer.

The perversion of grace into cheap grace exists only where there is still more or less close contact with church life. In this case, grace is generally connected with the "dear God" who spreads his mantle of love over the whole world and all mankind. This God who excuses everything becomes everyone's common possession. Grace becomes a matter of course, free of cost like the air that we breathe. Thus, grace logically becomes "cheap grace" and the "forgiveness of sins proclaimed as a general truth." "In such a Church the world finds a cheap covering for its sins; no contrition is required."[1] That is how Bonhoeffer characterized the cheap grace that becomes "justification of sin" and allows people to live a carefree life and eat, drink, and be merry while "Christ foots the bill." Cheap grace is not the "justification of the repentant sinner," but quite the opposite: "Cheap grace is the

1. *Cost of Discipleship*, pp. 45–46.

preaching of forgiveness without requiring repentance, baptism without church discipline, Communion without confession, absolution without personal confession. Cheap grace is grace without discipleship, grace without the cross, grace without Jesus Christ, living and incarnate."[2]

In Bonhoeffer's view, cheap grace had a long history: "As Christianity spread, and the Church became more secularized, this realization of the costliness of grace gradually faded. The world was Christianized, and grace became its common property."[3] Here Bonhoeffer looked beyond all confessional borders to the one great error of the Christian church as a whole. Thus Bonhoeffer registered a reformational demand: he called the church back to the costly grace of primitive Christianity, because through cheap grace the world had become Christian and Christianity secular. Here once again, Bonhoeffer's rejection of the "Christianization of the world" becomes clear. The thoughts in *Letters and Papers from Prison* are closely connected to the observations in *The Cost of Discipleship*.

Christendom has squandered the sacraments at dirt cheap prices among the people. In baptism, the Lord's Supper, and church weddings and funerals, everyone who thinks himself Christian is once again confirmed in his illusion through official ecclesiastical acts without really living as a Christian: "What are those three thousand Saxons put to death by Charlemagne compared with the millions of spiritual corpses in our country to-day?"[4] Bonhoeffer cried out against the everyday reality of the established church in which payers of church tax become recipients of cheap ecclesiastical grace and the blessing of the church is squandered. "We baptized, confirmed, and absolved a whole nation unasked and without condition. Our humanitarian sentiment made us give that which was holy to the scornful and unbelieving. We poured forth unending streams of grace."[5] Bonhoeffer's sad diagnosis from the 1930s is still valid. This everyday reality of the established church survived Bonhoeffer's death and still flourishes today. Nevertheless, Bonhoeffer's critique of cheap grace means the rejection of "established church" Christianity in its present form.

2. Ibid., p. 47.
3. Ibid., p. 49.
4. Ibid., p. 58.
5. Ibid.

Costly Grace

Real grace—costly grace—is not justification of sin, but of the repentant sinner. Costly grace demands repentance as a genuine change of direction that leads to discipleship. The Reformers lived this discipleship "in the midst of the world." Discipleship should not be relegated to monasteries and convents, but should be lived in the midst of everyday life. Thus once again a theme is taken up in *The Cost of Discipleship* that would be worked out further in *Letters and Papers from Prison*. However, "in the midst of the world" does not mean "canonization" or "justification" of the world. Rather, being in the midst of the world and at the same time living as Jesus' disciple means that the Christian has the responsibility to live daily under the forgiveness of the cross. Costly grace is lived-out grace: "For acquired knowledge cannot be divorced from the existence in which it is acquired."[6]

But does not an unreformational stringency lie in these words of Bonhoeffer? Did not even Luther speak of *pecca fortiter* (sin bravely), so that the Christian, all the more lively and joyful in his faith in God's love, can become certain of God's grace to him, even though he is a sinner? Cannot one then be carefree and "sin with impunity while Christ foots the bill"? Bonhoeffer's opinion on the reformational view of grace as expressed in Luther's *sola gratia* and *sola fide* was as follows. For Luther, *pecca fortiter* can only be "the consolation for one whose attempts to follow Christ had taught him that he can never become sinless, who in his fear of sin despairs of the grace of God. . . . those who from the bottom of their hearts make a daily renunciation of sin and of every barrier which hinders him from following Christ, but who nevertheless are troubled by their faithlessness and sin."[7]

Here once again, we see Bonhoeffer's dialectical understanding of sin and grace. Only those who are totally horrified by sin can live completely out of forgiveness and thereby take up the courage of *pecca fortiter.* As we will see in our discussion of *Ethics*, Bonhoeffer experienced this as he faced the bitterly serious question of whether a Christian can justify taking part in the murder of a tyrant. The serious business of discipleship will not be spared the pain of sin. However,

6. Ibid., p. 55.
7. Ibid., pp. 56–57.

neither will it be without the joy of grace and forgiveness. Justification of the sinner who "sins bravely" out of a profound sense of responsibility in the midst of the world also means the acceptance of guilt in discipleship to Christ. For there is no paradisical life of discipleship that is free of conflict. And conflicts can hardly ever be resolved without acceptance of guilt. There is no discipleship without grace, but also no grace without discipleship—there is no separation of justification and sanctification, righteousness and grace. If this integral relation is relinquished, there remains only cheap grace or grace-less moralism.[8]

In the 1930s Bonhoeffer was accused—even by voices from within the Confessing Church—of betraying the Lutheran heritage in his emphasis on discipleship and sanctification. Bonhoeffer's answer: "To be 'Lutheran' must mean that we leave the following of Christ to legalists, Calvinists and enthusiasts—and all this for the sake of grace. We justified the world and condemned as heretics those who tried to follow Christ. The result was that a nation became Christian and Lutheran, but at the cost of true discipleship. The price it was called upon to pay was all too cheap. Cheap grace had won the day."[9] Bonhoeffer wanted a concrete Christianity that is realized in actual discipleship.

What Is Discipleship?

Discipleship begins by listening to Christ's call. There can be no discipleship without obedience: "only he who is obedient believes."[10] But this is also true: only those who have the strength of faith can be obedient. Faith without obedience is mere assent to, or poetic empathy with, or even aesthetic enjoyment of, a falsely understood "Christianness." "Faith is only real when there is obedience, never without

---

8. Erich Mauerhofer, dogmatics professor at the FETA in Basel, took a very strong stand against "cheap grace" in his dissertation at the Theological College of Kampen, entitled *Der Kampf zwischen Fleisch und Geist bei Paulus*. In Mauerhofer's judgment the Christian already lives in a salvation-historical sense in the new eon. He is crucified with Christ in a singular and concluded manner, and God focuses directly on the sanctification of the Christian. Cheap grace, which overlooks the way of sanctification in the struggle between flesh and spirit, has become for Mauerhofer the distinguishing mark of Protestant churches. For a positive and critical discussion of Mauerhofer's view of sanctification, see Georg Huntemann, *Der verlorene Maßstab. Gottes Gebot in dieser Zeit*, 1983, pp. 140ff.

9. *Cost of Discipleship*, pp. 57–58.

10. Ibid., p. 69.

it, and faith only becomes faith in the act of obedience." Real faith "exists only in obedience, is never without obedience, that faith is faith only in the act of obedience."[11] Cheap grace and cheap faith amount to unbelief void of grace. Such unbelief is not put into action and changes nothing. Cheap faith remains nothing more than assent to some dogmatic propositions, or a form of elevated mood—an emotional or intellectual consumptive enjoyment of "Christianity." Cheap grace is religion. According to Bonhoeffer, whoever "believes cheaply" and is "religious" must be exhorted to obedience. "Only those who obey can believe."[12]

However, discipleship is not to be misunderstood ascetically. Discipleship occurs in the midst of the world. Later, in *Letters and Papers from Prison*, Bonhoeffer wrote the following about discipleship: "not in such a way as to injure or weaken our earthly love."[13] To be sure, discipleship calls one out of the world, but it does not drive one to contempt of the world. The *cantus firmus* and the counterpoint belong together as the human and divine natures of Christ belong together: "unseparated and yet distinguishable." Here again we have the dialectical structure in Bonhoeffer's theological thought. The Christian lives in discipleship in the world and with the world, and also delights in the world. Yet, he is not of this world and certainly not bound by this world.

Obedience does not mean that we "run man down in his worldliness."[14] Neither does a disciple of Christ run himself down through a kind of whiny self-pity about his sinfulness. Discipleship is not a self-fixated, egocentric perseverance, but a joyful, trusting, steady progression. Discipleship is not self-pitying. Rather, it trusts in forgiveness. Grace does not inhabit merely a corner of the world, but dwells in the midst of life. The issue in discipleship is to confront man with God at his strongest point.[15] A person is not rid of this world through discipleship; he is placed in this world. He is not rendered dysfunctional by discipleship but is made strong. The meaning of discipleship is to be experienced and recognized precisely in the strongest engagement in this world.

11. Ibid.
12. Ibid., p. 77.
13. *Letters and Papers from Prison*, p. 303.
14. Ibid., p. 346.
15. Ibid.

Discipleship is not an idea or a plan of action. Discipleship is Christ's call: "It is nothing else than bondage to Jesus Christ."[16] There is no grace without the commandment and no commandment without grace: "That is grace and commandment in one."[17] Discipleship is possible only because a now living and here present Jesus Christ exists. Because Christ exists, there must be discipleship. "Discipleship without Jesus Christ is a way of our own choosing."[18] The content of discipleship arises out of listening to and following the call: "And what does the text inform us about the content of discipleship? Follow me, run along beside me! That is all."[19] The content is Jesus Christ himself. Very clearly, we see here again the Bonhoefferian Christ-mysticism. And the ethical emphasis of his Christ-mysticism becomes clear, though, especially in the area of discipleship: The call to discipleship receives no other content than Jesus Christ himself, the relationship to him, community with him.[20]

The consequence of this call is that the caller takes over first place in the life of the one he calls. He is the deciding and ultimate factor to which everything else, as the penultimate, is subordinated: "Fellowship with Jesus and obedience to his commandment come first, and all else follows. Worldly cares are not part of our discipleship, but distinct and subordinate concerns. Before we start taking thought for our life, our food and clothing, our work and families, we must seek the righteousness of Christ."[21] When Bonhoeffer later, in *Letters and Papers from Prison*, emphasizes the "worldliness" of discipleship more, then this occurs in this framework of ultimate and penultimate. Bonhoeffer stresses that "the Christian is bound to the will of God alone, and that every other obligation is for the sake of Jesus conditional upon that will."[22]

In Bonhoeffer's day there was an immediate practical significance to the fact that this ultimate, which is the only thing to which we may tie ourselves without any reservation, is always and only God himself. At

16. *Cost of Discipleship*, p. 63.
17. Ibid.
18. Ibid., pp. 63–64.
19. Ibid., p. 62.
20. Ibid., pp. 62–64.
21. Ibid., p. 201.
22. Ibid., p. 154.

that time even pastors had to swear the oath of allegiance to Hitler, extending the totalitarian claim over people even in the church. For Bonhoeffer, there were political consequences of discipleship to Christ: "If his [the Christian's] own future is outside his own control, how much more is the future of the authority which demands the oath of allegiance! For the sake of the truth, therefore, and for the sake of his following of Christ, he cannot swear such an oath without the proviso, 'God willing.' For the Christian no earthly obligation is absolutely binding."[23]

Often, even in his own church, Bonhoeffer was not taken seriously. The overwhelming majority of pastors in Germany were prepared to swear the oath of allegiance (including, by the way, Karl Barth in 1934, as a Prussian civil servant).[24] The macabre solution to this problem came about through Martin Bormann. Bormann, the chief of

---

23. Ibid.

24. On this point, see Hans Prolingheuer, *Der Fall Karl Barth. Chronographie einer Vertreibung 1934–1935*, 1977. Barth originally wanted to swear the oath to Hitler only with an additional declaration. Later, Barth gave up the additional declaration, and the logical judgment of the Civil Criminal Division of Cologne on December 20, 1934, is as follows (p. 295): "It is decisive to the judgment of this court that the accused is now willing to take the required civil servant oath in the form of the law of August 20, 1934, without any addition." The debate on the issue of taking the oath became the cause of a general falling out within the Confessing Church. The Confessing Church was also divided regarding the broader issue of how to relate to National Socialism. In connection with this dissension, Goebbels had the opportunity to make the following statement in a speech at the District Conference of Berlin on June 29, 1935: "If I were our dear God I would find myself different spokesmen on earth than the ones that pretend nowadays to be his spokesmen. The dear pastors sometimes behave like quarrelsome fishwives. Sometimes one hears the phrase: 'Hitler is good, but the little Hitlers. . . .' One could far more justifiably say, 'Our dear God is good, but the dear little gods. . . .'"

Barth disapproved of the Confessing Church's attitude toward National Socialism just as much as Bonhoeffer. In a letter of June 30, 1935, to the Reformed theologian Hermann Hesse, Barth was very critical: "[The Confessing Church] still does not at all consider that it could possibly have something to say when directing a 'word to the authorities' besides the 'urgent request,' based on its political reliability, for the preservation of its existence as guaranteed by the Reich government. Neither does the Confessing Church consider that its prayer for the God-ordained political authority may have to prove its genuineness in that this prayer would also one day, when the Church sees that lying and illegality have been raised to a principle [of state behavior], be able to become the prayer intended in the Psalms for liberation from a tyranny worthy of the curse. For millions of people suffering injustice the Confessing Church still has no heart. It has not yet found words to address even the simplest questions of public integrity. The church still speaks—when it speaks—for its own cause alone. It still maintains the fiction that the state it is dealing with today is a state founded on the rule of the law as in Romans 13. And today we can expect less than ever that anything of this will soon change" (ibid., p. 349). That the church itself was thinking only of its own survival and thus was not being a church for others—that is exactly what Bonhoeffer deplored in his letters from prison just as Barth did.

staff in the party chancellery and the *Führer's* deputy, opposed requiring pastors to swear the oath of allegiance to Hitler. This happened after long, time-wasting, painful debates in the Confessing Church, which had ended with the majority of confessing pastors having decided to take the oath.

But these events make clear that suffering is a mark of discipleship to Christ: "Following Christ means *passio passiva*, because we have to suffer."[25] Discipleship means taking up one's cross. Affliction comes through the trials of the world, because the Christian suffers under his own fleshliness, his own sinfulness. But the Christian also suffers under the trials brought about by the guilt of others: "he too has to bear the sins of others."[26] In this sense there is in discipleship a quite distinct participation in the cross of Christ, even though we must never for a second dispute that the cross borne by Christ can never be compared to the cross borne by Christians in discipleship to Christ. The cross of Christ is unique.

Thus discipleship also means substitution, and substitution involves assuming guilt. We see that the crucial theme in Bonhoeffer's *Ethics* is already outlined in *The Cost of Discipleship*.

Suffering's meaning does not lie in itself. Suffering passes away through facing and bearing it. Bonhoeffer comments on Jesus' prayer in Gethsemane, that the cup may be taken from him (Matt. 26:39–42): "suffering will indeed pass as he accepts it. . . . The cross is his triumph over suffering."[27] Thus in discipleship suffering is never the ultimate. It has no meaning in itself. It is always the penultimate to the ultimate, and this ultimate is the overcoming of suffering in the resurrection.

How the National Socialists themselves, insofar as they still belonged to the church, viewed their "Christian religious faith" is shown in a "testimony" of Hermann Göring from the early summer of 1935. Göring asserted that for the faith of the [German] race [*Volk*] it is more important to be strong than to "have some imperfect recollection of catechism. We ask the servants of the word who have caused a race [*Volk*] to lose its faith: Where were you in that difficult time, where were the servants of the word when the dragon of Marxism wanted to devour Germany, where were they when Germany threatened to suffocate in unbelief? When a race [*Volk*] stops believing in itself then even the houses of God are no longer of any use" (ibid., p. 201).

25. *Cost of Discipleship*, p. 100.
26. Ibid.
27. Ibid., p. 102.

Bonhoeffer—A Theologian of Conversion and Rebirth?

It has certainly become clear that Bonhoeffer was not a pietist in the religious sense of the word. But if the real experience of being born again is a part of particularly pietist piety, then Bonhoeffer was a pietist. For Bonhoeffer, the real experience of being born again was an essential element of discipleship: there is no discipleship without being born again, but also no being born again without discipleship. His theology is a plea for the theology of regeneration. Being born again is not viewed here in a religious-emotional way. It is not the transformation from an emotional low to an emotional high, experienced as religious enjoyment. Understood Christ-mystically, being born again means participation in the suffering and death of Christ: "As we embark upon discipleship we surrender ourselves to Christ in union with his death—we give over our lives to death. Thus it begins; the cross is not the terrible end to an otherwise god-fearing and happy life, but it meets us at the beginning of our communion with Christ. When Christ calls a man, he bids him come and die."[28] Discipleship thus brings death, the break with all ties to the ego and the world. The disciple who has been born again depends neither on his ego nor on the world: he lives in and with Christ. He is crucified with Christ and has experienced powerlessness but also the resurrection to a new life with him. As Müller insightfully recognized, discipleship is not self-assertion but self-surrender.[29] Thus, discipleship does not result in "religious self-assertion." That would be the kind of religious aping that all too often marks historic pietism. Instead, discipleship brings self-surrender: "I no longer live, but Christ lives in me" (Gal. 2:20). This experience is precisely the experience of conversion and being born again.

28. Ibid., p. 99.
29. Müller, *Von der Kirche zur Welt*, p. 324.

18

Living According
to the Sermon on the Mount

In Bonhoeffer's understanding of discipleship, "Adherence to the law is something quite different from the following of Christ, . . . and any adherence to his person that disregards the law is equally removed from the following of him."[1] Thus there is no discipleship without the law of God, without the biblical revelation of the commandments in the Torah: "There is no new law. Only the one, old law."[2] Jesus does not want a better law. That is what the Pharisees wanted. Rather, "it is the one and the same; every letter of it, every jot and tittle, must remain in force and be observed until the end of the world."[3] But this law is always the law of God. It is the command of him who commands. Therefore, there is no "fulfilment of the law apart from communion with God, and no communion with God apart from fulfilment of the law."[4] Thus, there is no commandment without he who commands, but also no faith in him who commands without commandments.

It is not a matter of a schematic law that the Christian has to follow. Rather what is meant is the commandment of God to which we

1. *Cost of Discipleship,* p. 136.
2. Ibid., p. 137.
3. Ibid.
4. Ibid., p. 138.

194

respond in our relationship to this living God. The law is the law of God; thus God is greater than the law. For discipleship that means "genuine adherence to Christ also means adherence to the law of God."[5] But in Bonhoeffer's thought, this interaction with the law of God takes place completely within the context of his Christ-mysticism. The disciple fulfills the law because Jesus has already fulfilled it. The Christian follows after the one who has fulfilled this law of God as God wills it to be fulfilled. But there is still more: Christ as our substitute has lived out the righteousness that we who are his disciples can never realize: "He is the righteousness of the disciples."[6]

Thus Bonhoeffer remained completely within the camp of reformational Christianity: Christ leads us. In our place he bore our punishment and our curse for us. On this theme Müller writes:

> This orientation of discipleship to the cross is the hermeneutical principle by which Bonhoeffer interprets the Sermon on the Mount. The cross is the goal of the Sermon on the Mount, as the Sermon on the Mount is preparation for the cross. Thus, the Sermon on the Mount is not understood as positive law. That is, it becomes neither an Anabaptist structural principle of this world, nor does it become a series of excessive demands that release us from obedience because they are unfulfillable. The Sermon on the Mount is then neither the extraordinary possibility of a few, nor the guiding principle for a limited area of life that is basically outside of the everyday life of the Christian. . . . Because the cross is reality, Bonhoeffer understands the entire Sermon on the Mount not as imperative, but as indicative; and thus understood, the new commandment is at the same time the old law and the new Gospel.[7]

Whoever lives in discipleship is thus Christ-mystically included in Christ's destiny. It is not the Christian who bears Christ; it is Christ who bears the Christian. Just as we take part in Christ's suffering, cross, and resurrection because he includes us in them, so also do we take part in his righteousness, not because we are righteous, but because he allows us to have a part of his righteousness.

5. Ibid., p. 139.
6. Ibid., p. 141.
7. Müller, *Von der Kirche zur Welt*, p. 215.

This is how Bonhoeffer developed a Christ-mystical ethics or an ethical Christ-mysticism. Christ includes us in his striving for righteousness: righteousness is the essence of discipleship.[8] This righteousness is not done or made. Rather it is experienced. It simply comes over the Christian. The righteousness of the Christian is a righteousness that radiates from Christ, and the Christian radiates Christ's righteousness back. The righteousness that we live in discipleship to Christ is just as impossible to manufacture as are love and real affliction. Through this Christ-mystical understanding of discipleship, a moralistic or legalistic view of the Sermon on the Mount is ruled out once and for all. The natural man does not fulfill the law of Christ because he does not live in and with Christ. But neither can the Christian in discipleship ever fulfill the law of Christ and his righteousness. Somewhere, sometime, and somehow the Christian will always fail. But because he lives in discipleship, he also lives under the cross and thereby under the cross of forgiveness and reconciliation as well.

Fellow Human Beings

Bonhoeffer took the Sermon on the Mount quite literally, without any ifs, ands, or buts. He saw the root sin of all sin in the question: "Is God really supposed to have said?" [cf. Gen. 3:1]. For Bonhoeffer there was no doubt that Jesus did not mean only "the brother in the church" when he talked about loving one's enemies. The point for the life of the Christian with his fellow human beings is that the disciple of Christ cannot allow his actions to be determined by who the other person is, but only by the One Whom he follows in obedience.[9] Love for one's neighbor is an integral part of being in Christ. Loving one's brother is worship. Service to one's brother may not be separated from worship because "if we despise our brother our worship is unreal."[10] The Christian may not participate in the service of the Word or in the Lord's Supper if he is unreconciled with someone. The Christian lives with his fellow human beings, just as Christ lived among us.

But how did Christ live with his fellow human beings? Was his love a love that tolerated, allowed, and put up with everything? Jesus had

8. *Cost of Discipleship,* pp. 140–41.
9. Ibid., pp. 142–46.
10. Ibid., p. 144.

mercy on his fellow human beings; he loved them, but he also condemned and judged. He unified and he separated (Matt. 10:34–39; Luke 12:49–53). Thus love of fellow human beings can never mean a permissive tolerance or indifference to everything that another person does. In true discipleship, how I respond in each situation to my neighbor, my brother, or my enemy, cannot be regulated by laws. Rather, it arises out of spiritual knowledge, which grows out of discipleship.

This discipleship in love orients itself according to the love of Christ. We should love as Christ loved. We are indeed drawn into Christ's love through discipleship. And this love of Christ can be strict. It can reject, punish, and condemn as well as heal, help, seek, and forgive. The Christ of the Sermon on the Mount is the merciful and helping, but also judging Christ. The Christ who heals the sick and forgives sins is the Christ who at his second coming at the end of time will ride the white horse and tread the winepress of wrath (Rev. 19:11–16). Therefore, Jesus' statements in the Sermon on the Mount, such as those about loving one's neighbor and one's enemies, are not a "general ethical plan of action." That is how Gandhi and Tolstoy misunderstood the Sermon on the Mount.

The evil which one is not to resist (Matt. 5:39) is and remains evil. Bonhoeffer left no doubt that he understood this. But Jesus sees the possibility that "the right way to requite evil . . . is not to resist it."[11] For community can be preserved only if "evil is not added to evil." Bonhoeffer was of the opinion that evil should and can "run itself to a standstill,"[12] if it does not find what it seeks, namely, resistance. Then evil can no longer do what it really wants to do, namely, create a new evil. On this issue, Bonhoeffer wrote and interpreted in an unusually radical way. When he called for human beings to renounce revenge, he did not, as was customary in traditional theology, make a distinction between the private person and the office-bearer. But how should office-bearers such as judges and policemen renounce the use of force? To that question, Bonhoeffer said: "To make non-resistance a principle for secular life is to deny God, by undermining his gracious ordinance for the preservation of the world."[13]

11. Ibid., p. 157.
12. Ibid., pp. 157–58.
13. Ibid., p. 161.

How should we understand that? On the one hand we are called to renounce resistance against anything that is evil, so that the evil does not create new evil and community is preserved. And on the other hand Bonhoeffer clearly recognizes that the order of the world can only be preserved if power and revenge are practiced according to the measure of justice.

We are reminded that in the Advent of 1943 Bonhoeffer wrote: "It is only when one submits to God's law that one may speak of grace; and it is only when God's wrath and vengeance are hanging as grim realities over the heads of one's enemies that something of what it means to love and forgive them can touch our hearts. In my opinion it is not Christian to want to take our thoughts and feelings too quickly and too directly from the New Testament."[14] Thus the Christian may not speak the ultimate word of grace before the penultimate word of justice. Whoever does evil, does evil against God. Whoever is an enemy of Christ's church is really an enemy of God. This must always be made clear. Love does not renounce justice. Bonhoeffer confessed in this letter that he had not expressed clearly enough in *The Cost of Discipleship* that the ultimate of love and forgiveness follows the penultimate of justice and revenge. Out of this we conclude that law and vengeance are necessary in order that injustice can be controlled and law and order preserved. (We will see later how important this became for Bonhoeffer especially in his *Ethics*.) If justice is restored and the penultimate of law and order is fulfilled, then forgiveness and mercy are also possible. The real overcoming of evil, the triumph of the ultimate in love, can be accomplished only in the context of God's justice. That is why Christ died on the cross. Justice had to be fulfilled. He had to bear our punishment.

The nonresistance of evil does not mean surrender to evil. To surrender is not to overcome evil. It is also clear that justice limits evil but does not overcome it: "The will of God, to which the law gives expression, is that men should defeat their enemies by loving them." The enemy, whether a political or religious enemy, has "nothing to expect from a follower of Jesus but unqualified love."[15]

14. *Letters and Papers from Prison*, p. 157.
15. *Cost of Discipleship*, p. 164.

Once again, love does not invalidate justice. Love without justice would be love without the cross. At best, that would be sentimentality or eroticism. Guilt can be forgiven only if the guilty party recognizes his guilt and asks for forgiveness. Injustice cannot be covered by the mantle of love or simply brushed from the table. Guilt is a wound that must be overcome. The injustice of the enemy must be revealed. For only when the Christian confesses his guilt before God is he forgiven his guilt—otherwise it would just be cheap grace. Cheap grace does not just ruin man's encounter with God; it also ruins man's encounter with man.

We must keep in mind when considering Bonhoeffer's observations about the Sermon on the Mount that above all Bonhoeffer thought dialectically. The integral relation of love and justice is as impossible to fit into a system as God himself is. The Sermon on the Mount is about discipleship to Christ, and right decisions can be made only by trusting in the reality of this discipleship. To sum up: justice without love is brutality. Love without justice is sentimentality. The integral relation of love and justice is the essential thing in discipleship to Christ.

The "Extraordinary"

What Jesus calls surpassing righteousness (Matt. 5:20) in the Sermon on the Mount is according to Bonhoeffer "the extraordinary." He said: "The hall-mark of the Christian is the 'extraordinary.' The Christian cannot live at the world's level, because he must always remember the *perisson*."[16] What is this *perisson*? It is "the love of Jesus Christ himself."[17] This love is love unto death on the cross, because the "striking aspect" of Christianity is the cross that allows the Christian to be beyond-the-world and gives him the victory over the world.[18] Those who are blessed in the Beatitudes are "extraordinary ones" or "perfect ones" or "special ones" who in each situation always stand under the cross. By these blessed ones, Bonhoeffer did not mean ethical rigorists, eccentrics of a super morality or an ascetic lifestyle. Rather, he meant those who live simultaneously under the cross and in the midst of the world.

16. Ibid., p. 170.
17. Ibid.
18. Ibid.

Who are these blessed ones? They are those who mourn, those who are aware of their spiritual poverty; the meek, those who hunger and thirst for righteousness; the merciful, those who are pure in heart and love peace and who are persecuted for righteousness' sake. None of these mirror the normality of social existence. They are the extraordinary ones, the exceptions in every human society in the entire world. These extraordinary ones who are blessed by Jesus are the real disciples.

In *The Cost of Discipleship* the main stress lies on these "extraordinary ones." Later, Bonhoeffer criticized his own handling of that which should give direction to all human affairs, the righteousness of God as the ordering law of God (not as "natural conditions") in *The Cost of Discipleship*, remarking that he had not dealt with this theme sufficiently. In regard to the complete work of Bonhoeffer, but also and above all in regard to his *Ethics*, we should observe: the God-directed order, grounded in his righteousness, is the righteousness that is valid for us. It has to be. Only then can the extraordinary also become possible. But righteousness tends toward the extraordinary, in other words, toward mercy. Love "keeps no record of wrongs" and "it is not easily angered," but it "does not delight in evil but rejoices with the truth" (1 Cor. 13:5–6).

This integral relation between extraordinary and ordinary, between righteousness or justice and love cannot be synthesized or systematized.

The Christian in discipleship to Christ must act in responsibility toward the Lord who called him to discipleship. And then he will have to decide in each situation whether he should establish justice through the use of power and measured vengeance, or whether he should act in loving forgiveness and nonresistance to evil. But regardless of what the Christian decides, he always stands under the cross and he is always in need of forgiveness. No discipleship without forgiveness, no forgiveness without discipleship. Here once again Müller remarks aptly: "The peace of Jesus Christ is the cross. But the cross is God's sword on this earth. It cuts things in two. . . . As far as I can see Bonhoeffer is one of the very few in modern theology who have dared to be truthful enough to acknowledge the seriousness of natural man's contradiction of the cross. . . . Because he can take the cross seriously, he does not have to be surprised that the world also takes the cross seriously—and hates it."[19]

To put it in concrete terms: that person is mistaken who thinks that he acts completely in line with discipleship to Christ only when he loves his enemy and yields to him, or does not resist evil and allows it to happen to himself and others without assuming any guilt. Conversely, whoever practices reprisal and vengeance at any price because justice has been violated in his opinion also falls into guilt, since the ultimate, the extraordinary, is always love and forgiveness. Knowing how to act or how to decide in each particular case can only arise out of discipleship, out of the power of the Holy Spirit. And nevertheless, each decision is always so imperfect that it is in need of forgiveness. No discipleship without the cross, no cross without discipleship.

Discipleship as Political Opposition

Bonhoeffer finished the final version of *The Cost of Discipleship* in the years 1935–37. His thoughts on discipleship can be traced back as far as 1932. But *The Cost of Discipleship* as we know it arose in the time between 1935 and 1937, in the context of his teaching duties at the seminary in Finkenwalde. H. Strunk has the following observation about *The Cost of Discipleship* in the context of the political situation in Germany at the time: "For Bonhoeffer, discipleship entails not the saving of one's own soul from the condition of this world, but essentially 'protest,' opposition to the condition of the world; 'Hand-to-hand combat' under which one 'takes hold of the world.'"[20]

Bonhoeffer's *The Cost of Discipleship* stands in stark contrast to the events that ruled the day in Germany in the years between 1935 and 1937. These years were characterized by the triumph of the National Socialist movement. In January 1935, 90.5 percent of the population of Saarland decided in favor of annexation with Germany. The Catholic bishops of Germany stood on the side of reunification with National Socialist Germany. In an interview with the *Kölnische Zeitung* at the end of December 1934, even the former social-democratic minister of the interior of Prussia, Karl Severing, welcomed the possibility that the

19. Müller, *Von der Kirche zur Welt*, p. 217.
20. On this point, see the postscript to the original German edition of *Cost of Discipleship*, p. 293.

Saarland would be annexed to the German Reich. More and more, the opposition against Hitler was melting away. Thus, in March 1935, Hitler was able to announce the reintroduction of compulsory military service in Germany—a clear violation of the Treaty of Versailles. To begin, thirty-six German divisions were to be raised, and Hermann Göring announced proudly that Germany had a powerful air force at its disposal. Whoever spoke out against the Reich and its regime was put in a concentration camp. In 1935 the system of concentration camps was thoroughly reorganized. There were seven concentration camps with a total of about seven to nine thousand prisoners. They were guarded by the "SS death's head units" which as "SS guard units" no longer belonged to the overall general unit of the SS.

In May 1935 Leni Riefenstahl's film *Triumph of the Will* was premiered during a ceremony of the Imperial Chamber of Culture in the State Opera of Berlin. This film, which was full of vigorous men and the marching of massive military columns and which atmospherically accompanied the epic proportions of the National Socialist dictatorship with Wagnerian music, was in its entirety the exact opposite of that which Bonhoeffer expressed in his *The Cost of Discipleship*. The will to power, the man of power, the closed columns, the iron will— all of that in contrast to the person who wanted to live under the cross in discipleship to Christ, in the tension between love and justice. In May 1935 the compulsory Labor Service was introduced. The following may be found in the text of the law that was passed: "All young Germans of both sexes are obligated to serve the *Volk* in the Reich Labor Service. Those who are physically unfit and those who are non-Aryans, as well as those who are married to non-Aryans, will not be called to the Labor Service. By decree of the *Führer*, the period of service will be set at one half year."

In the month of June of that same year Hitler was able to celebrate perhaps his greatest triumph. The naval treaty between England and Germany was signed, thereby officially abolishing the Treaty of Versailles once and for all. With this, Hitler had established himself internationally. In September 1935 the Racial Laws were promulgated at the Party Congress in Nuremberg—"The Law for the Protection of German Blood and German Honor," which was also called the "Blood Protection Law" for short. According to this law, marriage and even sexual intercourse outside of marriage between Jews and official citizens having German or German-related blood were forbidden. Also, only people of German or related blood could be citizens of the German Reich. Already in November, the first regulations for implementing these Nuremberg Laws came into force. After that Jews could no longer be citizens of the Reich and no longer had the right to vote. They could not hold public office. Jewish public officials lost their pensions and exact regulations were enacted as to who was to be categorized as German, Jew, or half-breed.

In March 1936, in violation of the requirement of the Treaty of Locarno, German troops marched into the demilitarized zone of the Rhineland. The Reichstag was dissolved, new elections were called, and the voters given a single list of candidates that they could mark Yes or No. This vote was at the same time a vote of confidence for Hitler's policies: 99 percent of all Germans voted for these policies of Hitler. The Olympic Games in Berlin in 1936 were another brilliant hour in the history of the new German Reich, whose triumphs now generally appeared to be unlimited.

In March 1937 Pope Pius XI published the encyclical "With Deep Anxiety and Burning Indignation" in which he sharply criticized the practices and theories of National Socialist ideology without directly attacking the Nazi regime. These conflicts between church and state had no effect on the stream of events. Hitler had correctly assessed the insignificance of the churches of both great confessions. Thus, when he received the Italian head of state Benito Mussolini in Berlin in September 1937, Hitler was able to celebrate another great triumph. Unemployment had decreased substantially. In general, people were content.

To be in the opposition in those years required much sensitivity and steadfastness. The law was being violated, democracy was dead, the Jewish minority was being pushed into a realm where they had no rights, and a *Weltanschauung* was spreading that was carrying out the mobilization of the German soul in a way that did not make the future look very good. But who could have foreseen what this would lead to? Bonhoeffer was one of the very few who did. Against the neo-heroic militarization of the German soul in the years 1935–37, Bonhoeffer confessed the peace of Christ. Against the emaciation of the established church and its accommodation to the general political consciousness—against the "*Kasualienkirche*" with its cheap grace,

Bonhoeffer stood with the "confessing community" of faithful Christians in discipleship and sanctification.

Peters sees a yet stronger significance of the political in Bonhoeffer's *The Cost of Discipleship*. He maintains that Bonhoeffer developed his theology of the cross at a time when he "could not find an affirmative relationship to the political attempts to solve the problems of the years 1932–33."[21] Peters argues that Bonhoeffer experienced inner conflict instead of reconciliation with the political order of the national revolution, and that this inner conflict realized itself as the carrying of the cross in this world, this "cursed earth." The cross then became a rebellion against this world of the penultimate. However, Peters says, Bonhoeffer did not intend "cross" to mean "renunciation of the world" but resistance after the manner of Gandhi's pacifism.

But is discipleship really in that sense "a critical renunciation of society and the times"? It is true that Bonhoeffer decidedly renounced the Third Reich and was opposed to any accommodation to it. But that does not mean that his interpretation of the Sermon on the Mount in *The Cost of Discipleship* was merely an instrument of opposition to the Nazi regime. The issue is much larger than that. Discipleship is a renunciation of the world as world. That is completely clear, for Christ is not the confirmation but the overcoming of the world. It would be a misuse of Bonhoeffer to reduce *The Cost of Discipleship* to a political statement about the "work of opposition." *The Cost of Discipleship* is a protest against every satisfied-bourgeois or religious-ceremonial perversion of Christianity. The issue for Bonhoeffer was sanctification and concretization of faith in this world so that those who are called out of the world also become disciples in the world.

But precisely this logical view of Christian existence "automatically" had to lead to an inner confrontation with the this-worldly mythology of the 1930s as expressed in Nazi ideology. Bonhoeffer did not contrive the political consequences. They were simply given in his view of what is Christian. It is important, though, that one keep this background of the 1930s in view. The suffering of which Bonhoeffer spoke, this "nonresistance" to evil, is the enduring of the totalitarian dictatorship and a modus operandi for undermining this system through nonresistance. Bonhoeffer once said that the Sermon on the

---

21. Peters, *Die Präenz*, p. 114.

Mount was "the only source of strength that can blow all of the magic and horror [of nazism] to smithereens."[22] Clearly, discipleship is understood to be opposed to remilitarization and the oath of allegiance to the *Führer*.

Here, the emphasis on the ultimate becomes opposition to the penultimate. If the penultimate of the order and just working of the state has broken down, then this system can and should be overcome by means of the ultimate of suffering and nonresistance. Thus one certainly can and may understand Bonhoeffer without unduly politicizing him. Undoubtedly the Sermon on the Mount then becomes the opposition of the ultimate against the penultimate. But that does not then become a principle. Rather, it is a possibility in a totalitarian situation such as that with which Bonhoeffer was faced. That he later decided in favor of another possibility, namely, that of political opposition that included being ready to use force, simply shows that Bonhoeffer did not derive from the Sermon on the Mount an absolute pacifism that was valid for all times and situations.

22. *GS*, 3:25 (a letter to K. F. Bonhoeffer of January 14, 1935).

19

Discipleship and Community

In the World, But Not of the World

Sanctification is first of all separation from the world. Those who are saints in Christ are different from the world not because they want to be or contrive it to be so, but simply because they are. Nevertheless saints are in the world and live with this world. And they also carry "the world" within themselves. Saints remain sinners and need justification. Therefore, sanctification is a continuous process—not a "having" but a "being"—better yet, a becoming. But the basic process of sanctification is also a "being cut out" of the world. In the Hebrew, *qados* (holy) comes from *qadad* (to cut), and this undoubtedly incorporates the notion that something of the "profanity'" of the world is cut out so that one can be especially dedicated to God. The saint who has been "made holy" is the "one cut out of the world." It is significant what Bonhoeffer said about the "community of saints" in their relationship to the world: "Like a sealed train travelling through foreign territory, the Church goes on its way through the world. Its journey is like that of the ark, which was 'pitched within and without with pitch' (Gen. 6.14), that it might come safely through the flood. The saints are sealed so that they might have redemption, deliverance and salvation . . . at the second coming of Christ."[1] Bonhoeffer saw the community of Christ's disciples as the community of the endtimes.

1. *Cost of Discipleship*, p. 313.

During the years 1935 to 1937, in the *Führer's* "thousand-year kingdom" on earth, when the present was being lifted up and exalted jubilantly and when Protestant theologians strove for the melting of the church into the *Volk* as a whole, the lonely voice of Finkenwalde reminded people of the apocalyptic structure of the church, which is in this world but not of this world.

Thus Bonhoeffer sang a completely different melody from his contemporaries when he said about the community of saints: "Their sanctification will be maintained by their being clearly *separated from the world*. . . . Their sanctification will be *hidden*, and they must wait for the day of Jesus Christ."[2]

Sanctification Perfectionism

It was unusual for a Protestant theologian to put such emphasis on sanctification. That was not at all the song that Lutheran theologians were singing at the time. Some asked at the time if Bonhoeffer had acquired a Reformed or Catholic understanding of what a Christian is. (By the way, that was only asked in small circles, because at the time Bonhoeffer was not nearly so well known as he is today.) But we, too, ask: Is sanctification, in Bonhoeffer's view, possible as a "finished process"? Can sanctification in this sense become a kind of possession? Here once again, Bonhoeffer's answer reveals the dialectical structure of his thought: "The believer will be justified, the justified will be sanctified and the sanctified will be saved in the day of judgment. But this does not mean that our faith, our righteousness and our sanctification (in so far as they depend on ourselves) could be anything but sin. No, all this is true only because Jesus Christ has become our 'righteousness, and sanctification and redemption, so that he that glorieth let him glory in the Lord' (1 Cor. 1.30)."[3]

In his emphasis on the sanctification that is effected through Christ, Bonhoeffer really did lie more within the Reformed than the Lutheran camp. But he remained very much a reformational theologian because he always knew that sanctification does not come from us, but from him who effects it in us. The sanctified person is saved at the final judgment not because there are only a few "imperfections"

2. Ibid., p. 314.
3. Ibid., pp. 335–36.

that he still has to work out, but because the sanctified person lives from grace even in his sanctification—his real sanctification—namely, the actual experience of love, faith, and hope. Thus, sanctification is understood here Christ-mystically.

The Political Significance of Sanctification

The community of saints is a visible community. It is the "city set on the hill. . . . Hence there is a certain 'political' character involved in the idea of sanctification."[4] At that time, that was a slap in the face of all Lutheran theologians. That the church as community of saints is visible precisely because of and through its sanctification and that it has something to say to the world, including the *polis*; that it thus has a substantial message for the political realm—those were unusual ideas for conventional academic theology in Germany at that time. Thus, out of sanctification comes a "political ethics." Certainly the world is the world and the church is the church. But the Word has to go out from the church over the whole world as the message that the world and all within it is the Lord's.

Thus, the community of saints is not an unworldly idyll for the pious. The "pious wishes of the religious flesh . . . the 'deceitful arrogance and the false spirituality of the old man'" is salvation egoism, which Bonhoeffer decidedly rejects.[5] But sanctification, life in discipleship, in faith, in love, and in hope, can be realized only in community: "By pursuing sanctification outside the church we are trying to pronounce ourselves holy."[6]

With this idea of the integral relation between sanctification and the visible community of saints, Bonhoeffer undoubtedly set a direction that lay outside of traditional Lutheran theology.[7] In June 1936 he wrote a report for the Council of the Confessing Church of Pomerania with the title: "Irrlehre in der Bekennenden Kirche?" ["False Doctrine

---

4. Ibid., p. 314.
5. Ibid., p. 315.
6. Ibid.
7. See Bethge, *Bonhoeffer*, p. 573: "Curiously enough, Bonhoeffer's attitude was seen as 'infiltrated by the Reformed view.'" "Curiously enough" is a mistaken choice of words. Bonhoeffer was really on the way to thinking and writing in a Reformed manner, especially in theological ethics, and in his view of sanctification, of the integral relation of state and church, and of the independence of the individual congregation.

in the Confessing Church?"] In this report he wrote: "these accusations are accompanied by the popular-scientific assertion that the Confessing Church has long been infiltrated by 'Reformed' doctrine. It is claimed that the issue today for Lutheran pastors and congregations is the liberation from the enslavement to Reformed 'legalism.'"

This accusation of Reformed "legalism" is of course factually false, but formally correct. For the integral relation between sanctification and the community of saints as described by Bonhoeffer could not be found in the Lutheran confessions. That is why the official churches could not accept Bonhoeffer's position at that time, nor can they accept it now even if they would consider accepting it. But precisely this integral relation of sanctification and church, this visibility of sanctification, sanctification as a sign of the city on the hill—precisely this was Bonhoeffer's concern. It was a part of his struggle against cheap grace, against the secularization of the church.

Did Bonhoeffer hold to this opinion throughout his life? We find the decisive statement on *The Cost of Discipleship* in a letter of July 21, 1944: "I thought I could acquire faith by trying to live a holy life, or something like it. I suppose I wrote *The Cost of Discipleship* as the end of that path. Today I can see the dangers of that book, although I still stand by what I wrote."[8] Many theologians welcomed this statement of Bonhoeffer with great jubilation. They saw in it the step out of sanctification and the community of saints into the world: "From the church to the world"—this is where they believed they had found a mandate for the modernist interpretation of Bonhoeffer.

Now Bonhoeffer does speak here of a path. The path that he walked along at that time was the path of the isolated community in Finkenwalde, which at that time became his strived-for ashram (spiritual retreat). Then, in 1944, he took another look at this isolated life that he had tried to lead as a holy life, and wrote that he had learned "that it is only by living completely in this world that one learns to have faith. One must completely abandon any attempt to make something of oneself, whether it be a saint, or a converted sinner, or a churchman."[9] Now at that time Bonhoeffer did not at all attempt to make a saint or a churchman out of himself. He did not view himself as a con-

8. *Letters and Papers from Prison*, p. 369.
9. Ibid.

verted sinner either. But while in *The Cost of Discipleship* the accent is more on the ultimate of sanctification while the penultimate of the world remains in the background, now, in political opposition and then in imprisonment, the penultimate of political resistance has moved into the foreground. Not in a way that the penultimate has been detached from the ultimate, but just the opposite: Bonhoeffer lived in a world in which he could allow the ultimate of the Word of God to teach him what is possible when challenged by the penultimate of the world. "Then one throws oneself completely into God's arms." Now he no longer perceived his own suffering so much as a disciple in the world but rather as the suffering of the world itself and of God in the world. Then one is "watching with Christ in Gethsemane."[10]

That is exactly what is new—that the Christian does not bear his own suffering or the suffering of the church, but really bears the suffering of the world and of God in the world. From this point of view there is no break between *The Cost of Discipleship* and *Letters and Papers from Prison,* but only a broadening of knowledge that necessarily results in a shift of accent from the ultimate to the penultimate. But Bonhoeffer remained in his dialectical structure of the integral relation between "in the world" but not "of the world." *The Cost of Discipleship* was written when Bonhoeffer was surrounded by a crowd of seminary students who saw themselves as part of the Confessing Church. *Letters and Papers from Prison* was not written in the community of saints but in the community of the completely profane, in the powerlessness of a prison cell. In the midst of the world of the military prison in Tegel, with the prisoners and the crafty corporals who guarded them, Bonhoeffer really took part in the suffering not only of the saints, but also of the world as a whole.

In this context Bonhoeffer recalled a friend of his youth in his letters from prison, Jean Lassere, a French Protestant pacifist who later became known for his book *La guerre et l'évangelie* which came out in 1953. Bonhoeffer recalled a conversation in which Lassere had said to Bonhoeffer that he wanted to become a saint. Bonhoeffer replied that he wanted to learn to believe. Lassere did become a saint in the sense that he became a pacifist and desired to live out sanctification in the world in this way. Bonhoeffer decided differently as a part of the polit-

10. Ibid., p. 370.

ical opposition to Hitler. In this way he did not lead a "holy life," but "got his hands dirty" in his willingness to resist, rebel, and participate in the murder of a tyrant. It was the experience of Bonhoeffer that one must be ready to "take guilt upon oneself" when one is in the midst of the world, for sanctification in the world is something different from sanctification alongside of the world. All of this was somehow brought to expression already in *The Cost of Discipleship,* but it is accentuated differently in the letters from prison.

What is the break that many theologians tend to see between *The Cost of Discipleship* and *Letters and Papers from Prison,* written in the spring of 1944? Müller sees this break as the transition out of the church and into the world. Clifford Greens believes that the Bonhoeffer of the 1930s, in other words the Bonhoeffer of *Discipleship,* did not appreciate human strength as a good gift carrying the possibility of genuine strength, but only as something destructive, such as power in the totalitarian state.[11] David Hopper considers Bonhoeffer's thought in *The Cost of Discipleship* to be reactive—a defense against an insistently ideological and all-devouring world reality.[12] He sees *The Cost of Discipleship* as simply too negative. Rainer Strunk is of the opinion that Bonhoeffer in *The Cost of Discipleship* does not have a clear concept of the world.[13] But all of these interpretations fail to recognize not only the totality of Bonhoeffer's thought, but also the dialectical structure, his new way of thinking, which recognized and reflected upon reality in a bipolar way.

The Bonhoeffer of the 1930s concentrated on the ultimate against the secularization of the penultimate with which the church was currying favor. His stress on the wholly other is a condemnation of this-world fanaticism. His emphasis on compassion, bearing one another's burdens, and mercy stands against his time's obsessive affirmation of life and its "principle of selection." And his high praise of those who hunger and thirst for righteousness stands against the unrighteousness that was growing more and more at that time. But never, either

---

11. Clifford Greens, *The Sociality of Christ and Humanity,* 1972; translation by Bethge, *Cost of Discipleship,* p. 296.

12. David Hopper, *A Dissent on Bonhoeffer,* 1975.

13. Rainer Strunk, *Nachfolge Christi. Erinnerungen an eine evangelische Provokation,* p. 213. On this point, see also Bethge's postscript to the original German edition of *Cost of Discipleship,* pp. 296ff.

in *The Cost of Discipleship* or in the least bit in *Letters and Papers from Prison,* did he think even for a moment of placing the church at the sidelines of the world.

Bonhoeffer lived what he said. When he wrote *The Cost of Discipleship* he was the director of a seminary where his job was to train seminarians for the ministry. When he wrote his letters from prison he was a political prisoner who had been an informant in the political opposition. Thus, he was at one time more in the world of the ultimate and at another time more in the world of the penultimate. But just as Bonhoeffer did not neglect to speak of the penultimate of the world in his handling of the ultimate in *The Cost of Discipleship*, so also, in the penultimate of the political, he experienced the ultimate in the truth of the cross as the forgiveness of guilt (guilt he had taken upon himself) and as participation in the suffering of God in the world. We know that the letters in *Letters and Papers from Prison* unconditionally rule out any Christianization of the world or secularization of Christianity. We know that because Bonhoeffer wrote in those letters of the *arcanum,* the place in which the body of believers is hidden from the world and readies itself for the world under the Word. The dialectical tension between sanctification and world, church and politics, informs Bonhoeffer's entire life's work. His concern was always all of reality—the one reality—but it is always a bipolar, dialectically experienced reality that cannot be systematized. Today, one cannot understand *The Cost of Discipleship* without *Letters and Papers from Prison,* nor vice versa. *The Cost of Discipleship* speaks to the penultimate of the world out of the ultimate of the community of saints. In *Letters and Papers from Prison* Bonhoeffer speaks out of the penultimate of political experience to the ultimate of the truth of the cross. There are different phases, different positions, but they are all in one life process of being a Christian. Each time, there are variations on the one great theme in the thought and life of Bonhoeffer: the Christ-mystical understanding of this God-forsaken modern world.

PART 7

Bonhoeffer's Ethics of Order

20

The Dissolution of All Values

In the year 1940, Bonhoeffer had to lay down his work at the seminary for good. At that time the "Reich Ban on Speaking" was imposed on him, and the "Reich Chamber of Literature" forbade him all literary activity including the sending of circular letters or printed material.

The beginning of *Ethics* goes back to 1939. The individual fragments were written from 1940 to 1943 in the Ettal Monastery, the attic room of his parents' home, and the manor house at Kieckow in Pomerania. His work on *Ethics* was interrupted often by his activity as informant in the *Amt Canaris* or by other activity in the political opposition. Bonhoeffer did not leave behind a completed *Ethics*, but only fragments. On December 15, 1943, he wrote: "I sometimes feel as if my life were more or less over, and as if all I had to do now were to finish my *Ethics*."[1] As we know, he was never able to finish it. When Bonhoeffer was writing the various fragments, the Second World War was raging, first with the triumphs of Germany and later with its defeat beginning to emerge. The various fragments of his *Ethics*, which were received and collected by Bethge, should be understood as a unity: It was the one great challenge that Bonhoeffer experienced

---

1. *Letters and Papers from Prison*, p. 163.

in these war years and he responded significantly. Nevertheless one must keep the course of events of these years in mind if one is to understand the *Ethics* correctly.

On July 27, 1939, Bonhoeffer surprisingly returned to Germany from the United States. In his biography of Bonhoeffer, Bethge described the motives behind this sudden return. They play no role in understanding *Ethics*. In March 1939, German troops occupied Czechoslovakia and on March 16 the "Protectorate of Bohemia and Moravia" was announced in Prague. England and France answered this on March 31 with their declaration of guarantee for Poland. The onset of a World War loomed on the horizon. In August von Ribbentrop, Hitler's foreign minister, signed the German-Soviet Non-Aggression Pact with its secret additional protocol on the dividing up of Poland. On September 1 the German Army Squadron North and South under Colonel-General von Brauchitsch crossed the Polish border supported by two air units. In response, England and France declared war against Germany on September 3. Already on October 6, the so-called Polish Campaign was over.

In the spring of 1939 the decree implementing the Law of the Hitler Youth, the so-called Compulsory Youth Service for sixteen- to eighteen-year-olds, was issued. In the late summer of 1939 compulsory military service, which had not become law until the previous spring, was introduced in Great Britain. At that same time in Germany, the Main Office of Imperial Security of the SS was founded to combat domestic political opposition. In 1944 Bonhoeffer became a victim of this office. On December 28, 1939, the Soviet Union placed itself outside of the Geneva Convention, and all doors were opened for the atrocities of the war on the eastern front that began in 1941.

In Germany the Mother's Cross was introduced, depending on the number of children, in bronze, silver, and, for more than eight children, gold. Those who received the Mother's Cross were given preferred service by the authorities and were entitled to be seated at any time when using public transportation. Young people had to greet wearers of the Mother's Cross with the words, "Heil Hitler."

After the conclusion of the Polish campaign Hitler issued a decree, retroactive to September 1, authorizing a certain group of doctors to grant euthanasia to terminally ill people. The program of euthanasia began, and the methods used in this program were later put into practice in the death camps during the Holocaust. In December 1938, 550,000 Jews were deported out of the areas of Poland that had been declared German territory. After the Polish campaign 3.2 million Jews from the other occupied territories of Poland, the so-called Government-General, were sent to ghettoes where their extermination began, first of all in the form of unimaginable physical deprivation.

The extermination of unworthy life, the looming obliteration of Judaism, the cult of vitality and youth, the precedence of the party state above all other spheres of human life, and the militarization of existence—these were the challenges Bonhoeffer had to face in his *Ethics*. Throughout all of the fragments we find sensitivity to chaos and Bonhoeffer's opposition, on the basis of law and order, to the uprising from below. According to Bonhoeffer, not *Volk*, race, and blood, but the authority of the commandment "from above" is the standard for good and evil.

> We can no longer avoid the fact that the ethical realm demands clarity concerning above and below. Above and below are not simply interchangeable depending on the fluctuating worth of subjective accomplishment and manner. . . . Only through affirmation and perseverance in being above is there affirmation and perseverance in being below and vice versa. Wherever no one dares to be above any longer and no one "believes they need" to be below any longer; wherever being above seeks its justification solely from below; thus, for example, wherever the father derives his authority from the trust of the children, or the government from its popularity; correspondingly wherever being below is seen only as a candidacy for being above and thus as a potential explosive against everything above; wherever all of this is the case genuine ethical speech is no longer possible ethical chaos breaks in.

Thus Bonhoeffer raised the decisive question of the basis of the authorization for ethical speech in that he demanded inward affirmation of and perseverance in being above and below. With this question, the ethical reaches decidedly beyond itself.[2]

One can recognize roughly two phases in the development of Bonhoeffer's ethical fragments. In the first phase the issue was defense and resistance, the answer to the breakdown of ethics in the dark shadows

2. *Ethics*, pp. 274–75.

of the totalitarian state. In the second phase Bonhoeffer worked more or less on behalf of the resistance to Hitler as his coming defeat became more and more likely. Bonhoeffer also considered the new beginning after the fall of the Third Reich, which he was certain would come. Thus the positive engagement for a new political order, the hope of a new beginning in postwar Germany came to the fore.

But at the beginning of the war all signs seemed to point to anything but the fall of the Reich. The euphoria of success was everywhere. At 5:30 A.M. on May 10, 1940, the attack on the Netherlands and the invasion of Belgium and Luxembourg by German troops began. Already on May 15, the Dutch forces surrendered. The Belgians surrendered on May 28 and the French on June 22. While a more oppressive mood had spread through the German population at the very beginning of the war in 1939, now the military triumphs had led to a kind of victorious exhilaration. The success had proven the optimists correct. Bonhoeffer saw this mood and ethic of success for the challenge it was, and in his *Ethics,* he answered the challenge. At this time, in the summer of 1940, Lithuania, Latvia, and Estonia were made into Soviet republics. The dividing up of Europe between two totalitarian power blocs was rapidly gaining momentum. This process led to conflict, and on June 22, 1941, the German campaign against the Soviet Union began. Already by the beginning of December, this led the German armies into the catastrophe near Moscow, when Guderian's tanks had to retreat for the first time. On January 31, 1943, two months before Bonhoeffer was arrested on April 5, the sixth German Army division surrendered in Stalingrad. The German Reich was nearing its collapse when Bonhoeffer was taken to the military prison at Tegel and had to stop work on his *Ethics.*

In January 1939 the Jews were forbidden to visit the cinema, the theater, concerts, and art exhibitions. In addition, their driver licenses were taken away and they were debarred from all employment. As of September 1, 1941, they had to wear the Jewish star in public. By this time only 234,000 Jews still lived in the Reich. In 1933 500,000 Jews had lived in Germany. On January 20, 1942, the infamous Wannsee Conference began. The conference included representatives of the various ministries, the offices of the SS, and the Party and Imperial Chancellories. The Wannsee Conference was chaired by Reinhard Heydrich, the *SS-Obergruppenführer,* General of the Police and Deputy

Protector of Bohemia and Moravia. Here the foundation was laid for the systematic extermination of the Jewish people in death camps such as Auschwitz, Treblinka, Belzec, Chelmno, and Maidenek, under the unbelievably cynical catch phrases "final solution of the Jewish question" and "special treatment."

In September 1941, because of protest from the church and the military, Hitler had to stop his program of euthanasia temporarily, although the movie *I Accuse*, which premiered in August of that year, still passionately advocated active mercy killing. The methods and facilities used to get rid of sick people, as well as the "medical and technical specialists," were then adopted by the death camps. In May 1942 in Birkenau, a secondary camp for Auschwitz, the first selection took place. Jews capable of working were separated from Jews incapable of working who were then killed because they were considered unworthy to live. This was the first mass gassing—1,500 Jewish people were gassed—and the disaster had begun to take its course.

On February 18, 1943, about two-and-a-half months before Bonhoeffer's arrest, Goebbels proclaimed total war in the Sports Palace in Berlin. Total war also meant that the state was tightening its totalitarian grip. On April 26, 1942, in a speech before the Reichstag, Hitler had already claimed for himself the supreme judicial authority. The *Volk*, he said, does not exist for the judiciary, but the judiciary exists for the *Volk*. Since—as Bonhoeffer had correctly asserted in his 1933 essay "Der Führer und der Einzelne"—the *Führer* is only the mouthpiece of the masses, this meant the rulership of the collective over everything that had previously been understood as law and order. Hitler had proclaimed the final repudiation of the rule of law. Shortly before that the Jews who still lived in Germany had been resettled in the east. But instead of the triumphal feeling of 1940 and 1941, something akin to a fatalistic mood began to spread among the people.

On the rule of the totalitarian state, the collective, Bonhoeffer wrote:

> Here the individual is viewed only in terms of his utilizable value for the whole, and the community is understood only in its utilizable value for a higher institution or organization or idea. The collectivity is the god to whom individual and social life are sacrificed in the process of total mechanization. Life is extinguished, and the form which exists for

the purpose of serving life now assumes unrestricted mastery over life. Life is no longer in any sense an end in itself, and it is swallowed up in the void, for the mechanization draws its strength only from life and when it has killed all life it must itself collapse.[3]

The Church and the Challenge of the Time

In the 1920s, 1930s, and 1940s there were overwhelming political and economic upheavals in Germany. But with unwavering constancy the process of secularization progressed throughout these three decades. To be sure, over 90 percent of the population still belonged to either the Protestant or Catholic Church, in spite of the trend of leaving the church that began in the mid-1930s. The official Protestant churches still baptized, confirmed, married, and buried their members with the blessing of "cheap grace." But these official Protestant churches were in reality superchurches without Christian congregations to fill them. The National Socialist state assured both of these large churches, the Catholic as well as the Protestant, financial support that churches in the rest of the world could only dream of. In addition to these gigantic direct contributions, which included the financing of the theological faculties, the state collected the church tax for the churches. The theology professors, who were training the next generation of pastors in Germany, were officials of a state led by the *Führer*, who held both the office of chancellor and president of the Reich, and who was commander-in-chief of the armed forces. The church bowed to this state. Opposition was the exception. On July 20, 1944, after the assassination attempt against Hitler for which Bonhoeffer bore part of the ethical responsibility, official church office-holders sent downright Byzantine declarations of loyalty to the survivor.

In order to understand Bonhoeffer's *Ethics* as a work opposing the collapse of Christian values, we must remember that the Confessing Church, after its initial decisiveness in Barmen and Dahlem in 1934, fell prey more or less to inner ossification, quarreling, and paralysis. In the end, the Confessing Church was merely a ghetto within the official churches. The overwhelming majority of all Protestant pastors in Germany were neutral. They kept out of the immediate dispute with

3. Ibid., p. 150.

the National Socialist state. The insignificance of especially Protestant Christianity in Germany kept growing. There was no alternative to Nazi ideology.[4]

The Confessing Church was isolated in the ecumenical movement as well as in Germany. Bethge came to the following bitter realization: "Thus there is indeed not one single record in the ecumenical movement of any participation or membership of the German Confessing Church at any one of their conferences in the 1930's."[5] Either the Confessing Christians could not travel, or they did not want to attend or, if they were there, their presence was not noted in the minutes. The ecumenical movement simply did not know what to do about the church struggle in Germany. At the World Church Conference in Oxford of July 12–26, 1937, under the theme "Church, People, and State" there were no longer any representatives at all from the Protestant Church in Germany. Instead, a representative of the German Methodists thanked God that Hitler had averted the danger of Bolshevism and professed in Oxford that the freedom to proclaim Christianity was unlimited in Germany.

The Ecumenical Movement and the Totalitarian State

From July 12–26, 1937, 425 delegates from 40 nations assembled in Oxford. At this conference, "the life-and-death struggle between the Christian faith and the secular and pagan movements of our time" was acknowledged. The delegates realized that in all of Europe the foundations of community life were threatened and that the collapse of all values was on the horizon. Not only the cultures that were shaped by Christianity tottered precariously; the secular ways of life that had recently become dominant were also in danger. Thus, Oxford really did help to develop the awareness of crisis in regard not only to

---

4. The most comprehensive and objective account available on the topic of the church and the Third Reich is a monograph by Klaus Scholder (in two volumes up to now; the second volume by his students). Significant in this connection is also the so-called Stuttgart Confession of Guilt of October 19, 1945, which was written by members of the ecclesiastical resistance, and which states, among other things, "we accuse ourselves of not having confessed more courageously, prayed more faithfully, believed more joyfully, and loved more passionately." This confession does not imply a collective guilt of the German people, but rather asserts that through the guilt of the Protestant Church in its intellectual and spiritual confusion and weakness a people could be infiltrated, occupied, and led astray by an ideology.

5. Bethge, *Bonhoeffer*, p. 623.

Germany but also to all of Europe. Naturalism was rejected with unequivocal clarity. Any such attempt to exalt nation or race as the highest good above all other goods was condemned: "Nation or ethnicity is always simultaneously both God-given and influenced by sin." The delegates declared that "the revelation of God in Christ" should be the exclusive source of Christian proclamation. The subordination of the church to the "life of the people" and the "idolization of one's own ethnic group" were categorically rejected. War was condemned "without reservation or restriction."[6]

Oxford contributed substantially to the pacifism that was spreading at that time, especially in England. Already in Oxford, the churches were called to repent. Capitalism was condemned as "tyranny over the lives of countless people." It was argued that capitalist production views "human labor as a commodity" and that the capitalist system promotes inequality and injustice. Just as it characterizes the ecumenical world conferences today, the socialist bias clearly prevailed in Oxford. In this context one must remember that in typically Protestant industrial nations such as the United States, the Netherlands, and England, as opposed to Germany, there were still enormous numbers of unemployed who were suffering mass destitution (in 1936, 60 percent of the population of the United States lived below the poverty line). The Oxford Conference in 1937 recognized the problems and burdens of a capitalist society threatened by disintegration from the inside out that needed a very wide-meshed social net to keep the impoverishment under control. However, the conference did not see the threat of the totalitarian socialist state. Stalin's extermination of the Kulaks in the years 1930 to 1932 was not mentioned. The danger posed by radical socialism was simply not discussed at all. It was not recognized that Nazi ideology was a socialist ideology, an expression of the collectivism that Bonhoeffer so accurately grasped (witness the primary motto of National Socialist ideology—"You are nothing, your Volk is everything"). Neither did Oxford see that the roots of anti-Judaism lay in the revolt against God as Father. To be sure, Oxford saw the dangers of racism, but the delegates failed to recognize the

6. On this point, see "Kirche und Welt in ökumenischer Sicht. Bericht der Weltkirchenkonferenz von Oxford über Kirche, Volk und Staat," in *Kirche und Welt. Studien und Dokumente*, vol. 12, edited by the research department of the ecumenical council, 1938.

demonic power of anti-Semitism and the coming downfall of Judaism in Europe. The encyclical of Pope Pius XI, *Cum cura ardenti*, which was adopted on March 23, 1937, was clearer than anything that resulted from the Oxford Conference of 1937. Even if it did not directly name the National Socialist regime, the language was clear and straightforward and much of the content is very similar to Bonhoeffer's *Ethics*.

In regard to the discussion of social engagement and of the crisis of capitalism that took place at Oxford in 1937 it must be noted that National Socialist Germany had achieved more socially than any other western European country. Instead of 6 million unemployed males as in 1933, the Germany of 1937 had only one million unemployed males. The reduction in unemployment and the improvement in the standard of living of the masses was not at first significantly due to rearmament. The working class and the middle class in Germany were living in a kind of uplifted mood at this time. The social slant of National Socialist ideology appealed to the mass of the workers. In 1937, Germany began to mass produce radios (people's receivers). The Volkswagen, the car for everyone, seemed to be just around the corner, and the strength-through-joy trips made it possible for the first time for even workers to take vacations in far-away places. Kindergartens and various social institutions such as the National Socialist People's Welfare Service, the Imperial Labor Service, and the Hitler Youth, all promoted a solidarization effect among all social classes within the Germany of that time. And beginning in 1934, Germany was the only country other than the Soviet Union that celebrated May 1 as the Labor Day holiday. New texts were written to the old melodies of the socialist labor movements. The so-called Winter Assistance Work was depicted as "help through action" as opposed to the "doctrines" of socialism and the "dogmas" of Christianity. Thus, in the Germany of those years, there was an awareness of a "community of the *Volk*."

Thus there was a "positive mood" in the political landscape of Germany at the end of the 1930s. After all, the National Socialist movement had been from the very beginning always more "mood" than "doctrine." The mood was the mood of the people—their mouth was the mouth of the man who sensed and formulated this mood: Adolf Hitler. Finally, this mood became the standard by which one distinguished between good and evil. What was useful to the *Volk* was good, what was damaging to the *Volk* was evil. No one who has not experienced this positive mood of the people of those years can truly imagine the loneliness of a confessing theologian such as Bonhoeffer.

The result of this "ethics of mood" was an enormous uncertainty regarding the law, because written laws took in more and more the aura of the old-fashioned and untimely. Besides, emergency decrees, *Heimtückegesetze* [the Nationalist Socialist law against malicious gossip] and Enabling Acts lent all measures taken by the Nazi regime a sufficient air of legality. Thus, the "conscience of the *Volk*," as motivated by propaganda, was able to establish itself more and more. Who can imagine what it must have taken to write an *Ethics* unswervingly based on revelation, law, and order against this positive, sometimes downright hysterically jubilant will of the people?

Bonhoeffer's *Ethics* is closely related to Barth's theology. Both Bonhoeffer and Barth agreed that nature or creation could never provide the standard for good or evil. Their rejection of the naturalism of their time was absolutely clear. Only through an orientation toward the revelation of God is it possible to distinguish between good and evil. Thus true ethics is the ethics of revelation. In *Evangelium und Gesetz,* written in 1933, Barth made clear that the law of God is part of God's saving will as revealed in the holy Scriptures. The law of God is an integral part of the gospel—upon hearing such a statement the Lutherans could do nothing but throw up their hands in horror while tears rolled down their cheeks. Then in 1938, Barth brought out the political significance of the Gospel in *Reichfertigung und Recht*. If one speaks of justification one must also speak of justice and thus of law; if one proclaims Christ then one must be aware that this proclamation also has repercussions for the state. We should not passively accept political reality, but change it out of obedience to God. What Barth in effect did was to advocate the rights of the individual, which can only be realized in a democracy, against the collective tendencies that were emerging at the time. Because God's justification of his children brings about their freedom, Barth saw democracy as the legitimate state system—the one that corresponds to biblical revelation.

In Germany, many were horrified by these thoughts of Barth. The churchmen in Germany wanted no part of it. They wanted to live in peace with the state and to remain as undisturbed as possible within their own realm so they could ply their "proclamation." On September 19, 1938, when Czechoslovakia was being threatened with an attack by Hitler, Barth wrote an open letter to Josef Hromadka, a theology professor in Prague. This letter includes the following: "If the political order and freedom are threatened, then this threat indirectly concerns the church as well. And if a lawful state comes to the defense of these things, then the church indirectly takes part in this defense as well."[7] In the Munich Conference of September 29, 1938 between Chamberlain, Daladier, Hitler, and Mussolini, Barth—just as lonely a theologian as Bonhoeffer at that time—saw catastrophe for the liberty of Europe. Barth's admonishing words to the church: "He who has been justified by grace must also, in trust, profess the law. And an inseparable part of this law is liberty." Barth professed the claim of the truth of Christ over all of society. Bonhoeffer thought exactly the same.

Bonhoeffer too was shocked about the threat to the Occident posed by the revolution of nihilism that was being played out before his eyes. The elements of disintegration were technocratic organization, the uprising of the masses, nationalism, rationalism accompanied simultaneously by the outbreak of the irrational, the cult of blood and race, the idolization of death and the death-wish, and the general barbarism that was growing with the decline of morality and common decency. For Bonhoeffer, the cause of all of this was godlessness: "Only the church still tries to cover up godlessness: life, history, family, nation are all falling victim to nothingness. One could continue on indefinitely, because nothingness spares nothing."[8]

For Bonhoeffer the National Socialist revolution was only a moment in the vast process of secularization, in occidental civilization's growing alienation from Christianity. The conservative, Christian-Occidental ethicist of order Bonhoeffer fought the good fight against the nihilism of his time. Therefore, Bonhoeffer's *Ethics* is a living testimony against the nihilism and terror of the cultural and moral revolution that is also taking place right now. For the trend toward the dissolution of all values has continued right up to the present day. Even if left-wing theologians would like to close their ears to this,

---

7. See Karl Barth, *Eine Schweizer Stimme 1938–1945*, 2d ed., 1953. On the Hromadka letter, see *Kirchenblatt für die reformierte Schweiz* of November 24, 1938, under the significant title "Noch einmal: Friede oder Gerechtigkeit."

8. On this point, see *Ethics*, pp. 88–109.

Bonhoeffer was a man of law and order. Müller, who as an East German theologian would like to have monopolized Bonhoeffer's theology for the cause of socialism, admits that the ethicist Bonhoeffer "could perhaps be called the last honest Christian Occidental."[9] Müller is correct. But certainly Bonhoeffer will not have been the *very* last Christian occidental theologian—at least, let's hope not.

9. Müller, *Von der Kirche zur Welt*, p. 28.

21

Revealed Ethos

The ideology of National Socialism strove to be naturalistic. Ethos was supposed to be oriented toward nature, race, blood, national character, and the like. Here the Neo-Darwinist accents were impossible to overlook—the struggle for survival, the right of the stronger, the eradication of everything that is weak or incapable of coping with life. Praise be to whatever makes strong. The Christian view of the human being as sinner, the hope of redemption and reconciliation were seen as typical expressions of decadent humanity. Any attack against Judaism was in effect also an attack against Christianity. Basically Judaism and Christianity were equally "hostile to life" according to Nazi ideology.

The new man was not to be intellectually oriented or spiritually convicted, but racially bred. The law of blood was just as dominant over the individual as the law of the *Volk* or the collective. Thus the *Volk* or the state was placed above the family and marriage. This trend continues into our time as well. Consider that the second report on the family of the West German Ministry of Health and Family, published in the 1970s, also places society over the family.[1] Another indication that sub-

1. In the second report on the family of the Federal Ministry of Youth, Family, and Health, 1975. According to this report, parents should respond to their children's concepts of values according to a consensus (in the sense of the Neo-Marxist ethics of consensus) and in this regard new legal regulations should be adapted to "social and societal change." But "since social reality constantly changes in the course of time and since political measures themselves are also subject to processes of change, this cognitive process can at no time be considered closed" (IX and XI).

stantial aspects of Nazi ideology continue to be influential today is the fact that in the present debate about human rights, collective human rights take precedence over individual human rights. In Germany it has often been not only the same ideas as those of Nazi ideology, but the same people then and now promoting these ideas.

Protestantism in Germany was powerless in the face of this National Socialist "upheaval." One significant reason for this was that Protestantism also acknowledged "the natural order," the so-called creation order as the point of departure for ethical norms. Many— above all Lutheran—theologians had no trouble digesting and acknowledging the talk of race, national character, the right of the stronger, and so on. It fit their theology of the creation order—their "natural ethics."

But Bonhoeffer took up the challenge and made clear once and for all that ethics cannot be based on nature or on the so-called theology of the creation order. Bonhoeffer advocated a theology of revelation against theology based on the creation order.[2]

Neither, however, can ethos be based on convictions. Conviction was a catchword of the time. It was imperative that one have good convictions. But Bonhoeffer rejected "an ethics of conviction" just as he rejected "the ethics of success" that was also characteristic of those years in which everything that happened in the Third Reich was justified by pointing to the success of the system—success that was indeed unparalleled for a number of years. Bonhoeffer's objection to this "success" was not welcome in the exhilarating mood of the time. People who did not allow themselves to be ethically blinded by the political and military successes of 1930s and early 1940s were simply called whiners and complainers.

The following were some of Bonhoeffer's thoughts on basing ethos on success: "When a successful figure becomes especially prominent and conspicuous, the majority give way to the idolization of success. They become blind to right and wrong, truth and untruth, fair play

---

Thus, here the family has clearly become a mandate from below in a social, collective process. This is precisely what Nazi-ideology sought, and this is exactly what Bonhoeffer opposed with his ethics "from above." Here we see the immediate relevance of Bonhoeffer to the continuation of the struggle against the absoluteness of the biblical ethos and the structures ordained by it.

2. "The problem of Christian ethics is the realization among God's creatures of the revelational reality of God in Christ" (Ethics, p. 190).

and foul play. They have eyes only for the deed, for the successful result. The moral and intellectual critical faculty is blunted. It is dazzled by the brilliance of the successful man and by the longing in some degree to share in his success."[3] The accommodation to success, to the factual, is a pervasive sign of the crude worship of self-actualization in our time as well. Still today, the ethical arguments of politicians are often through and through arguments from success. In reality, there are—at least in the political realm—just as few ethical distinctions made today that disregard the question of success as there were when Bonhoeffer wrote his *Ethics*. The willingness to make basic ethical distinctions on what is really good and really evil, even when one must sacrifice and give up what one wants, is just as rare today as it ever was.

The mobilized technological man of the twentieth century believes in success. Whoever does not believe in success is a pessimist unfit for excelling in life. But the cross challenges this crude affirmation of the here and now. Thus Bonhoeffer wrote:

> The figure of the Crucified invalidates all thought which takes success for its standard. Such thought is a denial of eternal justice. Neither the triumph of the successful nor the bitter hatred which the successful arouse in the hearts of the unsuccessful can ultimately overcome the world. Jesus is certainly no apologist for the successful men in history, but neither does He head the insurrection of shipwrecked existences against their successful rivals. He is not concerned with success or failure but with the willing acceptance of God's judgement.[4]

Another catchword of Bonhoeffer's time was duty. Fulfillment of duty was the highest obligation. Duty had its meaning in and of itself.

---

3. *Ethics*, p. 76. According to Bonhoeffer the ethics of success leads astray because historical facts are falsified "in order to prove that evil has not been successful . . . that success is identical with goodness. . . . The figure of the Crucified invalidates all thought which takes success as its standard" (pp. 76–77) because even the good must be subject to the cross. Today it seems almost unimaginable how difficult it was to resist this success-oriented thinking. In regard to the year 1938, Joachim Fest asserts tersely in his Hitler biography: "If Hitler had been the victim of an assassination at the end of 1938, only a very few would hesitate to call him the greatest German statesman, perhaps the consummator of Germany's history. The aggressive speeches and *Mein Kampf*, the anti-Semitism and plan for world rule would probably have been forgotten as the works of a youthful imagination from the early years." See also Sebastian Haffner, *Anmerkungen zu Hitler*, 1984, p. 43.

4. Ibid., p. 77.

Kant's ethics had laid the necessary groundwork for this view. Bonhoeffer's opinion on this was as follows:

> It looks as though the way out from the confusing multiplicity of possible decisions is the path of duty. What is commanded is seized upon as being surest. Responsibility for the command rests upon the man who gives it and not upon him who executes it. But in this confinement within the limits of duty there can never come the bold stroke of the deed which is done on one's own free responsibility.[5]

Of course, neither can ethics be grounded in reason: "One is distressed by the failure of *reasonable* people to perceive either the depths of evil or the depths of the holy."[6] Good and evil cannot be grounded rationally. Good or evil is not a matter of rational substantiation, but of obedient acknowledgment. And this acknowledgment of what is good is always an act of trust and obedience. Neither are there for Bonhoeffer any "principles" that could provide a measure of good or evil. The standard of good in the rejection of evil has been revealed in God's Word alone. The good is the will of God as revealed in Scripture.

The Good as Revealed in Christ

"The problem of Christian ethics is the realization among God's creatures of the revelational reality of God in Christ."[7] At issue is "participation" in the reality of God as revealed in Christ. As will soon be made clear, even Bonhoeffer's ethics are integrated into his Christ-mysticism. Bonhoeffer devised the rule: what is really real is the good as it has been revealed in Christ. But evil as the anti-real stands in the way of that which is really real. The good is not an ethical proclamation only. Rather, the good is the law of that which is really real: "Only by participating in reality do we share in the good." For Bonhoeffer, the good is not only a matter for pious circles. Rather, in listening to

5. Ibid., p. 66.
6. Ibid., p. 65.
7. "This brings us to the only possible object of a 'Christian ethic,' an object which lies beyond the 'ethical', namely, the 'commandment of God.' . . . God's commandment is the only warrant for ethical discourse" (ibid., p. 277). The command of God comes "from above." It "establishes on earth an inviolable superiority and inferiority" (p. 279), independent of the time and "of earthly powers and laws" (ibid.). Therefore, "natural law can never lay claim to divine authority in opposition to the decalogue" (p. 310). One cannot expect a clearer formulation of an ethics of revelation and order.

revelation we recognize what the good is within the entirety of world and human reality. Bonhoeffer objected to the ghettoization of the revelation in the world. The good has to do with the whole of reality: "With respect to its origin this indivisible whole is called 'creation.' With respect to its goal it is called the 'kingdom of God.'"[8] It is a matter of receiving a share of the immediate whole of the reality of God. That is the sense of the Christian inquiry into the good.

This good reality has been revealed in Christ. Thus the point is to share in the reality of God, and in the world in Jesus Christ. With that, Bonhoeffer emphatically rejected the notion that "the autonomy of the orders of this world is proclaimed in opposition to the law of Christ." "The cause of Christ" must by no means become "a partial and provincial matter within the limits of reality." Bonhoeffer's fundamental principle was: "There are not two realities, but only one reality, and that is the reality of God, which has become manifest in Christ in the reality of the world."[9] The issue is the "realization of Christ" in this world, a world that we must understand "from this center," that is, from Christ.

Christ must take on "stature" in this world. He must "take shape among us here and now." Humanity and world should move toward "the figure of Jesus Christ" and be included in him.[10] Does that mean

---

8. Ibid., p. 193.

9. Ibid., pp. 196–97.

10. "Formation" (*Gestaltung*) is an exciting word in Bonhoeffer's *Ethics*. He understands formation (*Gestaltung*) in relation to the "figure" (*Gestalt*), thus, in relation to Christ. Formation means "One can speak of formation and of world only if mankind is called by name in its true form, which is its own by right, which it has already received, but which it merely fails to understand and accept, namely, the form of Jesus Christ, which is proper to man, and if in this way, in anticipation as one might say, mankind is drawn in into the Church. This means, then, that even when we speak in terms of the formation of the world we are referring solely to the form of Jesus Christ" (ibid., p. 84). Bonhoeffer's concern was that "Christ take form among us here and now" (p. 85). Not only the individual, but also human society (the Occident) should be formed (*gestaltet*) in response to Christ. His righteousness, his love, his power of reconciliation and redemption should radiate out as it were into the existing reality. After all, everything that is real is structured in relation to the Christ figure. By this, Bonhoeffer did not mean the Christification of the world as Teilhard de Chardin understood it—as a necessary, evolutionary, historical process, but as the ethical mandate of the Christian in the world, and also against the world until the second coming of Christ. Being formed (*Gestaltwerdung*) is a Christ-mystically understood incorporation of the Christian's being into the power that restrains chaos and preserves the world—until the end-times. Then and only then, will the Christian be formed to perfection. The Christian is integrated into the preserving reality of Christ in all of his life expressions—including the struggle for righteousness and the conflict with the secondary, technocratic world. However, all of this happens in struggle and conflict, namely, within the messianic suffering, dying, and victory of Christ.

that everything real is Christian and everything Christian is real, analogous to the Hegelian view of reality: everything real is reasonable and everything reasonable is real? Is the course of the world, nature, and history the self-revelation of God? To that, Bonhoeffer said very clearly: "what is Christian is not identical with what is of the world."[11] But that which is Christian and that which is of the world are not simply "statically independent" of one another. There are not two realities. Rather, it is a matter of that which is Christian being "employed as a polemical weapon against the secular, . . . in the name of a better secularity."[12] Thus, reality is understood processually. In this world, the reality that has been revealed in Christ, the reality of righteousness, mercy, and love, is to be established. Thus, the real reality, which is "given form" by Christ, stands in opposition to the unreality.[13] Therefore, there can be no retreat from the world into "Christian inwardliness." Neither does the church have its place or its space in this world, nor is it isolated from this world. Rather, "The only way in which the Church can defend her own territory is by fighting not for it but for the salvation of the world. Otherwise the Church becomes a 'religious society.'" Thus Bonhoeffer advocated an ethos on the offensive that calls for the reshaping of the world—an ethos against the unreality of evil and for the reality of the good. The point is not to lead a pious life but to be a witness to Jesus Christ before the world.[14]

The Good in the Struggle Against Evil

Bonhoeffer did not write a great deal about evil directly. Somehow it is clear on every page of his *Ethics* that evil is, and how it is. But Bonhoeffer did not want anything to do with an ethic of surrender before the power of evil. He did not want an ethic of resignation or retreat even though the 1940s perhaps more than any other period could eas-

11. Ibid., p. 199.
12. Ibid.
13. The reality of God is the ultimate in relation to the penultimate of all existing created reality (ibid., p. 189). In Christ, this ultimate reality of God has entered into the penultimate of world reality (p. 194), but the penultimate of fallen creation is always borne by the ultimate of the preserving and upholding common grace of God (p. 193). There is no neutral space, neither is there a dualism between heaven and earth, but only the one realm of Christ's self-realization. The body of believers fights for the realization of Christ in the world and for this world: Here the self-evident presupposition is that such a testimony of Christ's self-realization to the world can only properly go forth when it originates in the sanctified life of the Christian congregation.
14. Ibid., pp. 202–03.

ily have led one astray to such an ethic. Bonhoeffer saw the power of evil daily—that was no longer a problem; the power of evil was obvious. For Bonhoeffer the issue was how the good, which continues to be effective in Christ-with-us, asserts itself in this world. Bonhoeffer advocated an ethic on the offensive, out of which he knew that "yet the devil must serve Christ even against his will. . . . the realm or space of the devil is always only beneath the feet of Jesus Christ. . . . The world is not divided between Christ and the devil."[15] Thus Bonhoeffer's *Ethics* takes as its vantage point the triumph of the resurrected One: "The dark and evil world must not be abandoned to the devil. It must be claimed for Him who has won it by His incarnation, His death and His resurrection. Christ gives up nothing of what He has won. He holds it fast in His hands."[16]

Bonhoeffer did not entertain any illusions. He knew that "the world in and of itself" is involved in a life-and-death struggle with the body of believers. But the victory has already been won through Christ. The world has been "incessantly drawn into the event of Christ."[17]

Thus Bonhoeffer in his *Ethics* came to a Christ-mystical view of this world. Not only the individual Christian, but also the whole creation, all of world reality is included in Christ's struggle, messianic suffering, and death, but also in his resurrection. And what is good in this world is that which allows Christ to include it in his messianic life.

Now one can very easily read into these remarks of Bonhoeffer the delighted cry of a progressive, revolutionary theologian. If the world is included in the Christ-event, and especially in his resurrection, then the world is on its way to becoming a good world through liberation and revolution.

However, this jubilation from the wrong side needs to be countered, if by nothing else than by the fact that in Bonhoeffer's view the good, in contrast to the view of progressive theology, is revealed in God's commandments: "God's commandment is the only warrant for ethical discourse."[18] And Bonhoeffer did not relativize the command

---

15. Ibid., p. 204.
16. Ibid.
17. Ibid., p. 205. By this Bonhoeffer meant the incarnation, Christ becoming flesh, which not only reveals but also brings about the ultimate of the reality of God—to be sure, within the messianic reality of struggle, suffering, the cross, and the resurrection.
18. Ibid., p. 277.

of God: "If God's commandment is not clear, definite and concrete to the last detail, then it is not God's commandment."[19]

The world as such does not reveal God's will! Neither are the poor, the proletariat, or the persecuted the bearers of salvation in the sense that they could reveal the will of God. Bonhoeffer held that "the commandment of God does not spring from the created world. It comes down from above."[20] This idea of "from above to the world below" is already enough to horrify progressive theology. But precisely because of this movement from above to below the authorization to proclaim the divine command takes place.[21] Thus for the Christian it is a matter of "God's commandment, revealed in Jesus Christ."[22] Christ is the "centre and the fulness of life."[23] But for Bonhoeffer the truth, that is, Christ, is completely concrete. Bonhoeffer was concerned with this concretization from the beginning. He wrote: "It does not only interrupt the process of life when this process goes astray, but it guides and conducts this process even though there is not always need for consciousness of this fact."[24] Thus we encounter Christ in more than just the obvious interruptions and disturbances of our lives. In the Christian life, there is an unconscious sharing in the reality of Christ and thereby in the command of God. Without thinking about it hour by hour or day by day, the Christian lives in the reality that has been revealed in the commands of God. For the commands of God are more than an appeal; they are the emanation of a living reality that becomes the "daily divine guidance of our lives."[25] This direction of God leads us into the ordered life, a life of law and order:

> The commandment of God becomes the element in which one lives without always being conscious of it, and, thus it implies freedom of movement and of action, freedom from the fear of decision, freedom from fear to act, it implies certainty, quietude, confidence, balance and peace. I honour my parents, I am faithful in marriage, I respect the lives and property of others, not because at the frontiers of my life

19. Ibid., p. 278.
20. Ibid., p. 279.
21. Ibid.
22. Ibid.
23. Ibid., p. 280.
24. Ibid.
25. Ibid.

there is a threatening 'thou shalt not,' but because I accept as holy institutions of God these realities, parents, marriage, life and property, which confront me in the midst and in the fulness of life. It is only when the commandment no longer merely threatens me as a transgressor of the limits, it is only when it convinces and subdues me with its real contents, that it sets me free from the anxiety and the uncertainty of decision.[26]

Bonhoeffer emphasized the positive contents of the commandments of God: "The commandment of God permits man to live as man before God."[27] "The commandment of God . . . is concerned with the positive contents and with man's freedom to accept these positive contents. . . . God's commandment can be treated as the theme of a Christian ethic only by dint of keeping these positive contents and this liberty of man simultaneously in view."[28] Thus Bonhoeffer did not advocate a "hospital ethics" here. This is not an ethics of moaning and groaning—not an ethics of "No," of antipathy, of "suspicious self-observation" but an ethic of "Yes." It is the gospel in commandment, the freedom for human dignity and humanity.

God's Command and Law and Order

It is an unshakable fact that Bonhoeffer was an ethicist of order who held conservative values. This unambiguous realization has immediate significance for the cultural and moral revolution of our time. The challenges of such an upheaval, challenges that Bonhoeffer had to face in the 1930s and 1940s, continue in our time. That is why the Bonhoefferian ethic is so relevant. For the Protestant ethic as it presently represents itself can hardly be regarded as an ethic of order or revelation.

Bonhoeffer already thought in the categories of an ethics of order when he wrote the "Confession of Bethel," which was basically a precursor of the Barmen Theological Declaration of 1934. The preservation of state, law, the "normal" relationship of the sexes, marriage, family, property, and occupational calling as preservational ordinances was indispensable according to Bonhoeffer. The expression "preservational ordinance" was probably invented by W. Künneth.

---

26. Ibid., pp. 280–81.
27. Ibid., p. 282.
28. Ibid., p. 284.

But in this case Bonhoeffer "thought parallel" to Künneth and took the expression "preservational ordinance" instead of "creation order." The latter expression gave the impression that creation as such could provide ethical standards. The expression "creation order" could also have given the impression that there is a good and undamaged creation that brings good order out of its own working if man lives in obedience to "nature."

In Bonhoeffer's lectures on Genesis, which were published later under the title *Creation and Fall*,[29] it becomes clear that for Bonhoeffer creation is a fallen creation. Creation is partially undone by the power of evil and will not be fully restored and liberated until the second coming of Christ. Until then, it is the preservational ordinances that keep this creation from being destroyed by the chaotic powers of evil. Preservational ordinances are a defense against the power of evil. But Bonhoeffer also knew that any human, secular, or social order could be and had to be shattered "when it closes up within itself, hardens and no longer permits the proclamation of revelation."[30] Therefore the church of Christ must judge the structures of this world, because they do not have meaning in and of themselves. They are from God, through God, and directed to God.

In a lecture on July 26, 1932, in Cernohorske Kupele at the Youth Conference of the World Association of Interchurch Relations, Bonhoeffer emphasized that in discipleship one may have to do without certain ordinances such as family, marriage, or possessions, but that this doing without does not abolish the ordinances as such. Thus, order is God-given for the preservation of this world; but order can only be recognized under the Word of God. Also, order is fragile and may be rescinded if it stands in the way of the proclamation of the grace of God through Christ.

Bonhoeffer viewed his time as the time of the revolution of nihilism. For Bonhoeffer, "the western world is brought to the brink of the void." This is how Bonhoeffer saw his own situation: "Everything established is threatened with annihilation. This is not a crisis among crises. It is a decisive struggle of the last days."[31] Bonhoeffer saw him-

---

29. *Schöpfung und Fall. Theologische Auslegung von Genesis 1–3*, 4th ed., 1958.
30. *GS*, 1:153ff ("Zur theologischen Begründung der Weltbundarbeit"). The lecture was given on July 26, 1932, in Černohorske Kupele.
31. *Ethics*, p. 105.

self practically in the midst of the structures of the last days. Man come of age does not live in opposition to order, but in support of order. He is a man of order. This man of order represents the promise of overcoming the godlessness dressed up in "religious-Christian" clothing. A church that betrays the divinely ordained order in its proclamation is a guilty church.

Already in his day, Bonhoeffer noticed the rise of hedonism. He foresaw the so-called pleasure-oriented permissive culture that did not fully develop as a fundamental feature of life until the present day. Life swings back and forth "between the most bestial enjoyment of the moment and adventurous games of chance."[32] In the cultural and moral revolution of his time, Bonhoeffer sensed the destruction of reliability: "the collapse of the foundation of historical life, of trust in all its forms." Bonhoeffer understood "fear of the void" very well.[33]

Bonhoeffer saw the cause of occidental nihilism in the Occident's alienation from Christ: "The west is becoming hostile towards Christ. . . . it is genuine decay."[34]

In the face of this analysis of the situation Bonhoeffer arrived at a high assessment of the power of order. He called attention to 2 Thessalonians 2, where Paul speaks of the power that hinders or holds back the coming catastrophe, the way that leads into chaos and the disintegration of all orderly structures. It is the power that upholds (vv. 6–7). Bonhoeffer understood this power that upholds to be the ordering power of the state, "the force of order, equipped with great physical strength." This ordering power, this strength that restrains chaos, is the penultimate to the ultimate of the saving action of God that intervenes from above.[35] It is the penultimate to the ultimate of the second coming of Christ. This power that upholds is not God, and neither can this power remain without guilt—the state as ordering power will always be a guilty state—but "God makes use of it in order to preserve the world from destruction."[36]

Without a doubt, Bonhoeffer desired a strong law-and-order state. He sought the struggle for justice in "a time turned completely upside

32. Ibid., pp. 106–7.
33. Ibid., p. 197.
34. Ibid., p. 108.
35. Ibid.
36. Ibid.

down." He believed the gospel would prove itself to those who struggle for justice:

> Jesus gives His support to those who suffer for the sake of a just cause, even if this cause is not precisely the confession of His name; He takes them under His protection, He accepts responsibility for them, and He lays claim to them. And so the man who is persecuted for the sake of a just cause is led to Christ, so that it happens that in the hour of suffering and responsibility, perhaps for the first time in his life and in a way which is strange and surprising to him but is nevertheless an inner necessity, such a man appeals to Christ and professes himself a Christian because at this moment, for the first time, he becomes aware that he belongs to Christ. This, too, is not an abstract deduction, but it is an experience which we ourselves have undergone, an experience in which the power of Jesus Christ became manifest in fields of life where it had previously remained unknown. . . . The experience of our own time is that it is the good who find their way back to Christ and that the wicked obstinately remain aloof from Him. Other times could preach that a man must first become a sinner, like the publican and harlot, before he could know and find Christ, but we in our time must say rather that before a man can know and find Christ he must first become righteous, like those who strive and who suffer for the sake of justice, truth and humanity.[37]

The above is a clear point of departure for Bonhoeffer's ethic of order. This point of departure includes the following word to the church as well: "Her vision of the end of all things must not hinder her in the fulfilment of her historical responsibility." She must leave it to God's discretion whether the end is nigh, or whether history will continue its course.[38] Thus, Bonhoeffer did think apocalyptically. At no time in his life did he deny the second coming of Christ. But Bonhoeffer was concerned that as long as the world keeps on going the church should do everything imaginable through its proclamation to preserve the state as ordering power founded on the rule of law. The church and the ordering power are "allies." "Even the forces of order she compels to listen and to turn back."[39] For only the state that is

---

37. Ibid., pp. 60–61.
38. Ibid., p. 109.
39. Ibid.

prepared to listen to the proclaimed word of the church is a state founded on the rule of law.

God's Command and Our Responsibility

The command is the command of the Lord, the will of the personal God. But more than that: God was revealed in Christ and Christ came into the world that had been created by God. Here Bonhoeffer made a key observation: it does not say that "God became an idea, a principle, a programme, a universally valid proposition or law, but that God became man."[40] Thus the command cannot be separated from the Lord who revealed himself in Christ. Therefore, ethics is not an ethics of law, but an ethics of command. The Christian is responsible not to a law but to the Lord who has given the command. Bonhoeffer did not want an abstract, but a concrete ethic of responsibility to a person: "What can and must be said is not what is good once and for all, but the way in which Christ takes form among us here and now. The attempt to define that which is good once and for all has, in the nature of the case, always ended in failure."[41]

But isn't that situational ethics? Did Bonhoeffer mean by that that an ethical decision always depends on the situation or even that it is conditioned by the situation?

Bonhoeffer's ethic is not a situational ethic, but in essence an ethic of responsibility. He was concerned that in each particular, always unique situation the Christian perceives this distinct responsibility to the command of God. Bonhoeffer did not advocate a situational ethics, because his ethic is oriented toward God's command.

Every situation requires a decision and is subject to the command of God. At the end of 1942 and the beginning of 1943, in the report entitled *Nach zehn Jahren* in which Bonhoeffer took stock as it were of the collapse of the Occident, he asked the question: "Who stands fast?" The following was his answer: "Only the person whose final standard is not his reason, his principles, his conscience, his freedom, or his virtue, but who is ready to sacrifice all this when he is called to obedient and responsible action in faith and in exclusive allegiance to God—the responsible man, who tries to make his whole life an

40. Ibid., p. 85.
41. Ibid., pp. 85–86.

answer to the question and call of God. Where are these responsible people?"[42]

In each situation, the issue is responsibility to God and one's neighbor. Responsibility is not responsibility to the situation, but responsibility to God in the situation. Christ lived in a substitutionary capacity for us; therefore through him all human life is essentially substitutionary.[43] Only in this way and in no other way can we help others: "Deputyship, and therefore also responsibility, lies only in the complete surrender of one's own life to the other man. Only the selfless man lives responsibly, and this means that only the selfless man *lives*."[44] Thus, in the end Bonhoeffer understood the ethic of order and responsibility Christ-mystically also. The responsible decision is made not in relation to an abstract principle or in rigid conformity to law, but in relation to discipleship in Christ. And here the "absolute good" can be the "absolute bad" and vice versa. Bonhoeffer made clear in the fragment "What Does It Mean to Tell the Truth?" what the integral relation between command, situation, and responsibility means. In this fragment he gave such a clear and illustrative example that it bears citation in full:

> For example, a teacher asks a child in front of the class whether it is true that his father often comes home drunk. It is true, but the child denies it. The teacher's question has placed him in a situation for which he is not yet prepared. He feels only that what is taking place is an unjustified interference in the order of the family and that he must oppose it. What goes on in the family is not for the ears of the class in school. The family has its own secret and must preserve it. The teacher has failed to respect the reality of this institution. The child ought now to find a way of answering which would comply with both the rule of the family and the rule of the school. But he is not yet able to do this. He lacks experience, knowledge, and the ability to express himself in the right way. As a simple no to the teacher's question the child's answer is certainly untrue; yet at the same time it nevertheless gives expression to the truth that the family is an institution *sui generis* and that the teacher has no right to interfere in it. The child's answer can indeed be called a lie; yet this lie contains more truth, that is to say, it

42. *Letters and Papers from Prison*, p. 5.
43. *Ethics*, p. 225.
44. Ibid.

is more in accordance with reality than would have been the case if the child had betrayed his father's weakness in front of the class. According to the measure of his knowledge, the child acted correctly. The blame for the lie falls back entirely upon the teacher.[45]

A key idea to understand in this example is that the issue in this conflict that the child is trying to resolve is the issue of the preservation of an order, namely, the order of the family. Bonhoeffer's ethic of responsibility, a responsibility that must be discerned in each particular situation in a way proper to that situation, does not only include order, but is aware of its obligation to order.

Bonhoeffer knew that the solution to a conflict in responsibility to God's command cannot be achieved without guilt. The responsible person becomes guilty: "If any man tries to escape guilt in responsibility he detaches himself from the ultimate reality of human existence, and what is more he cuts himself off from the redeeming mystery of Christ's bearing guilt without sin and he has no share in the divine justification which lies upon this event. He sets his own personal innocence above his responsibility for men."[46]

Kant, in his ethical rigorism, thought quite differently. He would have branded the child's statement a downright lie and called upon the child to be unconditionally truthful, that is, to betray its family and its father. Kant would not have hidden an innocent victim of persecution if that would have made it necessary for him to lie. In Bonhoeffer's judgment, this ethical rigorism is totally unchristian and inhumane. For Bonhoeffer it was very clear that one can, may, and should lie if one has to in order to save an innocent friend from murderers. The persecution of the Jews in the Third Reich provided illustrative examples of this in abundance. But Bonhoeffer also knew that all decisions involve the taking on of guilt: "if, in other words, I refuse to bear guilt for charity's sake, then my action is in contradiction to my responsibility which has its foundation in reality."[47]

One should not say here that the ends justify the means in Bonhoeffer. To say the ends justify the means is ideology. Bonhoeffer saw through the "ideological ethic" very clearly: "The man who acts ideo-

45. Ibid., pp. 367–68.
46. Ibid., p. 241.
47. Ibid., p. 245.

logically sees himself justified in his idea; the responsible man commits his action into the hands of God and lives by God's grace and favour."[48]

Bonhoeffer took upon himself the ethical responsibility for the tyrannicide of Hitler. It is well known that Bonhoeffer belonged to the circle that desired the violent elimination of Hitler. However, it was clear to Bonhoeffer that the success of such a decision could not be foreseen. The removal of Hitler could very well have had terrible consequences. Everything could still have ended up much worse if, for example, other prominent Nazis would have succeeded Hitler and pursued his policies in a still more radical way. There could have been mass murder and chaos, vengeance and terror. In this situation it was apparent to Bonhoeffer, the responsible one, that ethical action is not legitimized by success. We all know that world history is almost exclusively written in such a way that the ethical must allow itself to be legitimized by the standard of success. Not so with Bonhoeffer. For him ethical action was action in responsibility to God, in obedience to his command. Thus here once again the Bonhoefferian dialectic is of significance: obedience and freedom, responsibility and guilt, action and forgiveness.

48. Ibid., p. 234.

22

The Biblical Ethos and This World

Through the fall man lost his beginning, his origin in God. He now lives in hatred against this origin, against God, the Creator of man's life and of this world. Bonhoeffer writes: "We do not rule. Rather, we are ruled over. Things, the world, rule over man. Mankind is a prisoner, a slave to the world. His rulership is illusion."[1] In other words, if man no longer shares in the lordship of God, if he is no longer the representation of the lordship of God, then man's lot is to be dominated by hostile powers. The domination of man over man also begins. Without God, man becomes a slave.

Shame is what announces the falling away from God, the hostility toward the Father in heaven. The behavior patterns of German society in the 1920s and 1930s tended toward shamelessness. The breakdown of sexual taboos was not an invention of the 1960s and 1970s. Already in the 1920s and 1930s, shame was moving into the realm of the out-of-date. For the "enlightened" of that time, shame was already something that belonged somehow to the morality of a past age. But basically what this shamelessness made clear was that man, in his ever-growing alienation from Christ and God, had lost his consciousness of guilt before God. Bonhoeffer understood shame in the following

1. *Schöpfung und Fall*, p. 126.

way: "Shame arises only out of the knowledge of the breaking up of mankind, of the breaking up of the world in general, and thus also of the breaking up of oneself. Shame is not the expression of no longer accepting the other as a gift of God, but of the obsessive desire for the other and thereby of the accompanying knowledge of the other as someone for whom it is also no longer enough to belong to me, but who wants something from me. Shame is the veiling of myself from the other, for the sake of my own and his wickedness."[2]

Thus, shame is a sign that man has become guilty not only in relation to God, but also in relation to his fellow human beings. In this connection the dignity of the individual was important to Bonhoeffer. The individual is to be protected against being "figured out" and manipulated. Every individual bears his own unique secret that no one may unveil. In this context Bonhoeffer spoke of the veiling that was so very important to him.

Here we must once again be aware that already in the 1930s in the so-called Third Reich, shame was rejected as a remnant of a Jewish-Christian morality. The naked heroic man and the naked Nordic woman were ideals of beauty of that time. Shamelessness is the radical denial of the integral relation between God and man. Shamelessness denies the fall of man and the fall of nature and rejects reconciliation. Where there is shamelessness, man has lost sight of the holiness of God (see Isa. 6 and Luke 5). Shamelessness not only in talk of God (the shameless denial of God), but also in man's general portrayal of himself, destroys the reverence of man for man since man is no longer exalted as a creature of God. Creation is stripped of its mystery and becomes a manipulable thing. The intellectual atheism of the nineteenth century is naive and harmless compared to the atheism of shamelessness that is being pumped into our present-day civilization through print and electronic media. There is no more radical atheism than that of shamelessness. Shamelessness is the most radical denial of God because it is comprehensive in scope.

The "Natural" and the Fallen Creation

Bonhoeffer's ethic is an ethic of revelation. Bonhoeffer rejected the idea of a natural ethic. But he did not reject the natural as such: "We

2. Ibid., p. 75.

speak of the natural, as distinct from the creaturely, in order to take into account the fact of the Fall; and we speak of the natural rather than of the sinful so that we may include in it the creaturely."[3] In other words, the good creation of God is partially undone by the power of evil. Everything that is—earth, plants, animals, and humans—lives in the shadow of evil. But everything that lives in the shadow of evil does not stop having its origin in God and his creative power. Therefore creation is not evil, but only partially undone by evil: "Through the Fall the 'creature' becomes 'nature.'"[4] But the natural is determined through God's preserving will and the natural's alignment with Christ.[5] The natural safeguards our life from the unnatural, which sets itself against God's will, for life itself is on the side of the natural. The unnatural destroys life.

In the endtimes the natural will be destroyed. Even "vitalism" the greed for life, "cannot but end in nihilism, in the disruption of all that is natural."[6] When in our present-day, pleasure-based society vitalism in the form of emotionalism rises up against the natural, against the God-ordained relationship between the sexes, for example, when things become perverted—the natural is destroyed.

Individuality is also part of the "nature of man." Bonhoeffer saw that this was threatened by the collectivism of his time. There is such a thing as the right of the individual that is rooted in what is naturally given.[7] For Bonhoeffer it was clear that "the existence of a natural right of the individual follows from the fact that it is God's will to create the individual and to endow him with eternal life."[8] The individual is immortal as an individual, not as a collective. Exactly the opposite view prevailed in National Socialist ideology: You are nothing, your *Volk* is everything. The individual is transitory, so that the *Volk* may live on. In complete contrast to this collectivist tendency of the twentieth century, Bonhoeffer elevated the individual. Individual human rights come before collective human rights.

3. *Ethics*, p. 144.
4. Ibid., p. 145.
5. Ibid.
6. Ibid., p. 149.
7. Ibid., p. 153.
8. Ibid., p. 154.

Bonhoeffer was a sharp-eyed prophet of the threat of collectivism: The collective is the god to whom both individual and community life is sacrificed. Here life is snuffed out.[9]

Bonhoeffer saw the danger of the false path of collectivism above all to German society:

> And indeed there can be no doubt that in our modern social order, and especially in the German one, the life of the individual is so exactly defined and regulated, and is at the same time assured of such complete security, that it is granted to only very few men to breathe the free air of the wide open spaces of great decisions and to experience the hazard of responsible action which is entirely their own. In consequence of the compulsory regulation of life in accordance with a definite course of training and vocational activity, our lives have come to be relatively free from ethical dangers; the individual who from his childhood on has had to take his assigned place in accordance with this principle is ethically emasculated; he has been robbed of the creative moral power, freedom. In this we see a deep-seated fault in the essential development of our modern social order, a fault which can be countered only with a clear exposition of the fundamental concept of responsibility. As things stand, the large-scale experimental material for the problem of responsibility must be sought for among the great political leaders, industrialists and generals; for indeed those few others who venture to act on their own free responsibility in the midst of the pressure of everyday life are crushed by the machinery of the social order, by the general routine.[10]

The natural, the law, and the command of God are all related to each other. The law protects the "natural from arbitrary revolutionary outbreaks," for "if right is sought for in what is naturally given, then

---

9. Ibid., p. 153. "Social eudemonism" destroys, according to Bonhoeffer in his critique of socialism, the rights of the community, because "the right of the individual is the power which upholds the right of the community, just as, conversely, it is the community that upholds and defends the right of the individual." Therefore, "the existence of a natural right of the individual follows" (ibid., pp. 153–54). "Social eudemonism" overestimates the power of the will over against the reality of natural life itself (p. 154). Therefore, reason is the natural adversary of social eudemonism. The conservative Bonhoeffer opposes social eudemonism with the old Prussian rule: The principle of *suum cuique* is the highest possible attainment of a reason which is in accord with reality (p. 154). Therefore, according to Bonhoeffer the individual may also fight for and defend his natural right (p. 155).

10. Ibid., pp. 250–51.

due honour is being rendered to the will and to the gift of the Creator, even in a world which is involved in conflict; and attention is being drawn also to the fulfilment of all rights when Jesus Christ through the Holy Ghost shall give to each his own."[11] Thus, fallen creation is not devilish creation. Nature is the fallen creation but at the same time also the preserved and upheld creation of God. This upheld and preserved nature is basically what Kuyper meant by the effect of common grace. God will not allow his creation to sink in the floods of chaos until the second coming of Christ. Nature is upheld by God, but also, again and again, attacked, challenged, yes even "partially undone" by the voidness of evil. Bonhoeffer and Kuyper viewed nature and history dynamically, in a way that does justice to the above-described reality.

Christ-Mystical Understanding of Creation

For Bonhoeffer, the inquiry into the good was the inquiry into Christ: "The problem of Christian ethics is the becoming real of the revelatory reality of God among His creatures." This eccentric sentence, one could justifiably say this "theological jargon," which dominated the theological scene in Germany from the 1920s to the 1960s, means that God reveals himself in Christ. Christ is not a remembered ideal like Goethe. Rather, in Christ the true will of God, who is at work right now in creation, is revealed. And this will of God that has been revealed in Christ preserves creation from chaos and directs itself against the power of evil. That is why Bonhoeffer could call Christ the "antilogos." This antilogos protests against any and every absolutization of creation.

Because of the fall there may be no absolutization in the realm of creation, because all visible things live in the shadow of evil. Christ is the antilogos against these absolutizations in creation. He is life against death, good against evil, order against chaos. In Christ we recognize what God wants: He wants to preserve, to heal, to save. He wants reconciliation and forgiveness. It is very clear: it is useless to try to recognize God's will in creation outside of Christ. God's will, which works itself out even where we do not recognize it, can be recognized only through the revelation of Christ. This cosmos is on the way to redemption in spite of its hostility to God. All things are by him,

11. Ibid., p. 153.

through him, and to him. "This means that no created thing can be conceived and essentially understood without reference to Christ, the Mediator of creation. All things were created by Him and for Him, and have their existence only in Him (Col. 1.15ff.)." In creation, Christ is life, light, peace, joy, fear, death, struggle for survival, sickness. There is no divine world just as there is no Christian world. God and the world are not identical, and neither are Christ and the world identical. Neither is there a Christian or divine society. But throughout nature and throughout the history of human society, God is at work through Christ. The preserving, liberating, and redeeming power of God stands behind everything. Bonhoeffer's conviction was that there is no real Christian existence outside of the reality of the world and no real reality outside of the reality of Jesus Christ. The person who declares allegiance to Jesus Christ as the revelation of God is in the same breath declaring allegiance to the reality of God and to the reality of the world. Müller makes the following observation on the above quote: "with the incarnation of Jesus Christ, we are forbidden to separate God and man, divine and secular, holy and profane, supernatural and natural, Christian and unchristian into two spheres."[12] Yet it is also not permissible simply to intermingle these unseparated things as a function of the relation between God and creation as has been tried again and again in the one-dimensionality of theological modernism.

Bonhoeffer thought dialectically and processually. The processual character of his theological thought is made clear through the categories of "ultimate" and "penultimate." The ultimate is the redeemed world at the second coming of Christ, the new heaven and the new earth. In relation to this ultimate of the redeemed world in which God is all in all, this world is merely the penultimate. But the penultimate points to the ultimate, and the ultimate is already having a tangible effect on the penultimate. The ultimate is already present in the penultimate of this world: the kingdom of God is already in our midst.

In this context, Christian ethics must guard against two things: radicalism and compromise. Radicalism

> sees only the ultimate, and in it only the complete breaking off of the penultimate. Ultimate and penultimate are here mutually exclusive

12. Ibid., p. 197; see also Müller, *Von der Kirche zur Welt*, pp. 305f.

contraries. Christ is the destroyer and enemy of everything penultimate, and everything penultimate is enmity towards Christ. Christ is
the sign that the world is ripe for burning. There are no distinctions.
Everything must go to the judgement. There are only two categories:
for Christ, and against Him. . . . No matter if the whole order of the
world breaks down under the impact of the word of Christ, there must
be no holding back. The last word of God, which is a word of mercy,
here becomes the icy hardness of the law, which despises and breaks
down all resistance.[13]

The opposite extreme of this radicalism that renounces the world
is that compromise which is deeply involved in the world:

Here the last word is on principle set apart from all preceding words.
The penultimate retains its right on its own account, and is not threatened or imperilled by the ultimate. The world still stands; the end is not
yet here; there are still penultimate things which must be done, in fulfilment of the responsibility for this world which God has created. . . .
The ultimate remains totally on the far side of the everyday; it is thus,
in fact, an eternal justification for things as they are; it is the metaphysical purification from the accusation which weighs upon everything
that is. The free word of mercy now becomes the law of mercy, which
rules over everything penultimate, justifying it and certifying its worth.

Compromise means the secularization of Christianity.

Bonhoeffer fought against the escapist character of radicalism, that
is clear. But neither did he desire any secularization of Christianity,
any world-bliss. By his oft misunderstood worldliness Bonhoeffer
meant only that the penultimate should not be maliciously betrayed
in favor of the ultimate: "It is the same germ that disintegrates the
world and that makes the Christian become radical."[14]

The crucifixion of Christ does not "simply mean the annihilation
of the created world, but under this sign of death, the cross, men are
now to continue to live, to their own condemnation if they despise it,
but to their own salvation if they give it its due." Furthermore,
"already in the midst of the old world, the resurrection has dawned"
and "even the resurrection does not annul the penultimate, but the

13. *Ethics*, p. 127.
14. Ibid., pp. 127–29.

eternal life, the new life, breaks in with ever greater power into the earthly life and wins its space for itself within it."[15]

Here it is absolutely clear that Bonhoeffer thought apocalyptically. Thus, according to the catchwords of progressive theology, Bonhoeffer was an "apocalypticist." But the "apocalypticist" Bonhoeffer thought dynamically. The "already now" stands beside the "still to be." The Christ-mystic Bonhoeffer knew about being in Christ; he knew about the reality of redemption that is given through this being in Christ, even if only in hope. There is no penultimate in and of itself because the penultimate is already moving toward the ultimate and is affected by the ultimate. "It is the ultimate which determines the penultimate"[16] and "for the sake of the ultimate the penultimate must be preserved," because "the state in which grace finds us is not a matter of insignificance."[17] Thus the penultimate, namely, "to give bread to the hungry," has significance for the way in which grace comes to us.[18] But—and let this be written into the memory of all Christo-Marxists—"what is happening here is a thing before the last. To give bread to the hungry man is not the same as to proclaim the grace of God and justification to him, and to have received bread is not the same as to have faith."[19]

The Mandates of God

The ethics of contemporary modern Protestantism does not want to be an ethic of order, but an ethic of love. It recognizes itself in Tillich's words: "Only love can change itself according to the concrete demands of every individual and social situation without losing its eternity and dignity and unconditional validity."[20] According to Robinson, only love "can allow itself to be directed completely by the situation."[21] Through love man becomes God's stand-in, the substitute for Christ. Love, as the ultimate, overrules the penultimate of all laws and ordinances. Yes, love is opposed to law and opposed to order.

15. Ibid., p. 132.
16. Ibid., p. 133.
17. Ibid., p. 136.
18. Ibid., p. 137.
19. Ibid.
20. P. Tillich, *Der Protestantismus—Prinzip und Wirklichkeit,* 1950, p. 202.
21. Robinson, *Honest to God,* p. 115.

In modern ethics, something akin to an ideology of love has developed. But this love is structureless and formless and subjective to the highest degree. What is love here? Is sentimentality or self-actualization confused with love? Is love *eros* in the Platonic sense of self-actualization, or is it rather *agapē* in the sense of Christian mercy? The ethic of love is arbitrary like the ethic of conscience or the ethic of conviction: love without order is sentimentality, order without love is legalism.

Bonhoeffer countered this vague ethic of love with a clear ethic of order. He concretized this ethic of order by speaking of mandates. By "mandates" Bonhoeffer meant God's standing provisions for man so that in the name of God he could fully discern what God expects of him in the spheres of the created order with which he is entrusted. Mandates are the conferring of divine authority on earthly institutions.[22] In this way Bonhoeffer set order against emotionalism and against the arbitrariness of society and the subjectivist spirit of the age. Bonhoeffer recognized four mandates: work, marriage, state, and church.

For Bonhoeffer, marriage was the oldest human order: "Marriage was given already with the creation of the first man. Its right is founded in the beginnings of mankind."[23] Therefore, marriage may not be qualified by any other order, because it is in fact not qualified by any other order. There is no authority in this world that stands above marriage. Furthermore, there may be no confessional limitation of marriage because marriage is an order of nature and not of grace. Bonhoeffer held to his view of marriage until the very end, as well as to his view of the relation between man and woman according to which the man is the head of the woman. This is apparent in his "Traupredigt aus der Zelle" ["Marriage Sermon from a Prison Cell"] of May 1943. In this sermon Bonhoeffer says—certainly to the horror of modern progressive ethicists—the following:

> *God makes your marriage indissoluble.* "What therefore God has joined together, let no man put asunder" (Matt. 19.6). God joins you together in marriage; it is his act, not yours. Do not confound your love for one another with God. God makes your marriage indissoluble, and protects

22. See Peters, *Die Präsenz*, p. 108.
23. *Ethics*, p. 174.

it from every danger that may threaten it from within and without; he wills to be the guarantor of its indissolubility. It is a blessed thing to know that no power on earth, no temptation, no human frailty can dissolve what God holds together; indeed, anyone who knows that may say confidently: What God has joined together, *can* no man put asunder. Free from all the anxiety that is always a characteristic of love, you can now say to each other with complete and confident assurance: We can never lose each other now; by the will of God we belong to each other till death.

Here Bonhoeffer is clearly on a collision course with feminism. In this sermon he said: "You may order your home as you like, except in one thing: the wife is to be subject to her husband, and the husband is to love his wife."[24] These sentences did not simply happen to be said without thought. Neither are they remembrances of traditions or familiar customs from Bonhoeffer's youth. How seriously Bonhoeffer took the special responsibility of the husband in marriage, and how clearly he rejected feminism, is clear in the following sentences from the wedding sermon from prison:

> It is an unhealthy state of affairs when the wife's ambition is to be like the husband, and the husband regards the wife merely as the plaything of his own lust for power and licence; and it is a sign of social disintegration when the wife's service is felt to be degrading or beneath her dignity, and when the husband who is faithful to his wife is looked on as a weakling or even a fool. The place where God has put the wife is in the husband's home.[25]

That Bonhoeffer spoke in this context of the "unhealthy times" in which he lived shows that the emancipation of women as it is being carried too far today had already begun in the 1930s. And it is just as clear that Bonhoeffer saw this development as a rejection of the biblical ethos and condemned it.

Naturally, Bonhoeffer believed in the primacy of the family before the state. The rights of parents superseded the rights of society. In the half-year courses in Finkenwalde between the summer of 1935 and

24. *Letters and Papers from Prison*, p. 43.
25. Ibid., p. 44.

the winter of 1939/40 and later in the *Sammelvikariat* Bonhoeffer consistently defended this primacy against the claim of the totalitarian state: "Neither is the parental order a part of the political order, but separate from it. . . . The order of marriage and of parents has its own right before God and limits the right of the state."[26] Who would want to dispute that Bonhoeffer was a conservative ethicist of order?

Marriage and work are original ordinances: "The Bible discloses both of these to us already in Paradise, and thereby shows that they are part of God's creation, which is through and for Jesus Christ. Even after the Fall, *i.e.* in the only form in which we know them, both are still divine institutions of discipline and grace, because God desires to show himself to the fallen world as the Creator. . . . Marriage and labour are from the beginning subject to a definite divine mandate."[27] As part of this mandate of work Bonhoeffer included agriculture, commerce, industry, art—in other words, the entire creative activity of humankind. Work and marriage have "their own origin in God, an origin which is not established by government, but which requires to be acknowledged by government."[28] That means that commerce, the arts, and science may not be derived from the will of society or the state. In notes for *Ethics* that Bonhoeffer left behind, he writes of the "natural right to work and property."[29]

All mandates are mandates of the Lord. Therefore working out his ethic of responsibility Bonhoeffer states that "in and through" these mandates "God . . . desires to be honoured and adored."[30]

Bonhoeffer rejected the separation of the Sermon on the Mount and the Ten Commandments, for "precisely in the renunciation of one's own right, of property and of marriage, for the sake of God, one may be rendering higher honour to the true origin of all these gifts, to God Himself, than by an insistence upon one's own right. . . . When Jesus calls upon men to follow Him in renouncing their own right, and to give up life, marriage, honour, and property for the sake of fellowship with Him, He is not establishing a new table of absolute values." That which is sacrificed, namely family, marriage, property or life, are by no

26. *GS*, 5:412.
27. *Ethics*, p. 344.
28. Ibid.
29. Ibid., p. 186.
30. Ibid., p. 358.

means thereby disparaged. Already in the Old Testament, that which is sacrificed was always the good in creation.[31] According to Bonhoeffer, there is no "double standard" for "Responsible acceptance of the institution of property in faith in God is not essentially different from renunciation of property in faith in God."

Bonhoeffer's doctrine of mandates was developed as a part of his ethics of order in the context of struggle against a spirit that is not only similar to the spirit of our time, but can also be thought of as something like a penultimate that preceded the ultimate that is our time. In fact, the challenge to the ethics of order and responsibility as understood by Bonhoeffer has grown in intensity since his time. Thus, Bonhoeffer's ethics of order is all the more significant precisely for the present day.

31. Ibid., pp. 358–59.

PART 8

Bonhoeffer
in the Resistance

23

The National Socialist Revolution

The Hostility of National Socialist Ideology Toward Christianity

The relationship between National Socialism and Christianity was not easy to figure out in the early days of the Nazi "movement." Point 24 of the twenty-five points of the National Socialist German Workers party platform of February 24, 1920 (put together by Drexler, Feder, and Hitler) was as follows: "We demand the freedom of all religious confessions as long as they do not endanger the existence of the state or offend the ethical or moral sense of the Germanic race—the Party itself takes the viewpoint of a positive Christianity without binding itself to a specific confession. The Party opposes the Jewish-materialist spirit within us and outside of us and is convinced that a lasting healing of our people can only occur from the inside out, on the basis of: public before private good." If one looks carefully one may feel considerable critical misgivings against this point of the party's very socialistically slanted platform:

1. Race, in this case the Germanic race, is the final and decisive standard for the preservation of the ethics and morality. In fact, race is the supreme measure, above all other values.
2. In the end, the objection to the Jewish spirit implies the objection to Bible-believing Christianity, because the writings of the Old and New

Testaments, with the possible exception of the works of Luke, were all written by Jews. In the final analysis, therefore, Christianity, which according to these racial-biological standards arose out of the Jewish race, must also be of the Jewish spirit. One can follow from the beginning of Hitler's career to the end how seriously he took this matter. In 1919, Hitler followed this train of thought: "First stage: cleansing of the Bible—what of it is of our spirit. Second stage: critical examination of the remains."[1]

On April 12, 1922, in the Bürgerbräukeller in Munich, Hitler gave a political speech with the title "Die Hetzer der Wahrheit" ["Agitators for Truth"]: "I tell you: my Christian feeling points me to my Lord and Savior as a fighter. . . . It points me to the man who, at one time lonely and surrounded by only a few followers, recognized these Jews and raised the battle cry against them; the man who, as true God, was not at his greatest as a patient sufferer, but as a fighter! In boundless love I read as Christian and human being through the passage which proclaims to us how the Lord finally gathered himself up and took hold of the whip in order to drive the usurers, the nest of vipers and adders, out of the temple. . . . But today after two thousand years, deeply moved, I recognize His immense struggle for this world against the Jewish poison most powerfully in the fact that he had to bleed to death on the cross for this struggle."[2] In his book *Mein Kampf* Hitler wrote: "Thus I believe I am acting today according to the will of the almighty Creator: by warding off the Jews I am fighting for the work of the Lord."[3] Here, the God-man Jesus becomes the fighter against the Jewish spirit. The death of Jesus on the cross is understood as the consequence of this struggle against the Jewish spirit. This is a radical reevaluation of the cross and of Christianity in general. German Christian Protestant theologians following in Hitler's train would try every trick in their historical-critical bag to make Jesus into an Aryan.

1. See Scholder, *Die Kirche*, p. 108.
2. Speech by Hitler on April 12, 1922, in the Bürgerbräukellar in Munich. See ibid, p. 109.
3. Hitler, *Mein Kampf*, 17th ed., 1943, p. 70. Reports of the Bavarian police on Hitler's public speaking activity around 1920 show that Hitler was mostly engaged in anti-Semitic agitation at this time, and that anti-Semitism was often the main content of his speeches. This anti-Semitic agitation was always accompanied by the unusually loud applause of his listeners. On this point, see D. Irving, *Hitlers Weg zum Krieg*, 1978, p. 29.

Already in the year 1932 the Lutheran theologian Hermann Sasse, who had at first worked together with Bonhoeffer but later, because of his exclusively Lutheran confessionality, broke with Bonhoeffer, recognized the immediate challenge to the church that Article 24 of the National Socialist party platform posed. Sasse was of the opinion that according to this article of the party platform the church was "a deliberate and permanent offence to the ethical and moral sense of the Germanic race" because this party article stood in utter opposition to the Christian doctrine of sin and reconciliation. Precisely this doctrine left open no possibility "that the Germanic or Nordic or any other race is able by nature to love God and do His will. Rather, a newborn child of noblest Germanic heritage is . . . just as captive to eternal damnation as the hereditarily severely polluted half-breed of two decadent races." In addition to this Sasse recognized that, with Article 24, the state as "omnipotent state" wanted to watch over even "the souls of its citizens."[4]

3. The talk of positive Christianity with the socialistic slogan "public before private good" forces Christianity into a socialistic plan of action. The German Christian, according to this, would have to be a national and socialist Christian.

But only a few saw the radical consequences of this point of the NSDAP's party platform. Several interpretations of Article 24, including official interpretations from the Party itself, gave the impression that the large established churches in their traditional form met the requirements of Article 24 fully. Since the Party itself wanted to fight against Bolshevist atheism, a mood arose within the Party organizations that many understood as promoting the possibility of a religious or perhaps even Christian revival. Already in 1932 the group commanders of the SA hired chaplains. Many theologians joined the SA, and, to the horror of foreign observers, assembled as German-Christian theologians at the general synod of the old Prussian Union Protestant Church dressed in SA uniforms with the full regalia of belt and dagger. The district leader of Berlin and Reich propaganda minister Goebbels were married in the church, and Hermann Göring did the

4. *Kirchliches Jahrbuch*, 1932, pp. 65–67. See also Scholder, *Die Kirche*, p. 180.

same. When Göring walked to the altar at his sumptuous wedding in the Cathedral of Berlin in 1935, 30,000 soldiers formed a guard of honor. Two years earlier, on the Day of Potsdam in March 1933, when the venerable Reich President von Hindenburg shook the hand of the newly appointed Reich Chancellor Adolf Hitler, the reconciliation between the modern National Socialist movement and the Christian tradition seemed ensured. Hindenburg was regarded as a believing Lutheran Christian.

In these years mood was everything. Name was just sound and fury. The feeling of unity as a whole *Volk* in spite of all class differences, the invocation of the Lord God who seemed to be bringing about a momentous turnabout in the German nation, the youthful Jesus hero as *Lichtmensch* [man of light] who had "fallen" in battle against the Jews, the proclamation of a new moral order with the affirmation of marriage and family and a "reforestation program of the German race" so to speak, the rectifying of poverty and social need, and "Christianity of the deed" as social obligation—all of these things stimulated the impression of a religious-Christian-racial awakening.

Utterly lost in all this was the understanding of sin, justification, and substitutionary suffering on the cross. Suffering and sins in general were elements that offended the Germanic race's sense of worth. People wanted to set sail for new shores; to do that they needed courage, and they wanted Christianity's Jesus of Nazareth as the man of light to be the bearer of this courage.

The National Socialist movement found a mood that had been long in the making. Already from 1930 on, the name of God became more and more a metaphor for the renewal of the people and the state. Conservative predecessors of Hitler, such as von Papen, who was also Reich Chancellor for a short time, wanted to save Germany through God and Christianity. The outwardly still intact churches offered themselves as an instrument of national renewal. Bonhoeffer realized this. In a sermon on June 12, 1932, at the time of von Papen's government, Bonhoeffer said:

> We read that a government proclaims that an entire people should be saved from collapse—by means of the Christian world-view. . . . Do we believe that we would allow ourselves to be taken in a second time by this "in the name of God, Amen?" . . . Or is there hiding behind our

religious tendencies the ravenous urge for arbitrariness, the urge to do in God's name what pleases us, to play off and incite one nationality against the other in the name of the Christian world-view? . . . Our disobedience is not that we are hardly religious, but that we would actually so much like to be religious . . . supremely reassured when some government or other proclaims the Christian world-view . . . the more pious we are, the less we put up with being told that God is dangerous, that God does not allow Himself to be mocked.[5]

That is exactly what people wanted—to be religious. And the National Socialist revolution was able consciously to tie into this religious mood. In those years Hitler's great concern was not to challenge the churches. He could then continue unimpeded on the road to power. The Protestant Church, which was in a permanent identity crisis, was only too glad to allow itself to be sucked into this mood. This was so much the case that Bonhoeffer wrote his grandmother the following on August 2, 1933: "It is becoming more and more clear to me that we are going to have a great racial national church that will no longer bear Christianity in its essence."[6]

The religious mood of that time actually served to cover over a deep hostility toward Christianity that had asserted itself in the process of Germany's secularization. The National Socialist movement was also able to tie into this hostility to Christianity in the name of religion. Even if certain Nazi ideologues who were very critical of Christianity, such as Arthur Dinter and Alfred Rosenberg (whose influence on Nazi ideology has always been overestimated), were on occasion called off from their attacks, the fact remains that hostility toward Christianity was at the heart of the National Socialist movement, and was tended and looked after as something akin to a "holy flame."

Although this was not recognized until later, the man who more and more came to function as the point of crystallization between the Nazi movement and its anti-Christian essence was none other than Martin Bormann, who had moved up from Chief of Staff of the Deputy of the *Führer* (Rudolf Hess), to Head of the Party Chancellory, and finally to Secretary of the *Führer.* This man was a fanatical opponent of Christianity who had totally banned from his family life all writings

5. *GS*, 4:65f.
6. Bethge, *Bonhoeffer*, p. 354.

and practices that had anything in the least to do with Christian tradition. He soon also put an end to the dream of SA-chaplains and SA field worship services. The idea of a synthesis between a racially or racistically interpreted Christianity and the National Socialist movement held no water with him. In February 1937 Bormann instructed all party offices "to refrain from the admission of members of the clergy into the party."[7] Party orators were instructed to avoid formulations that indicated that the Party should take care of this world, but the church should take care of the next world. After all, argued Bormann, "in reality the clergy knows just as little about the next world as we do."

Bormann also skillfully took care of details. For example, he ordered that clergymen no longer be called "servants of God," but rather "servants of the church" or "church officials." In addition, the expression "church service" (Kirchendienst) was no longer to be equated with "worship service" (Gottesdienst). The reason for this was that genuine worship would not be only a matter for the church, but also for the Party. Also, in public speeches there was no longer to be talk of the "Christian worldview" but of "Christian denominations." Then, at the end of June 1938, Bormann secretly ordered that "pastors immediately be relieved of their party status as state officials." In other words, pastors no longer were allowed to exercise any function in the Party, and "as of immediately, it is forbidden to entrust pastors with positions in the Party, its divisions and related associations." Along the same lines, it was prescribed "that clergy as well as other comrades of the German race who have strong ties to any Christian denomination cannot be admitted into the Party." Bormann's plan for the future was that "Party members who enter the clergy or take up the study of theology must leave the Party."[8]

Those who argue about whether Bormann acted on his own authority behind Hitler's back or with Hitler's consent fail to recognize Hitler's true intentions. Bormann was not only an absolutely faithful follower of Hitler but also, since he was practically closer to Hitler than anyone else—especially during the war years—Bormann knew

---

7. On Bormann's hostility toward Christianity, see Jochen von Lang, Der Sekretär—Martin Bormann: Der Mann, der Hitler beherrschte, 3rd ed., 1987. On the quote, see ibid., p. 137.
   8. Ibid.

more than any other man in Germany about Hitler's thoughts and intentions. Thus one would have to agree with Reich press officer Otto Dietrich[9] when he says that Hitler not only did not rein in Bormann, but also encouraged him in his action against the church. When the Reich Minister of Ecclesiastical Affairs Hans Kerrl attempted to build a bridge between Christianity and National Socialism and wanted to write a book about it with the title *Weltanschauung und Religion,* Bormann saw to it that Kerrl was prohibited from doing this. That happened in 1939. When Kerrl died toward the end of 1941, Bormann informed the Party apparatus via memorandum that from that time forward, he alone was responsible for the ecclesiastical policy of the Party.[10] And since in the view of National Socialism—by the way, just as in the view of communism—the state does not determine the Party, but the Party the state, the entire ecclesiastical policy of the Third Reich lay in the hands of Bormann.

Certainly, many National Socialists who still believed in the relation between "positive Christianity" and the Party could not follow so quickly in Bormann's footsteps. This was the case, for example, with the District Leader Josef Wagner, a strict Catholic who had fought hard for the Party in Westphalia. When the Wagner family wanted to forbid their daughter to marry an SS-officer because he had left the church, Josef Wagner was tried before a Party court. The supreme Party judge acquitted Wagner because Wagner appealed to the concept of "positive Christianity" during the trial. This acquittal, however, was of no use to Wagner because Hitler refused to put this court decision into force by signing it. Wagner was then expelled from this *Führer's* choir masquerading as a political party.

Friedrich Heer's extensive and sensitive monograph, *Der Glaube des Adolf Hitler,* informs us superbly about Hitler's attitude toward Christianity. It is very evident that in the course of time, especially during the war, Hitler put aside the more racial-biologically accented opposition to Christianity in favor of a more Enlightenment-oriented, rationalist opposition. Heer analyzed especially the table conversations of Hitler, from which the following picture arises.[11]

9. Ibid., p. 139.
10. Ibid., p. 180.
11. On the following statements of Hitler, see F. Heer, *Der Glaube des Adolf Hitler,* pp. 182ff.

Hitler was of the opinion that the church should bow to the progress of natural science. No one who was familiar with the findings of scientific research could any longer take the teachings of the church seriously. Christian faith contradicted the laws of nature, according to Hitler, and the church would die off painlessly as a general intellectual enlightenment took hold: "The time of the downfall of the church has come. It will take another few centuries, and then what will not happen through revolution will happen through evolution." Nevertheless, Hitler still saw the subversive spirit of Christianity as the religion of decadence: "Rome was broken by Christianity, not by Germanic tribes and Huns. What Bolshevism is putting into practice today on a materialist-technological basis, Christianity has achieved on a theoretical-metaphysical basis." Hitler believed he would be able to get rid of pastors and ecclesiastical organizations very soon after the war.

How much Hitler was in conflict with the central concern of Christianity is shown by the following remarks: "God creates human beings; characteristic of human beings is sin which renders them liable to death. But it was God who gave human beings the predisposition to sin. Then for 500,000 years he watches them dig a hole for themselves. It finally occurs to Him to send His only begotten Son. A murderous detour; the whole process is tremendously arduous. Others do not believe all of this. It has to be imposed on them by force. If our dear God had an interest in our knowing these things, then why the knee splints and thumbscrews?"

Hitler's total rejection of salvation history is clear. Christianity is a religion hostile toward life. Christian faith is superstition that contradicts the enlightened knowledge brought about through natural science. Hitler did not believe in eternity. He was not attracted by a heaven in which one could find only "unattractive and intellectually boring women." In contrast to that Hitler saw National Socialism as on the side of the affirmation of life, of tolerance, of belief in a meaning to life, and above all on the side of science. He contrasted the full-blooded vitality of National Socialism with Christianity's morality of renunciation. In the end, Hitler thought, the Finns had been intellectually crippled by reading the Bible. That was the real reason there were so many mental illnesses in Finland. "The droppings of Jews and the babbling of priests" were all the same to Hitler. They led to insanity and had to be opposed through a general enlightenment of the people. For the rest, Hitler comforted himself with the thought that the churches would collapse if the state no longer supported them or collected church tax: "If the church were supported by donations it probably wouldn't manage to rake in even 3 percent of the current state subsidy. Then every bishop would come crawling to his regional governor to ask for the elimination of the concordat so that he could get his legal tender again."

Bonhoeffer and the Challenge

The aristocratic Bonhoeffer saw in National Socialist ideology a creature from the deep, an uprising of the masses, of the collective, of the ordinary, of rampant disorder. Already during the summer semester of 1932, in his lecture course on the essence of the church, Bonhoeffer said prophetically: "There has always been a demand for the church's services. But today the origin of this call in secularity is very obvious. In a direct and immediate way people want community as a means of overcoming individualism (in communist ideology and in National Socialism). People want authority and *Führertum* (leadership). The church is merely secondary; it has become a means to other ends."[12] Thus Bonhoeffer recognized that ideologies, especially National Socialism, were seeking to use the church as an instrument to help them achieve their goals. Bonhoeffer also allowed himself no illusions as to how much the church was not only caught up in a process of disintegration from the inside, but also had basically lost its significance: "In the flight from itself, the church of today has become the object of profound contempt."[13]

Bonhoeffer at first reacted in an ecclesiastical way to the challenge of Nazi ideology as a theologian of the Confessing Church. Politically, he reacted as a man of "conservative values." Bonhoeffer did not "come to advocate" resistance. He *was* resistance in the depths of his very being. He personified it.

Only a few in the Protestant Church saw through Nazi ideology from the beginning as Bonhoeffer did. Reinhold Niebuhr recalls Bonhoeffer's opinion at that time of totalitarian repression in Germany: "The Christians in Germany must now decide whether they desire the

12. *GS*, 5:230.
13. *GS*, 5:231.

victory of their people and the downfall of Christian civilization, or the defeat of their people and the continuing existence of Christian civilization."[14] And Helmut Traub remembers an encounter with Bonhoeffer: "I objected: didn't he see that everything was lost; either way, hardly any of us would get out of this alive. He replied that he saw it the same way, but for that reason—and this was Bonhoeffer's real answer—for that reason each of us would have to come to the clear realization that he is faced with a choice: If he desires Germany's victory, then he also must desire the complete end of his freedom and of Christianity within him." Certainly, these were later remarks, but they are of a piece with what Bonhoeffer had said about National Socialism from the very beginning.[15]

In 1941, at the time of the greatest triumphs of the Nazi regime, an article was published under the guise of a book review that discussed a future reordering of Europe after the war. Bonhoeffer was one of the writers of this article. In it he says that it was difficult for the Germans to evaluate the Nazi regime correctly: "And it may not be left unsaid that the statesmen of other nations become Hitler's helpers against the resistance groups in Germany by making concessions to Hitler that had been refused to his predecessors. Because of this it is understandable that it became more and more difficult for the German nation to understand the true character of the regime. It is understandable that only relatively few remained unshaken in their conviction, that this regime was Satan disguised as the angel of light."[16]

In reality, Hitler's remarks as quoted by Heer—remarks that come mainly from Hitler's table conversations at the Führer's headquarters during the early part of the war—were the expression of the general Enlightenment consciousness that dominated not only Germany but all of Europe. After all, were people not generally convinced that the era of Christianity was over, and that science and enlightenment contradicted the propositions of Christianity as to the origin and purpose of the world? Were people not generally of the opinion, not only in Germany but in all of Europe also, that Christianity, with its tendency

14. In *Begegnungen mit Bonhoeffer*, p. 132.
15. Ibid., p. 127.
16. Bonhoeffer's discussion of September 1941 with Visser't Hooft of the book by William Paton, *Die Kirche und die neue Ordnung*, contains Bonhoeffer's basic thoughts on the reordering of Europe after the war. See *GS*, 1:480ff.

toward self-denial, stood in the way of life's full potential, in other words in the way of "happiness"?

Precisely because of this alienation from Christianity that dominated all of Europe, only very few saw and recognized how Satan disguises himself as an angel of light. After all, the foreign policy victories and then the military triumphs were fascinating to the masses. In 1940 and 1941 many, not only in Germany but also in Europe as a whole, were asking themselves whether National Socialism was indeed preparing the way for a reordering of Europe.

In this Nazi state, Bonhoeffer did not lead a "normal life." He was not a pastor in the Protestant Church, and he had to give up his position as an instructor in the Department of Theology at the University of Berlin. He lived on the edge of illegality—all the more during the war. Then, as an informant for the *Amt Canaris*, he came into immediate contact with the resistance movement against Hitler, and even started to perform tasks for the resistance. Officially, Bonhoeffer was still a kind of roving teacher or theological consultant for the Confessing Church, and because of his duties for the *Amt Canaris* he obtained release from military duty. The Anglican bishop of Chichester, George Bell, describes Bonhoeffer's inner attitude as witnessed at an encounter with Bonhoeffer in Sweden in 1942. According to Bell, Bonhoeffer was of the opinion that Hitler was the Antichrist and that everything possible must be done to remove him regardless of whether success was likely or not.[17]

It is debated whether Bonhoeffer thought Hitler was the Antichrist or not, because another statement of Bonhoeffer exists: "No, he is not the Antichrist. Hitler is not great enough for that. The Antichrist is using him, but the Antichrist is not as dumb as Hitler."[18] However Bonhoeffer may have judged the demonic in Hitler, he saw in Hitler such a challenge to church and state that he joined the resistance that later planned the assassination attempt of July 20, 1944, and undertook trips to other countries on behalf of the resistance in order to ascertain through his ecumenical contacts what kind of peace or cease-fire offers the Western powers would offer a new German government after Hitler's removal. Bonhoeffer saw the situation quite

17. See Bethge, *Bonhoeffer*, p. 811.
18. Ibid., p. 812.

simply as follows: either the collapse of National Socialist Germany, be it through a military defeat or through a rebellion, or the collapse of Christian civilization. The radicality of this assessment was nearly unique at that time. Bonhoeffer saw himself in a battle not only for the Confessing Church, but also for Christian Western civilization; that is, for Christian Western world order.

Many Confessing pastors did not share Bonhoeffer's view. There is no longer any use in arguing whether even the majority of members of the Confessing Church failed to follow Bonhoeffer on this point. I think it must simply be concluded that Bonhoeffer was a lonely man in this view within the Confessing Church. Many men within the Confessing Church believed quite strongly that the war was necessary and hoped for the victory of National Socialist Germany. Many Confessing pastors served as reserve officers and paid a heavy toll in blood. Of the 150 students trained at Finkenwalde, 80 died in the war.

Many Confessing Christians opposed the political struggle against Hitler. With their high respect for the state, they favored only the spiritual or ecclesiastical fight against ideology in so far as it was a threat to the church. Ecclesiastically organized demonstrations against government policies as we have today were totally out of the question at the time. Although there are such demonstrations today, even supported or initiated by ecclesiastical office-bearers, these demonstrations are not for the preservation of Christian Western values or law, but for a revolutionization of society in a sense that contradicts Bonhoeffer's conservative intention.

Bonhoeffer was confident that the Nazi regime could be brought down. In 1941, during a trip to Switzerland for the *Amt Canaris*, he even expressed the opinion that a Germany in the borders of 1939 with a new government and a new state system could be saved.[19] Bonhoeffer was one of those in the German resistance movement who unflinchingly considered the violent removal of Hitler. He felt close to the politicians who wanted to bring about the restoration of the monarchy under Prince Louis Ferdinand of Prussia.[20] Bonhoeffer was prepared to carry out the assassination of Hitler himself. Before he did this he wanted to leave the Confessing Church in order not to draw

19. Ibid., p. 833.
20. Ibid., p. 857.

them into a battle, into a state of political resistance, which they in the end could not endorse, considering their views on the matter.

This brings us to a critical question. Was Bonhoeffer really executed as a martyr or "only" as a member of the political resistance? Pietists and Lutherans could not actually affirm Bonhoeffer's decision as a Christian decision, and to this very day neither group has done so. But Bonhoeffer saw only one possibility—resistance. He did not think it possible to convert Hitler. Bonhoeffer wrote about this in a letter to his friend Sutz already at the beginning of the 1930s: "Hitler has very clearly shown himself to be who he is, and the church must know whom it is dealing with. Isaiah did not go to Sennacherib. We have tried often enough—too often—to make Hitler hear what he should hear. It may be that we have not yet gone about it correctly. If that is so, Barth will not be able to go about it correctly, either. Hitler is not meant to be allowed to hear. His heart is hardened. He is precisely the one who should force us to hear—that is how things really stand. . . . We should be converted, not Hitler."[21] Bonhoeffer ruled out the possibility of "Christianizing" the Nazi regime. While the established church surrendered before Hitler, Bonhoeffer became acquainted with men in the resistance who hardly had any contact with the church anymore, but who, often living more or less outside of the church, had taken up the fight against evil as "people come of age." These men of the resistance were people who were doing the penultimate without necessarily having experienced the ultimate. This was a new and bitter, but finally also a liberating realization for Bonhoeffer. He was able to assimilate this realization in his *Ethics*.

Bonhoeffer as Martyr

Again we pose the question: Was Bonhoeffer hanged as a martyr or as a fighter in the political resistance? The German Protestant Church has still not arrived at a consensus. In 1985, on the fortieth anniversary of Bonhoeffer's death, yet another passionate disagreement flared up about it. In this context, a letter by Detlev Dädelow, a member of the Confessing Church during the Third Reich, is interesting and typical. The letter was written to the magazine *Evangelische Sammlung*:

---

21. *GS*, 1:43.

In my parents' house, top churchmen who have since died consulted with each other as to whether Dietrich Bonhoeffer's request to the Confessing Church for its blessing and ecclesiastical absolution was biblically justified. After examining the Holy Scriptures, they decided that this was not biblically justified. However, Bonhoeffer was not denied human understanding and pastoral consolation. Whoever had to live through the Third Reich will be able to understand Bonhoeffer's action from a secular point of view. But from a biblical point of view Bonhoeffer is not an ecclesiastical, but a political-secular martyr. The ecclesiastical martyrs of the Third Reich have for the most part been forgotten by today's church. But the political martyr Bonhoeffer has been used by ecclesiastical movements for purposes that do not comport with the gospel and that are certainly against Bonhoeffer's will as well.[22]

One can agree with everything in these last sentences. But whether Bonhoeffer sought pastoral comfort for his intentions in the political resistance movement from "top" churchmen seems very doubtful. It is also interesting that this letter completely separates the political, social-ethical task on the one hand from the Bible, the "ecclesiastical task," on the other hand. George Bell said in a memorial worship service in Holy Trinity Church in London on July 27, 1945, that Bonhoeffer represented both: political resistance and faith in the one revealed God, the political and the moral revolt against injustice and cruelty.

It is clear: Bonhoeffer was motivated by his obedience to the Word of God. His Christian faith, his Christian ethos of order, stood against the ideological-totalitarian challenge. As a Christian witness he took political action. After all, Christian witness and political action do not exclude each other! Did the prophets of the Old Testament act any differently? Bonhoeffer was a Christian martyr. Whoever denies that, denies the integral relation of Christian faith and political-ethical responsibility. Even the "No" of the early Christian martyrs was undoubtedly a political "no," for the offering of incense before the portrait of Caesar was a political act. Is a Christian who dies for the justice that has been revealed in the ethos of the Bible and who fights the battle for the structuring of justice in discipleship to Christ perchance not a martyr?

22. In *Evangelische Sammlung*, Berlin, January 5, 1986, ed. H. Fuhrmeister, G. Küppers, and K. Motschmann, 1986.

24

The State under God's Grace

Christ as Lord of the State

Bonhoeffer's experience with the totalitarian state in the 1930s and 1940s led him to the realization that the collective is the destruction of the state when the collective will asserts itself against law and order: "The collectivity is the god to whom individual and social life are sacrificed in the process of their total mechanization. Life is extinguished."[1] The collective bursts out from below, out of fallen, godless mass-man. Bonhoeffer saw the originally biblical and reformational meaning of political authority or of the state as follows: The basis and origin of the state are not understood as coming from below, from race or culture or the like, but from above, from the one who in the proper sense "governs" all.[2] And for Bonhoeffer, from above meant from Christ: "So long as the earth continues, Jesus will always be at the same time Lord of all government and Head of the Church, without government and Church ever becoming one and the same."[3] Jesus Christ, who justifies the sinner, wills that law prevail in the world. But in the political reality, this law always exists in struggle. It never comes to completion. Until the endtime the state (*polis*) and the

1. *Ethics*, p. 150.
2. Ibid., p. 335.
3. Ibid., p. 338.

church will be separate. Not until the heavenly world will state and church be one. For Bonhoeffer, an ecclesiastization of the state or a nationalization of the church would be just as heretical as the Christianization of the world or the secularization of Christianity.

Why and how is Christ the head over political authority?

1. Everything that is created—and this includes the political authority—has its existence in Christ alone. The Resurrected One has been given all authority in heaven and on earth (Matt. 28:18). Thus, according to Bonhoeffer, He is also "Lord of government."[4] John 19:11 and Colossians 2:15 emphasize expressly that the political authority is subject to Jesus Christ.

2. In Bonhoeffer's view, Jesus Christ has "restored the relation between government and God" through the reconciliation on the cross.[5] Nevertheless, one must distinguish here between possibility and realization.

3. The political authorities are included in salvation history. There are no morally neutral areas in politics. John 18:38 teaches us that the state recognized Jesus' innocence but then condemned him anyway because of pressure from below. Jesus was crucified with the permission of the political authority: The political authority became guilty, it is subject to God's judgment. Yet in its guilt before God, it can also be reconciled with God.

Bonhoeffer understood Romans 13:4 to say that those who possess political power are God's representatives. As such it is their duty not only to punish evil, but to reward good. Thus, the state authority has "a right to educate for goodness."[6] It is also obligated "to commend those who do right" (1 Pet. 2:14), regardless of the religious faith of those persons who hold political authority. "Indeed it is only in protecting the righteous that government fulfils its true mission of serving Christ."[7]

The political authority takes its direction "from the preaching of the Church."[8] Only in that way can it find the standard for political action. But what about pagan (i.e., non-Christian) political authority? How about when political authority is exercised by people who have broken

---

4. Ibid., p. 337.
5. Ibid.
6. Ibid., p. 340.
7. Ibid., p. 342.
8. Ibid., p. 341.

with the body of believers? Or what about a state authority that has never encountered the body of believers? According to Bonhoeffer, duly constituted pagan political authority possesses a natural right to authority. But this natural right is to be viewed in the context that "natural law has its foundation in Jesus Christ."[9] All spheres of reality inside and outside of the church stand under the headship of Christ— that is true of both society and nature. But in all of these spheres the possibility is given of resisting Christ's justice and justification, his command and his grace. Thus state and church must always be understood processually, always and only in the process of being realized until the second coming of Christ, when God will again be all in all.

For this reason there can be no static, unconditional relationship of obedience between the Christian and the state. The Christian must not—in fact, may not—be obedient to every governmental authority. "(The Christian's) duty to obey binds him until the political authority directly forces him to violate the divine command." Thus the Christian is not only released from his duty to obey if he is forced to deny his faith unto salvation; he is already released if God's justice is being violated. However, in such a case the Christian cannot reject everything that this authority decrees. Even an anti-Christian authority is an authority. Only "an apocalyptic view of a specific political authority would have to result in total disobedience." Thus total disobedience as total refusal can only be conceived of in an endtimes scenario. Until then there is a case-by-case disobedience in which the Christian is disobedient, always as "a risk taken on his own responsibility," where a divine command is being violated.

Bonhoeffer denied the right to revolution: "According to the Holy Scriptures, there is no right to revolution, but there is a responsibility of every individual to keep his office and his task in the *polis* pure."

Bonhoeffer did, however, see the possibility of the individual refusing all allegiance to the totalitarian state "out of obedience to the Lord of the church and of political life." Thus, resistance is always a matter of an individual or of a group based on personal responsibility, with the command of God as the final standard. The church as church can-

9. Ibid. All quotes on the right to resistance should be read in relation to one another (ibid., pp. 343–44). The statements about the penultimate of the state in relation to the ultimate of the reality of Christ are found in ibid., pp. 133, 322–25.

not foment revolution. The Christian, though, can join a political movement or a political resistance movement that does not rise up against the political authority as such, but against the perversion of the political authority.

For the Christian, the state is not the ultimate, but only the penultimate. But the state is not a "penultimate in itself." The state is subject to the ultimate, thus, to Christ: For Christ's sake and subject to Christ there is and should be a secular order in the state, family, commerce. For Christ's sake the secular order stands under the command of God. Thereby we must recognize that we are not speaking of the Christian state or Christian commerce, but of the just state and of just commerce, the secular order that serves Christ's purposes. Thus there is a Christian responsibility for secular institutions. Bonhoeffer emphatically did not give up the distinction between the spiritual and the secular. On the contrary, he was very concerned to see this differentiation maintained. The ultimate is salvation that overcomes this world; the penultimate is the reality of this world as God wills it to be.

There does exist a secularity to be ordered according to God's command. A secular order is to be recognized as a just secular order if it, as the legitimate penultimate of the world, does not hinder the salvation-bringing ultimate. That is why Bonhoeffer had understanding for Paul's judgment about slavery. Paul did not want slaves to break out of their slavery because they had become Christians. On this subject, Bonhoeffer wrote that Paul did not regard the form of slavery then present to be an institution that violated God's command. Ancient sources that indicate the relative mildness of that slavery could be cited here.

> Above all, St Paul was able to observe that the slave was clearly not prevented by his actual situation as a slave from living as a Christian. An order of the world which left room for the congregation of Jesus Christ and for life in accordance with the commandments of God was not in itself unacceptable; it required to be corrected from within. It may well have been much the same with the political and economic situation; here it is necessary to remember that the Roman Empire was precisely at this time characterized by a certain stability and legal security. It must also be borne in mind that it was only very much later that the Apostle came in contact with the sometimes far harsher form of slavery which was practised in the western part of the Empire, and that he

could have taken up a position with regard to these questions only within the context of his proclamation of Christ.[10]

Whether Bonhoeffer is correct in all this is not the point. What he asserts is that repressive conditions in a social situation do not establish the right to resistance as long as being a Christian is possible within these conditions. That does not change the fact that on the other hand the Christian is to do everything he can to make the state a really just state, or human society a really just society as it should be according to God's command. The Christian must work toward this goal—practically and persistently—when the possibility is given him. The penultimate of the political reality may never be trivialized, for "there is a depth of human bondage, of human poverty, of human ignorance, which impedes the merciful coming of Christ."[11] If the penultimate of social reality is destroyed the body of believers will have to open up a way for itself in order to somehow shoulder its share of responsibility for worldly conditions.[12]

The Community of Believers and the Community of Citizens

The conservative Bonhoeffer wanted to see the world structured in such a way that "the state as the upholder of order" finds an ally in the church. According to Bonhoeffer the ideal situation would be that the church (the community of believers) and the state (the community of citizens) would join in a common struggle against life- and order-destroying chaos. The struggle is the common goal of state and church. But the state cannot engage in this struggle if there is no church, because "only the Church brings government to an understanding of itself."[13]

In this context the issue of ecclesiastical office was significant for Bonhoeffer. Ecclesiastical office is not subordinate to the political authority. On the contrary, genuine political authority will support the church. "A government which fails to recognize this undermines the root of the true obedience and, therefore, also its own authority."[14]

10. Ibid., p. 324.
11. Ibid., p. 135.
12. Ibid., p. 324.
13. Ibid., p. 347.
14. Ibid., p. 348.

Bonhoeffer saw the common obligation of the community of believers and the community of citizens to the command of God as so crucial that he called to mind the relevance of the first commandment for both groups. Both should recognize that there can be no authority without faith in the Lord: "Government will fulfil its obligation under the first commandment by being government in the rightful manner and by discharging its governmental responsibility also with respect to the Church. But it does not possess the office of confessing and preaching faith in Jesus Christ."[15]

Here, Bonhoeffer's thought lies completely within the Western Christian tradition. His thought does correspond more to the Reformed rather than the Lutheran tradition. As stated in Article 36 of the Dutch confession of faith of 1562 about the task of the political authority: "Its task is not only to implement and oversee public order and the police, but also to protect the holy religion of the church (to repulse and wipe out all idolatry and false worship in order to destroy the kingdom of the Antichrist) and to promote the kingdom of Jesus Christ, to see to it that the Word of the Gospel is preached everywhere and God is served and taught by everyone as He commands in His Word." The words of this article that are in parentheses were not adopted by many Dutch Calvinists and were eliminated from the confession of faith of the Reformed churches in the Netherlands. How conservative Bonhoeffer's thought on the state was is shown by his view of the political authority's being based in God's grace: "That form of the state will be relatively the best in which it becomes most evident that government is from above, from God, and in which the divine origin of government is most clearly apparent. A properly understood divine right of government, in its splendour and in its responsibility, is an essential constituent of the relatively best form of the state."[16] Here it becomes clear that Bonhoeffer at that time considered the possibility that the monarchy would be the best and most ideal form of government for the German Reich after the fall of the Hitler regime.

But whatever form government takes, it should always understand itself on the basis of the law that is grounded in God. It should view its power as carried and secured "by the proclamation of the gospel of

15. Ibid., p. 349
16. Ibid., p. 352.

Jesus Christ."[17] Then, what is best for the state will also be best for the church. "It will be found here that what is best for government is also best for the relationship between government and church."[18] All of this of course presupposes that the church is really a believing church. Naturally, Bonhoeffer was aware of the spiritual disintegration of the Protestant Church. He saw the disintegration of the state and church, but he nevertheless, even in the war years, did not give up the hope that a believing church in a state founded on the rule of law and a state founded on the rule of law alongside a believing church would once again be possible in Germany. Thus, when he was writing his *Ethics*, Bonhoeffer believed in a future Christian state founded on the rule of law in Germany.

The Survival of Western Civilization

For Bonhoeffer, the peoples of Europe were "Western peoples" bearing features of Christ's influence.[19] Notice that Bonhoeffer wrote this during the war. During the World War, when the inner turmoil of Europe had reached its climax, Bonhoeffer was still concerned with the preservation of the West:

> Jesus Christ has made of the west a historical unit. The epoch-making events of history affect the whole of the west. The unity of the west is not an idea but a historical reality, of which the sole foundation is Christ. The great movements in the life of the mind are henceforward the property of the entire western world. Even the wars of the west have the unity of the west as their purpose. They are not wars of extermination and destruction like the wars of pre-Christian times and those which are even today still possible in Asia. . . . It is only when Christian faith is lost that man must himself make use of all means, even criminal ones, in order to secure by force the victory of his cause. And thus, in the place of a chivalrous war between Christian peoples, directed towards the achievement of unity in accordance with God's judgment in history, there comes total war, war of destruction. . . . Only with the advent of total war is there a threat to the unity of the west.[20]

17. Ibid., p. 353.
18. Ibid.
19. Ibid., p. 91.
20. Ibid., p. 92–93.

When Bonhoeffer wrote this, the unity of the West was indeed threatened—but only threatened, not destroyed. He still believed in the future of the West because he saw the West in a salvation-historical context. For Bonhoeffer, Western history was tied to the history of Israel in "genuine uninterrupted encounter." Western history is the continuation of Israel's history. Israel is the sign of the "free mercy-choice and of the repudiating wrath of God." The promised Messiah of Israel is the Messiah of the West: "An expulsion of the Jews from the west must necessarily bring with it the expulsion of Christ. For Jesus Christ was a Jew."[21]

When he wrote his *Ethics*, Bonhoeffer was not a dreamer. As no other, he grasped the realities, the anti-Christian challenges of his time. He was not unaware of the phenomenon of "Western godlessness." "Western godlessness ranges from the religion of Bolshevism to the midst of the Christian churches. In Germany especially, but also in the Anglo-Saxon countries, it is a markedly Christian godlessness. In the form of all the possible Christianities, whether they be nationalist, socialist, rationalist, or mystical, it turns against the living God of the Bible, against Christ."[22] The specifically Western godlessness is the godlessness of the church. It is active in ideologies; it idolizes man or it worships society. All European peoples are guilty of this Western godlessness: "The guilt of the apostasy from Christ is a guilt which is shared in common by the entire western world. . . . No attempt can succeed which aims at saving the west while excluding one of the western nations."[23]

Bonhoeffer saw this possibility of saving the Occident.

1. through "divine renewal of the church";[24]
2. through the restoration, one way or the other, of law, order and peace;[25]
3. through a European peace arrangement that would end the internecine struggle among the Occidental peoples.

---

21. Ibid., pp. 89–90. Bonhoeffer's unusually positive assessment of Judaism deserves a portrayal of its own. It is obviously related to Bonhoeffer's putting the biblical ethos of revelation above nature and race.
22. Ibid., p. 102.
23. Ibid., p. 119.
24. Ibid., p. 117.
25. Ibid., p. 119.

Bonhoeffer never gave up his ethos of order nor his ethics of order. To the end of his life, his letters testify to his opposition to everything uncouth and disorderly, to superficial this-worldliness, to primitive enlightenment-derived attitudes, to impudence, to all of these things that set themselves against law and order. It is said that during his time in prison Bonhoeffer abandoned the integral relation between Christianity and Occident, faith and the world. That is not true. What is true is that Bonhoeffer believed that the body of believers could only be protected from secularization in the *arcanum*, that is, closed off from public view and protected from debilitating worldly influence. It is part of the dialectic of Bonhoefferian thought that he believed that the body of believers can have an effect in this world only if it withdraws from the world and thereby from secularization. Man come of age in this world is the responsible human being who takes responsibility over against God's order and carries it through in the struggle against chaos.

The state of having come of age that Bonhoeffer meant is an aristocratic state. Its content affirms the Christian-Occidental order against the uncouth uprising from below. The less Bonhoeffer could set his hopes on the contemporary form of church life and Christianity, the more he trusted in common grace that preserves this world and, as a reflection of its prototype special grace, calls "man come of age" in his hunger and thirst for righteousness to responsible action as a co-worker with God against the power of chaos. Man come of age, who is occidental man, works as an element of "that which holds back" [2 Thess. 2:7] at the precipice of a Europe tearing itself apart. In the paradoxical thought of Bonhoeffer lies this insight: The body of believers withdraws from the world into the *arcanum* in order to find its identity and come to its real Christian-ness. Only out of this identity can it be there for others and work in the world conscious of its responsibility. On the other hand the secularity that has been liberated from facade-Christianity and from the control of ideology is genuine secularity, in which the order of God shines through. Thus the political ethic of Bonhoeffer is equally opposed to both the National Socialist and the Marxist-Leninist distortions of reality. Secular man come of age is not Marxist man, as many Bonhoeffer interpreters would so much like to believe. Genuine secularity as Bonhoeffer understood it is always the secularity that is free of both pseudo-Christianization and ideology.

PART 9

Bonhoeffer and the Established Protestant Church

25

Bonhoeffer's Christ-Mystical Church

Bonhoeffer became a member of the Protestant Church in Germany through infant baptism. There is no story of Bonhoeffer's conversion. Bonhoeffer's turning to the Christian faith lies "veiled" in the same way that much of God's work is, in Bonhoeffer's view. His very being would have deeply resisted a dramatic tale of his conversion like so often occurs as an expression of religious subjectivism. He probably did not experience a sudden conversion, but more—as it was expressed in Reformed Dutch Protestantism—a change of direction to the Christian faith that occurred gradually. Bonhoeffer began his university studies in 1923 and completed his study with the second comprehensive theological examination and then also with his inaugural dissertation in the summer of 1930. On November 11, 1931, he was ordained a pastor.

After World War I, the Protestant Church in Germany changed from a state church to a church of the German people. The Weimar Republic (based on Article 137 of the Weimar Constitution of 1919, which was adopted almost word for word into the Basic Law of the Federal Republic of Germany in 1949) granted the two great confessions, Catholic and Protestant, the status of public corporations with the significant right "to levy taxes on the basis of the civic tax lists in accordance with the provincial legal requirements." These taxes were then collected for the churches by the state. To what extent this institution was really a church according to the understanding of the Scripture and the reformational confession, and how one could really address this mass institution for the "administration of cheap grace" as the church of Jesus Christ—these questions were left open. The responsible churchmen thought (and still think today) pragmatically. Thus, Otto Dibelius, who in 1925 at the age of forty-five became the youngest-ever general superintendent of the Prussian Church, said at that time: "We are not to develop or restructure a Protestant church according to the basic principles of the Reformation. Rather, we are to accept from God's hands what happens, and what has happened now—not in order to make observations about it, but in order to act."[1] One could hardly conceive of a statement bringing ecclesiastical pragmatism to such clear expression as this declaration of Dibelius.

As a successful private lecturer in Berlin Bonhoeffer by this time had a network of foreign contacts and had studied more than a half-year at Union Theological Seminary in New York. Thus he had gained deep and broad insights into the Protestant theology of more than just Germany. Surprisingly and suddenly he wanted nothing other than to be a pastor in the German Protestant Church. He wanted out of the abstraction of the "academic life" in order to live the Christian faith "concretely" in a church congregation. And so Bonhoeffer applied to pastor the St. Bartholomew Church in Berlin in 1932—and lost the election. The congregational representatives gave twenty-five votes to Bonhoeffer and forty-seven to the opposing candidate.

Bonhoeffer never held the office of pastor in a congregation of the Protestant Church of Germany. But as a lecturer, student chaplain, intern, pastor in London, and then later as the head of education of the seminary of the Confessing Church, Bonhoeffer gained deep insights into the essence of the Protestant Church. He thought about the many church "events" and "celebrations," about the institutional duties like weddings and funerals, about the "church groups" and "holidays" that the congregations organized and experienced. He looked for true community of believers, genuine congregational life, and did not find it.

Bonhoeffer began to grieve over the state of this church. In a sermon of November 6, 1932, given for an academic worship service in

1. *Nachspiel. Eine Aussprache mit Freunden und Kritikern des Jahrhunderts der Kirche*, 1928, p. 29.

which the Reich President von Hindenburg also participated, Bonhoeffer said:

> No one who knows today's church will want to complain that the church doesn't do anything. No, the church does immeasurably much, and also with much sacrifice and seriousness; but we all do precisely too many second, third and fourth works, and not the first works. And exactly because of this, the church is not doing what is crucial. We celebrate, we represent, we strive for influence, we start a Protestant movement, we do Protestant youth work, we perform charitable service and care, we make propaganda against godlessness—but do we do the first works which are the basis of absolutely everything? Do we love God and our brother with that first, passionate, burning love that risks everything—except God? Do we really allow God to be God? Do we leave ourselves and our church to Him completely? If that were the case, things would have to look different, there would surely be a breakthrough.[2]

Christ as the Body of Believers

Precisely this, that "there would surely be a breakthrough" was Bonhoeffer's expectant attitude. Without being able to formulate it more precisely and more elaborately, he felt that this Protestant Church was lacking what was crucial. Bonhoeffer pondered the church. He reflected upon the "essence of the church." It does not surprise us that his view of the church became very much a Christ-mystical view. Being in Christ, sharing in his struggling, suffering, and dying—and in his resurrection—means being a Christian. And Christians who experience this, or to put it another way, a Christian community that experiences this and in this way knows that it is joined with Christ, is the Christian body of believers. The body of believers exists in Christ, or as it was then phrased: "Christ existing as the body of believers." In the Christology lecture course in the summer semester of 1933 Bonhoeffer said: "The body of believers does not *mean* the body of Christ; the body of believers *is* the body of Christ (emphasis added). The concept of the body as applied to the community of believers is not only a functional concept which would refer solely to the members of this body. Rather, this concept is all-

---

2. Sermon preached on Reformation Day, November 6, 1932, in *GS*, 4:100.

encompassing. It is the central concept for the mode of existence of Him who is present as both the exalted and the humbled One. This Christ existing as the body of believers is the whole person as the Exalted and the Humbled One . . . Christ is not only the head of the body, but also the body itself."[3]

Thus for Bonhoeffer it was important that the body of believers be included in the real event of Christ. The main point is here again the Pauline being in Christ. Bonhoeffer went beyond the view of the church expressed in Article 7 of the Confession of Augustine. There it is stated that the church is the community of believers in which the gospel is taught truly or purely and the sacraments are administered as they were intended. Bonhoeffer wanted to be more concrete. He was concerned with the difference between Christians and all other people. He was concerned with the fact that Christ is really present in the community of believers in his death and resurrection. To be sure, for Bonhoeffer the whole world is included in the suffering, death, and resurrection of Christ, but the community of believers holds a special place in this process, which Bonhoeffer describes as follows:

> All men are "with Christ" as a consequence of the Incarnation, for in the Incarnation Jesus bore our whole human nature. That is why his life, death and resurrection are events which involve all men. But Christians are "with Christ" in a special sense. For the rest of mankind to be with Christ means death, but for Christians it is a means of grace. Baptism is their assurance that they are "dead with Christ," "crucified with him," "buried with him," "planted together in the likeness of his death." All this creates in them the assurance that they will also live with him. "We with Christ"—for Christ is Emmanuel, "God with us." . . . The Christian who is baptized into Christ is baptized into the fellowship of his sufferings. Thus not only does the individual become a member of the Body of Christ, but the fellowship of the baptized becomes a body which is identical with Christ's own Body. The Christians are "in Christ" and "Christ in them."[4]

This Christ-mystical view of the church does not at all mean that a congregation as such, as a collective so to speak, is a Christ and that

---

3. *GS*, 3:194.
4. *Cost of Discipleship*, p. 268.

the name "Christ" is only a label or symbol for that mode of existence or community. Again and again Bonhoeffer made it clear that Christ is also distinct from the body of believers. Thus he said in a lecture during the summer semester of 1932: "Naturally Christ is also distinct from the body of believers. Humanity always remains Adam's humanity as well. . . . The body of believers can never point to itself. . . . The church is the presence of God through Christ on earth."[5] In this connection Bonhoeffer's view of representation also brings clarity: "The substitution of Christ means that He does that which puts Him in our place where otherwise we would have to stand before God."[6] This Christ-mystical view of the church in Bonhoeffer means:

1. Christ is the body of believers himself, but Christ is also the Lord of the body of believers.

2. Christ is also the brother in the body of believers. Thereby, the body is "structurally determined by the concepts of unity, lordship and community."[7]

Bonhoeffer could define his view of the body of believers in a very focused way in that he included it in the real Christ-event. But there is also a great openness in the dialectical structure of Bonhoeffer's thought. From the beginning to the end of his theological life, Bonhoeffer fought against the ghettoization of the church. For him, Christ is the Pantocrator who encompasses the whole world. In Bonhoeffer's inaugural lecture at the University of Berlin on July 31, 1930, he said: "In His death, however, the old, raped, battered world of the ego dies along with the ego, and in His resurrection and in His life the new aeon, the aeon of Christ, begins. The humanity of Adam is overcome by the humanity of Christ, not in a way that the former is now simply exterminated but in a way that it is fundamentally robbed of its power. Just as the world of Adam assaulted Christ, so it assaults the new humanity of Christ; however, just as Christ breaks the power of the world of Adam by His death, so he breaks it on behalf of man through the new humanity of Christ, for man in Christ."[8]

5. *GS*, 5:248.
6. Ibid., p. 249.
7. Ibid.
8. *GS*, 3:82.

26

Bonhoeffer's Striving for Community

Bonhoeffer thought it a quite impossible situation that theologians were trained to be pastors in the anonymity of university life. He wanted to make theology students part of a real Christian community. He published his experiences of this communal life in 1939 in the book *Life Together.*

Bonhoeffer's hunger for concretization of what is Christian corresponded to a longing for community. For him, Christian life could only be life in community. In this connection, he wanted to make use of experiences with Anglican communities that he had had in England while serving the German congregation in London in 1934.

In May 1935, Bonhoeffer assumed the leadership of a seminary that trained pastors for the Confessing Church. This seminary was first located in Zingst on the Baltic coast, and then in Finkenwalde near Stettin. How Bonhoeffer envisioned this life with theologians and which goals he pursued with this training in a "life together" become clear in a letter he wrote to the Council of the Protestant Church of the Old Prussian Union about the "Establishment of a Communal House at the Seminary in Finkenwalde." This letter includes the following passage:

The pastor, especially the young pastor, suffers under his isolation. Today the burden of proclamation for the individual pastor, who is not a prophet but an office-bearer of the church, is especially great. . . . The question of the Christian life has newly awakened among the theologians. . . . The answer to this question, however, will not be able to be given abstractly but only through a concrete, sober life together and through common reflection on the commandments. . . . They must be ready, under all outer circumstances and in renunciation of all financial and other privileges of the office of pastor, to be wherever their service is needed. . . . The pastor in his isolated official capacity stands in constant need of an intellectual refuge in which he can strengthen himself for his office in strict Christian living, in prayer, meditation, study of the Scriptures and brotherly discussion. Such places of refuge should be created, whereby at the same time the question of substitute pastors will be easily settled by providing substitutes from the brotherhood. . . . The brothers in this brotherhood house will live together in strict, worshipful ordering of the day. Not cultic forms, but the word of the Bible and prayer lead them through the day. They will be joined to each other through brotherly admonition and discipline and free confession.[1]

These are thoughts that point beyond a seminary to a communal house for pastors and brothers that was to become a home for isolated pastors in the cold and impersonal, institutionalized established churches. Bonhoeffer wrote all of this before he began his work. It is interesting to see what he wrote about his experiences after about three or four years of service in the book *Life Together* (1939). In this book Bonhoeffer established the following fundamental principle: *"Let him who cannot be alone beware of community. . . . Let him who is not in community beware of being alone."*[2] Here once again, the dialectical structure of Bonhoeffer's thought is significant. By no means did he want the individual to be swallowed up by the community. And by no means did he consider it possible that the Christian can live isolated as an individual. The individual and the community are related to each other dialectically—by no means without tension. But above all it was significant for Bonhoeffer that community is not from below, but rather "that in Jesus Christ we have been chosen from eternity, accepted in time, and united for eternity." Because of that it is true "that a Christian comes to others only through Jesus Christ," and that

---

1. "An den Rat der Evangelischen Kirche der Altpreußischen Union, Berlin-Dahlem," in *GS*, 2:145ff.
2. *Life Together*, p. 77.

therefore "a Christian needs others because of Jesus Christ." What is crucial: "It can only come from outside." Through God, through Christ and only through him can Christians be joined with one another: "When God was merciful to us, we learned to be merciful with our brothers. . . . I have community with others and I shall continue to have it only through Jesus Christ."[3]

At that time as well as today, these sentences are directed toward two types of recipient. On the one hand, these sentences speak to those who want to "make" community, to "build it up" from below. These are today's and yesterday's adherents of "religious group dynamics." To be sure, the concept of group dynamics as we know it did not yet exist in the 1930s. But Bonhoeffer very clearly rejected the notion that community is built by the one holding on to the other, and that the community as such has value in itself (even if it comes about, for instance, through psychological manipulation). Christian community is a community of brothers and sisters who have a Father in heaven. This community only works through a third party. Only in this way is the individual safeguarded from being sucked up by a community turned collective. The other recipient of these Bonhoefferian statements on the nature of community is religious pietism. Here the statement about "from the outside" applies. The basis of community is not the common experience of a subjective religiosity, but the encounter with the other, with Christ.

Thus Bonhoeffer fought against the "we-feeling" of a purely human solidarity, be it religiously or ideologically motivated: "God hates visionary dreaming; it makes the dreamer proud and pretentious. . . . So he becomes, first an accuser of his brethren, then an accuser of God, and finally the despairing accuser of himself." What he is saying here is that when one holds on to the community or his brother, he will inevitably lose faith in this community and his brother and become their accuser. This will then lead him into inner conflicts with himself and with the basic issue—yes, the issue of Christianity. At the end waits something akin to a human self-annihilation as we all too often observe with those who have been overrun by a religious and ideological feeling of community. Community as Bonhoeffer meant it is possible only if every individual who belongs to this community has

3. Ibid., pp. 21–26.

had Christ-mystical experience, if he has struggled with Christ, suffered with him, been powerless with him, and been resurrected with him to a new life.

Religious Community and Real Christ-Mystical Community

Bonhoeffer had suffered through "the very hour of disillusionment with my brother" and this had been "incomparably salutary." In this hour of disappointment he was taught that a Christian can live "only by the one Word and Deed which really binds us together—the forgiveness of sins in Jesus Christ."[4] This "forgiveness of sins in Jesus Christ" may sound formulaic—precisely because these words hardly have meaning anymore after their ecclesiasticized use. Nevertheless, they do have great meaning, namely, that community is possible only out of humility over against God and in renunciation of religious self-actualization. Always, community can only be community of the humble. And thereby Bonhoeffer hit upon a distinction that the Swedish theologian A. Nygren worked out in the 1930s: Christianity is not *eros*—love that focuses on self-realization, love for oneself, but *agapē*—the love that is merciful and understanding and does not come from man, but from God himself, and has been revealed on the cross.

Analogous to this distinction of Nygren's, Bonhoeffer used the expressions "emotional" and "spiritual" to refer to nongenuine and genuine Christian community.

> The community of the Spirit is the fellowship of those who are called by Christ; human community of spirit is the fellowship of devout souls. In the community of the Spirit there burns the bright love of brotherly service, *agape*; in human community of spirit there glows the dark love of good and evil desire, *eros*. In the former there is ordered, brotherly service, in the latter disordered desire for pleasure; in the former humble subjection to the brethren, in the latter humble yet haughty subjection of a brother to one's own desire. In the community of the Spirit the Word of God alone rules; in human community of spirit there rules, along with the Word, the man who is furnished with exceptional powers, experience, and magical, suggestive capacities.[5]

4. Ibid., p. 28.
5. Ibid., pp. 31–32.

The man who wrote these lines must have had had some first-hand experience with "emotional" conversion and "emotional" love of neighbor. Only someone who has gone through the deviancies of religious subjectivism can write as Bonhoeffer wrote. Bonhoeffer was an enemy of hypocritical piety—long before his imprisonment at Tegel. Already in the 1930s Bonhoeffer recognized the religious perversion of the Christian faith. From that time on Bonhoeffer was a sworn enemy of the religious-fleshly piety that clings to the ego and not to God. On "emotional" conversion, Bonhoeffer wrote:

> Thus there is such a thing as human absorption. It appears in all the forms of conversion whenever the superior power of one person is consciously or unconsciously misused to influence profoundly and draw into his spell another individual or a whole community. Here one soul operates directly upon another soul. The weak have been overcome by the strong, the resistance of the weak has broken down under the influence of another person. He has been overpowered, but not won over by the thing itself. This becomes evident as soon as the demand is made that he throw himself into the cause itself, independently of the person to whom he is bound, or possibly in opposition to this person. This is where the humanly converted person breaks down and thus makes it evident that his conversion was effected, not by the Holy Spirit, but by a man, and therefore has no stability.[6]

Emotional conversion brings about emotional community:

> Likewise, there is a human love of one's neighbor. Such passion is capable of prodigious sacrifices. Often it far surpasses genuine Christian love in fervent devotion and visible results. It speaks the Christian language with overwhelming and stirring eloquence. But it is what Paul is speaking of when he says: "And though I bestow all my goods to feed the poor, and though I give my body to be burned"—in other words, though I combine the utmost deeds of love with the utmost of devotion—"and have not charity [that is, the love of Christ], it profiteth me nothing" (I Cor. 13:3). Human love is directed to the other person for his own sake, spiritual love loves him for Christ's sake. Therefore, human love seeks direct contact with the other person, it loves him not as a free person but as one whom it binds to itself. It

6. Ibid., p. 33.

wants to gain, to capture by every means; it uses force. It desires to be irresistible, to rule. . . . Human love desires the other person, his company, his reciprocal love, but it does not serve him. . . . Human love is by its very nature desire—desire for human community. . . . But where it can no longer expect its desire to be fulfilled, there it stops short—namely, in the face of an enemy. There it turns into hatred, contempt, and calumny.[7]

What Bonhoeffer later wrote in *Letters and Papers from Prison* about the veil of discretion and distance is already thought through and expressed in *Life Together.* Even the relation of the body of believers to the world, the secularity of Christian life, this being "in the midst of the world" that is touched on again and again in *Letters and Papers from Prison* is already worked out completely in *Life Together.* Bonhoeffer, who at the beginning of his pathway through life expected everything of community, saw at the end of his life the great dangers of community. Community in itself and for itself not only means nothing, but it can also be a threat to Christian existence.

Any congregation with its many social groups, household Bible study groups, social evenings, and events should take heed of Bonhoeffer's warning:

A purely spiritual relationship is not only dangerous but also an altogether abnormal thing. When physical and family relationships or ordinary associations, that is, those arising from everyday life with all its claims upon people who are working together, are *not* projected into the spiritual community, then we must be especially careful. That is why, as experience has shown, it is precisely in retreats of short duration that the human element develops most easily. Nothing is easier than to stimulate the glow of fellowship in a few days of life together, but nothing is more fatal to the sound, sober brotherly fellowship of everyday life. . . . It is not the experience of Christian brotherhood, but solid and certain faith in brotherhood that holds us together. . . . We are bound together by faith, not by experience.[8]

Bonhoeffer reminded us that "Christian community is not a spiritual sanatorium." He admonished: "Only dwelling in community can

7. Ibid., pp. 33–34.
8. Ibid., pp. 38–39.

we be alone, and only he who is alone can abide in community. Both belong together.[9] Community as such is emphatically not salvation. Bonhoeffer did not, then, promote "religious" community. He rather called for nothing less than Christ-mystical community, in the sense that he saw community as integrally related to the real Christ-event. A community does not receive its life out of itself, but out of the "Other," out of Christ himself. Therefore, no Christian can live in a community that is not aware from the very start of the danger of a community that alienates itself from Christ and loses itself in religious subjectivism. Community as such is nothing at all; community in Christ, on the other hand, is everything.

9. Ibid., pp. 77–78.

27

The Secularized Church

Bonhoeffer had occasion to experience the reality of life in the established church as an intern seminarian in the working-class quarter in Berlin. There he was given the task of supervising a confirmation class. Among other things, house visitations, about which Bonhoeffer wrote in a letter to his friend Erwin Sutz on February 26, 1932, showed him that the reality of life in the established church meant that "in order to make such a visit, I could really have just as well studied chemistry. Sometimes it seemed to me that all of our work failed at the point of pastoral care. How torturous those minutes or hours often are when I or someone I visit attempt to bring about a pastoral conversation, and how haltingly and lamely it then progresses. . . . One has the feeling that if one would say something, one would simply not be understood at all. . . . But maybe our failure here really means the end of our Christianity."[1] The honesty with which Bonhoeffer not only saw the situation but also described it is compelling. However, at that time he knew of no alternative.

In his theological dissertation, which he finished in 1927 and which appeared under the title *Sanctorum Communio*, Bonhoeffer still argued strongly in favor of the established church. Bonhoeffer

1. *GS*, 1:27ff.

believed at that time that one should not separate the wheat from the chaff, but should bear with people as long as "no conscious rejection (of the gospel) has occurred. . . . The church should let the weeds grow on its field, for where would it derive its standard of knowledge by which to recognize weeds?"[2] Thus, he could even write the following about the celebration of communion in large cities:

> The critical observation has been made that when celebrating the Lord's Supper large-city congregations must suffer under the fact that the participants do not know each other; it is said that the seriousness of the brotherly ideal of community is weakened and that the celebration loses personal warmth. But isn't the confession of community of believers and love for one's brother the most unequivocal precisely where it is fundamentally protected from being mistaken in any way for some kind of community based on merely human sympathy? Isn't it precisely here that the real seriousness of the *sanctorium communio* is maintained where Jew remains Jew, Greek remains Greek, laborer remains laborer and capitalist remains capitalist, and where they are nevertheless all the body of Christ? Isn't the *sanctorium communio* better maintained here than where that harshness is thinly veiled? . . . Herein lies the fruitfulness of large-city communion celebrations, a fruitfulness which should not go unmentioned in the Lord's Supper sermon.[3]

In regard to this point, it must be admitted that there was a break in Bonhoeffer's thought. For he came to think quite differently by the mid-1930s, when he recognized in the established church's administration of the sacraments the practice of cheap grace.

In the lecture on the essence of the church during the summer semester of 1932 before the faculty of the University of Berlin we already hear very critical words about the established, tax-supported churches. Bonhoeffer spoke of "bogus conservatism" as opposed to "serious conservatism." The latter is aware of the relativity of all human social forms, while the former is conservatism of accommodation from the world of the petty bourgeoisie. This conservatism's worship services "know only the needs of the petty bourgeois . . . the

2. *Sanctorum Communio*, 4th ed., 1969, p. 166.
3. Ibid., p. 186.

needs of the leaders of commerce, of the intellectuals, of the unchurched, of the revolutionaries do not come out in this type of worship. . . . Church becomes the exception to everyday life, a celebration outside of daily routine . . . as a result the churches are becoming empty and the cinemas full. You see, the cinema satisfies the need for celebration better than the church."[4] A Christianity that presents itself only in celebration lies on the periphery of life. Solemn festivities bring religious satisfaction to those seeking protection. But this religious satisfaction does not bring the ability to overcome, to say nothing of reconciliation and redemption.

But if some quarters of the church erred in hallowing bourgeois religion, others strayed into glorifying the secular. The emphatically sought after secularity practiced particularly by theologians "open to the world" was for Bonhoeffer an evil thing. Here one seeks the approval of the world, the affirmation of society. Already in his sermon "Moses und Aaronkirche," preached on May 25, 1933, in the Kaiser Wilhelm Memorial Church in Berlin, Bonhoeffer said: "The world church, the church of the priests, wants to see something. She no longer wants to wait. She wants to get down to work herself." This church wants to do itself "what God does not do."[5] The actively secularized church is the church without the cross. This type of functionalism evaporates in the world through secularization. On July 27, 1933, Bonhoeffer wrote to Erwin Sutz that he was observing "a constant crumbling decline . . . because the strength to bring an action to completion is no longer there."[6]

But for all this critique of established church life, Bonhoeffer by no means advocated flight into the monasteries. One feels the dilemma, one senses Bonhoeffer's discomfiture in the face of the reality of established church life. On the one hand he rejected secularization as accommodation to society, but on the other hand he was worried about the danger of the ghettoization of the church. The office of pastor disappointed Bonhoeffer—there is no doubt about that. Perhaps it even horrified him. He never really got over his first direct experience with this church. Bonhoeffer's pain over the church caused him to

4. *GS*, 5:233.
5. *GS*, 4:124ff.
6. *GS*, 1:38f.

raise the question of another kind of church without at first knowing an answer. Not until his letters from prison did Bonhoeffer express his radical break with this kind of churchliness.

In the mid-1930s, accompanied by his seminarians and associate preachers, Bonhoeffer had additional bitter experiences. People who were estranged from the church desired on the one hand official ecclesiastical acts (such as baptism, marriage, funerals, etc.) which they dismissed as ridiculous on the other hand. Bonhoeffer observed how ecclesiastical office-bearers were disparaged by Nazi functionaries. He saw the quiet martyrdom of lonely pastors of the established church who had to live their lives on the sidelines of, or even in opposition to, secularized public opinion. Bonhoeffer stumbled onto the demonic nature of "cheap grace" precisely because of his experience in the established church. The rituals of the established church were used on the one hand as the cultivation of tradition and as family rituals. At the same time, however, this consumption of ritual took place in a downright cynical attitude of inward distancing; and the "worship servant" was denigrated as a kind of head waiter serving up the required ritual recipe.

Gradually Bonhoeffer recognized the dilemma: The religionless human being makes use of religious forms—in doing so, he collides with a contradiction within himself that he works off through cynicism. And the victim of this contradiction is the pastor, who is punished with the contempt of his religionless "customers." Bonhoeffer sensed strongly how words that once held power lose force.[7] in this ecclesiastical assembly line of official acts.

And what kind of congregations were they that as a small minority of church members, as "core congregations," actually bothered to come to worship services of the established church? Bonhoeffer's observation:

> Church is an organization of people who have a religious disposition, are interested and who strangely enough like to practice their religiosity in this type of church. These people belong for the most part to a social class that possesses neither a particular intellectual liveliness nor a particular creative power that points into the future; instead, their

---

7. *Letters and Papers from Prison*, p. 300.

most positive striking characteristic appears to be an exaggerated contentment in their own uprightness. The air here is rather used up, and the horizon very narrow. Not much seems to happen here. More happens in a movie theater. It is really more interesting.[8]

Then What Should Church Be?

Bonhoeffer was dismayed by the secularization of the church. At first, he did not at all have in mind the ideological infiltration of the Nazi period, although as we shall see in the next chapter, this was certainly a severe problem. But Bonhoeffer was not only troubled by how biblical words were ideologically hijacked by "German Christians." He also sensed that biblical words such as God, Jesus, reconciliation, redemption, faith, and love were being emptied in a much more dangerous sense. He sensed that their meaning had become useless and their use obsolescent. Through the Christianization of the world, biblical words had been robbed of their original meaningful content.

But secularization also means that biblical statements are religiously subverted. Religious subversion of biblical words means the superimposition on them of moods or emotional and subjective associations that do not come from real being-in-Christ. In various situations biblical words are equated with an attitude or form of expression or a solemn state of mind into which one shifts for a moment. Now genuine, premodern naive religiosity was the true experience of the mystery of faith; it was not limited to special moments. In the modern world this has changed. Today the religious experience is a marginal experience—the extraordinary alongside the normality of life, the unessential next to the essential. When Bonhoeffer strove for the non-religious interpretation of biblical words, he did not in any way mean that he wanted to change or reinterpret their original meaning. Rather, his concern was to allow the meaningful content of biblical words to find entrance into human life again, to see their meaning truly fleshed out in everyday life. Bonhoeffer's concern was Christ-mystically real existence, being drawn into Christ's life, struggling, suffering, and overcoming.

8. See the essay by D. Kraft, "Der Friedensgedanke," in *Bonhoeffer-Studien*, ed. D. Schönherr and W. Krötke, 1985, p. 89.

Finally, Bonhoeffer wanted Word and sacrament to be protected from the world. The biblical Word should not be squandered publicly throughout the whole world through ecclesiastical acts, events, or ceremonies. Bonhoeffer wanted to go back to the original *arcanum* as it was practiced by early Christianity. He wanted to detach the core processes that mark the body of believers from secularization. Christianity cannot be spread by demonstration or propaganda, for "noisy clamor will never produce quiet conviction."[9] Biblical words may not—in spite of what we are told today—be extolled and squandered as cheap goods through a form of "electronic evangelization." On the other hand Bonhoeffer also fought against the typical indulgence of theologians in a special language, a kind of theological concept-shamanism that they practice in their own religious or theological ghetto. He did not want the body of believers to cultivate a churchly manner of speech that is torn out of all earthly contexts and no longer comprehensible to the world.

Christianity in the discipline of the *arcanum*, the order that protects from the outside world, does not mean an idyll: "The discipline of the *arcanum* protects the world just as much from forceful and inappropriate imposition of religion."[10] The *arcanum*, the worshiping community closed off from the outside world, is not an island for the blessed ones taking refuge from the world. The *arcanum* and the world exist in a dialectical tension that is not resolvable. Only one who lives in the *arcanum* can also live in the midst of the world, and only one who lives in the midst of the world can also be in the *arcanum*. In the *arcanum* the body of believers lives out its worship services as it has always lived them: prayer, song, Word, and sacrament.[11] But their worship gatherings gain their compelling meaning, not through ceremony, through a type of religious suggestion, but because the words are backed up by genuine experiences. The idea of community, as it was developed in the first half of the 1930s and lived in the second half, was with Bonhoeffer to the end. However, he wanted this community of brothers and sisters to experience and live out again and again its being sent out into the world. The *arcanum* stands in correlation to the world: "The

9. Bethge, *Bonhoeffer*, p. 990.
10. Ibid.
11. See J. Glenthöj, *Was hat D. Bonhoeffer zur Frage des Gottesdienstes im säkularen Zeitalter gesagt?* 1969.

discipline of the *arcanum* without secularity is ghetto and secularity without the discipline of the *arcanum* is nothing but city streets."[12] The community of Christians among each other and with each other must become community with the world: "The fellowship between Jesus and his disciples covered every aspect of their daily life."[13]

The difference between the situations envisioned in *Letters and Papers from Prison* and *The Cost of Discipleship* is that in the latter, the community in its sanctified life stood somewhat parallel to the world, while in the former Bonhoeffer was concerned to see this community lived out in the midst of the world. The body of believers should no longer travel through the world "like a sealed train in a foreign land," but rather the saints should prove themselves in the dialectical tension with the world. Only one who cordons himself off from the world and experiences the Christian-communal life in the *arcanum*, only one who knows that he is different from the world, can encounter God and Christ in the midst of the world. Here we see the dialectical thought of Bonhoeffer, which very clearly leads to dialectical structures in his architecture of the body of believers.

The consciousness of sin is then no longer a licking of one's own wounds. It is not the self-denigration brought on by religious-masochistic torment, or by denouncing someone else as a sinner to get him "saved," thus making him a son of hell [see Matt. 23:15] out of envy or resentment. Rather the consciousness of sin is the Christian's real experience of guilt in the midst of the world, a guilt experienced because he faces up to and deals with his conflicts in the midst of the world and knows that he, as one who acts in the awareness of his responsibility, takes on guilt and needs forgiveness. Only the Christian who lives in the midst of the world and engages the world can really experience how abysmally world-bound the world and human beings are. Not imagined, but real sin; not self-induced, but Christ-mystically experienced sanctification—such was Bonhoeffer's concern in the integral relation he posited between the body of believers and the world.

In this context, Bonhoeffer's notion of "existing for others" is important. Once again let us remind ourselves that this is not to be

12. Bethge, *Bonhoeffer*, p. 992.
13. *Cost of Discipleship*, p. 284.

understood in the sense of a vacuous "moral rearmament"—a perhaps even religiously understood "be nice to each other." We are not dealing here with moralistic regulation but with discipleship to Christ, in which one bears up the other, suffers with him, laughs with him, and even helps him shoulder his load. But to be there for others also means to reprimand the other, to encounter him if need be with hardness and decisiveness, and to say "No" to him when he is hoping for a yes. This "being there for others" means the ability to suffer, certainty about future, the ability to handle stress. It means persistence, patience, hope, love, and friendliness. Above all, Bonhoeffer was concerned that Christianity not become religious self-aggrandizement and self-actualization. He opposed religious egoism, the mania for religious self-gratification. Neither did Bonhoeffer want community to become an organization of those who enjoy communal satisfaction of their religious needs. Bonhoeffer contrasted this religious community intent on need gratification with the community of believers based in true love that does not seek its own.

Precisely because modern industrial society no longer knows the natural relation between life community and Christian community as it existed in rural society, there is a danger that people in urban society come together solely for the purpose of mutual gratification of religious needs. Bonhoeffer, however, wanted the community of Christians to live in Christ in such a way that they would know, at the moment in which they go out into the world again, that they are included in the messianic suffering, death, and resurrection of Christ. Thus, everything depended for Bonhoeffer on his Christ-mystical view of the church, "that we do not let things come and go as they are; that our faith really is not opium."[14]

Already in his doctoral dissertation *Sanctorum Communio* Bonhoeffer emphasized that the church should not leave society to itself: "The church must become embroiled in interaction with the masses. It should listen when the masses call for community."[15] The church should not live "passively and introvertedly" in the world, but "demonstratively." Of course, later on, Bonhoeffer would not have been able to formulate it that way. Later, Bonhoeffer's concern was no

14. *Bonhoeffer-Studien*, p. 91.
15. Peters, *Die Präsenz*, p. 28.

longer that the church be demonstrative as church, but that the individual Christian, stepping out of his *arcanum,* interpret Christian faith through the living of his life and thereby not leave the world to itself.

From the ultimate of the *arcanum,* the pathway leads to the penultimate of the world, which is underway to the ultimate of the second coming of Christ at the end of time.

The Christian recognizes in faith what Christ wants for this world. While the racial, ideologically subverted Christians thought that the light fell on Christianity through Adolf Hitler, the really Christ-mystically existing Christian believes that it is the other way around—through Christ, the light falls upon the course of the world. The Christian does not go out of the *arcanum* into the devil's kitchen, but into the realm of tension between God and the devil. But under the Word and under the cross the Christian recognizes his place in salvation history. He knows why, how, and for what purpose he is included in the messianic Christ-event.

What Is to Happen?

Bonhoeffer did not expect the established church in the form he knew it to survive the war. For him, a possible new beginning after the war also meant a new beginning for the church. Bonhoeffer desired the radical separation of state and church. He wanted the church to renounce its possessions—a continuation of the church-tax system was unthinkable for him. He was also against any form of clericalism. The career-mindedness he had observed among the Protestant clergy must have permanently repulsed him.

Bonhoeffer conceived of the body of believers as a community come of age, totally in discipleship to Christ. Only in such a body was infant baptism conceivable for Bonhoeffer: "As far as infant baptism is concerned, it must be insisted that the sacrament should be administered only where there is a firm faith present which remembers Christ's deed of salvation wrought for us once and for all. That can only happen in a living Christian community. To baptize infants without a Church is not only an abuse of the sacrament, it betokens a disgusting frivolity in dealing with the souls of the children themselves.

For baptism can never be repeated."[16] Infant baptism, though, was no longer the rule for Bonhoeffer, but the exception.

The German established church as it is today contrasts with everything that Bonhoeffer hoped for in the future of the church. Quite certainly, he did not want to do away with the office of pastor—but just as certainly he rejected hierarchy. For Bonhoeffer, there were no offices, but rather ministries. In the churches, or core groups in churches, that now comprised a small minority of the overall population, there was no place for hierarchical bureaucracy. In August 1944, he wrote the following about the future form of Christianity:

> The church is the church only when it exists for others. To make a start, it should give away all its property to those in need. The clergy must live solely on the free-will offerings of their congregations, or possibly engage in some secular calling. The church must share in the secular problems of ordinary human life, not dominating, but helping and serving. It must tell men of every calling what it means to live in Christ, to exist for others. . . . It will have to speak of moderation, purity, trust, loyalty, constancy, patience, discipline, humility, contentment, and modesty. It must not under-estimate the importance of human example (which has its origin in the humanity of Jesus and is so important in Paul's teaching); it is not abstract argument, but example, that gives its word emphasis and power.[17]

In connection with these thoughts, it also became clear to Bonhoeffer that infant baptism cannot be legislated: "The New Testament lays down no law about infant baptism; it is a gift of grace bestowed on the church, a gift that may be received and used in firm faith, and can thus be a striking testimony of faith for the community; but to force oneself to it without the compulsion of faith is not biblical. Regarded purely as a demonstration, infant baptism loses its justification."[18]

Thus, the body of believers that Bonhoeffer foresaw as the body of the future was not to have any connection to the state and was not to be a church of cheap grace. In this future church, the power of the religious was to be broken. It was not to be a church of ceremonies. It was

---

16. *Cost of Discipleship*, p. 261.
17. *Letters and Papers from Prison*, pp. 382–83.
18. Ibid., p. 237.

to be a body of believers separate from the world, but precisely so that it might be all the more able to work its influence the world.

A church that lusts for publicity—like the church we see today—be it through "electronic evangelization" or through a flood of paper or through the rapid establishment of "public relations offices," would have been for Bonhoeffer the final consequence of the secularization of Christianity.

The least we should do, if we wish to do justice to Bonhoeffer's legacy to the church, is adopt the aims he set and begin to walk a path toward a church that no longer desires state-supported theological faculties, church tax, and hierarchies operating in cool remoteness from local congregations. We should rather think in terms of independent congregations that join together voluntarily in synods for purposes such as common support of seminaries. This is Bonhoeffer's vision of the church of the future. All offices can only be ministries, regardless of whether elder, deacon, servant of the word, or teacher of the church. Such a body of believers would not be one of cheap grace, but one of discipline—not by hierarchical decrees, but by the spiritual and intellectual strength of community that expels everything that is not spiritual. All in all, what that means is the self-dissolution of the Protestant Church in Germany in its present structure. This goal is the unavoidable, inexorable consequence of Bonhoeffer's legacy. But all of that is not "a matter of form." It is not merely a result of a mere "structural change." "Reorganization" will accomplish nothing. The future church cannot be realized through a new type of organization. A new identity must spring forth. The congregations would not only have to throw organizational and economic ballast overboard, but also concentrate on what is crucial and essential. The more the body of believers concentrates, the more it will be possible for it to expand into the world—and not as church, not as institution, not with its "claim to its place in public society." Rather, it would expand as the testimony of these who have concentrated on Christ in order to interpret Christianity in the world that belongs to Christ by means of a responsible life in faith, love, and hope.

28

The Confessing Church

The Internalization of Ideology in the Established Church

In the parliamentary election of March 1933 Bonhoeffer voted for the Center party because it was there that he saw the most of Christian-Occidental tradition being preserved. In that election the NSDAP (the Nazi party) received 44 percent of the vote and had to form a coalition with the German National Peoples party (DNVP). At that time there were 15 million unemployed in the United States (not receiving unemployment compensation). In contrast, there were 6 million male unemployed in the German Reich. They were receiving government unemployment compensation. Economic decline, unemployment, the near self-dissolution of most of the parties represented in the *Reichstag* (parties who no longer believed in their mission), street battles between radical political groups, and grave social unrest were all leading the Weimar Republic to the brink of collapse.

In the first months of 1933 there was a very sudden change. With the "Ordinance for the Protection of People and State" of February 28, the Enabling Act of March 24 ("Law for the Limitation of the Distress of People and State"), and the "Ordinance of the Reich President for the Defense against Malicious Attacks against the Government of the National Recovery" of March 21, Germany became a totalitarian state within one month. These laws made it legal for the government to rule Germany however it wanted.

It was not easy at that time readily to recognize the danger of National Socialist ideology. Within Protestantism (in complete contrast to Roman Catholicism) there was a great uncertainty and lack of clarity especially as to the effect National Socialism might have on the churches.

The NSDAP, or at least its leading figures, understood their movement at the beginning as the attempt to bring about a racial-Nordic renewal of faith. This situation changed, though, proportional to the attempts of the NSDAP at political realization. At that point the racial-religious element was superseded by political engagement. Klaus Scholder sees this prioritization of politics before racial-religious renewal as the original conception of Hitler.[1] How the situation developed can be seen in the official commentary on the NSDAP party platform, written by Gottfried Feder. The title of this work was "Das Programm der NSDAP und seine weltanschaulichen Grundlagen" ["The NSDAP Program and Its World-View Foundations"]. In the fifth edition of February 1929, Point 24 of the Party platform was explained as follows: "Certainly the German people will someday find a form for its knowledge of God, its experience of God, that is demanded by a Nordic bloodline." In the later editions, especially after 1931, this was changed to: "All questions, hopes and wishes as to whether the German people will one day find a new form for its knowledge and experience of God do not belong here." In the introduction to the 1931 edition we also find the explicit assurance that nothing is further from the intention of the NSDAP than "to attack the Christian religion and its worthy servants."[2]

1. Of course, Hitler never gave up his racist worldview, as his so-called political legacy of 1945 proves. He did not think, however, that the hour for a racial (völkisch) religious movement had come. At a reception of the Protestant bishops Meiser and Wurm in March 1934 in Berlin, Hitler made it clear to them that the Protestant Church would be left behind in the sweep of time if it chose to ignore the "facts that are given in blood and race." Nevertheless, Hitler was not impressed by the mysticism and cultic ceremonies of the SS (e.g., the Yule ceremony, etc.). Nor did Rosenberg's Myth interest him. However, that a racial (völkisch) religiosity would one day assert itself was beyond all doubt for Hitler. Until then his strategy was to proceed tactically with the churches, since a fight was not worth it to him because, among other reasons, he thought the era of the church was quickly coming to an end anyway.

2. Scholder, Die Kirche, 1:241.

A speech by a member of the Bavarian state parliament, Dr. Butmann, who had been a member of the National Socialist movement
since its very inception, provided an additional official statement of
this new line. On April 29, 1931, Butmann explained National Socialism's position on religion and church in the Bavarian state parliament.
This speech was printed in the Nazi newspaper *Völkischer Beobachter*
on May 1 under the title "Das positive Christentum der NSDAP." In
this speech Butmann declared that the National Socialist movement
did not want to interfere in the internal affairs of the Catholic or Protestant Church. The removal from office of the *Gauleiter* Dinter,[3] who
had seen the development of a racial religiosity as the foremost task of
the movement, had shown, in Butmann's view, that the NSDAP did
not desire any new religion. When the Party declared in Article 24 that
it took "positive Christianity" as its starting point, it meant Christianity as it is presented in the large established churches of the day, said
Butmann. The restrictions in Article 24 were to be applied only to new
faith communities, which the National Socialist state, in contrast to
Article 137 of the Reich constitution, did not want to allow without
review. In no way was the Protestant or Catholic Church to be
reviewed in order to see whether it met the requirements of Article 24
of the Party platform. Butmann said: "For us as a Party there is thus
no further searching for doctrine based on a new world-view, for a
new religion. The *Führer* has said this often enough and it is the guiding principle of our action. Rather, for us as a Party positive Christianity is the foundation."[4]

Of course that did not mean that the movement as such had given
up its long-term goal of contributing to a religious renewal in the
sense of a Nordic-racially based faith. But this goal became a long-
term goal, and the political tasks, as the most urgent tasks, were given
precedence.

Many within German Protestantism had not quite been able to keep
up with these twists and turns. Thus a movement formed within German Protestantism—starting in Thuringia—which attempted to tie

---

3. On this point, see A. Dinter, *Die Sünde wider das Blut. Ein Zeitroman*, 16th ed., 1921. See
also idem, *197 Thesen zur Vollendung der Reformation. Die Wiederherstellung der reinen Heilands-
lehre*, 1926. Because of his persistent equating of his religiosity with Nazi ideology, Dinter had
to give up his office as *Gauleiter* of Thuringia in 1927. Later, he was expelled from the party.
4. Scholder, *Die Kirche*, 1:550.

Christianity into a type of racial-Nordic belief in God after all. Thus the young pastor Siegfried Leffler from Thuringia, a German Christian, asserted that through Hitler "the light has fallen upon the history of Christianity." For Leffler, Germany had now become "the rival people to the Jews." The German people had been chosen "to take the veil of night from the cross and to render the truly redeeming service to the world which to this day no people on earth has accomplished."[5]

This German Christian religious movement did not really gain momentum until the 1930s. On June 6, 1932, in Berlin, this movement made itself public for the first time, and set up guidelines. These guidelines were concerned with the believing German person, with a new ordering of life, with a life profession of allegiance to the Germanic ethnic nation. They were concerned with recognizing God in the visible conditions of nature, and above all with establishing that only people who were Germanic by blood, not baptized Jews, could belong to the church. In addition, the German Christians wanted to do away with the old and—as they saw it—decrepit established churches with their obsolete bureaucracies and develop a new German Reich church out of a racially appropriate belief in Christ in the spirit of Luther. The synodical system was to be replaced by a *Führer* principle, the leaders in this case being German-Christian bishops. Of course, evangelism to the Jews was rejected and marriage between Germans and Jews repudiated. It is significant that in 1931, before the Nazis were in power, the Prussian Head Officer of Church Administration did not make any objections to these guidelines and allowed them as an ecclesiastical election manifesto. Scholder observed: "It has never been answered why the Prussian ecclesiastical leadership never protested against the guidelines before 1933."[6]

However, because this religious movement of the "German Christians" did not at all lie within the Party line—the Nazis had decided on a completely different strategy for dealing with the churches—the "German Christian" movement had no substantial significance beyond the year 1933. After a tremendous flourishing that had its effect on the ecclesiastical elections of the summer of 1933, this movement quickly faded into insignificance.

5. Ibid., p. 247.
6. Ibid., p. 265.

At that time, the core of the opposition to the influence of Nazi ideology on Christianity was the "Young Reformational movement" to which men such as Hanns Lilje, Walter Künneth, Hermann Sasse, Karl Heim, and others belonged. But even this "Young Reformational movement" said its "joyful Yes" to the new state. Undoubtedly, therefore, the Young Reformational movement approved of certain aspects of National Socialism; their objection was that they thought that the church should remain the church. The National Socialist state was not justified in influencing the church and its order. The Lutheran doctrine of the two kingdoms fit this position quite well. Church must remain church, and state must remain state.

From the church, there were hardly any direct attacks on the National Socialist movement as a whole. Nevertheless it is worthwhile to note the points of opposition that Scholder has summarized in his *Die Kirche und das Dritte Reich*.

There were indeed people who had gained deep insight into the neo-pagan essence of National Socialism. Bonhoeffer was one of them. Bonhoeffer saw in the Nazi movement the dance around the golden calf, the worship of naturalism and vitalism.

The purpose here is not to depict, even in outline form, the struggle between church and state that has been described so often and depicted finally with classical skill by Scholder. For Bonhoeffer's position it is important that he, Sasse, and a very few other theologians were invited by von Bodelschwingh to Bethel in the summer of 1933 in order to formulate quietly an answer to the challenge of the indoctrinated German Christians. Sasse, who later as a Lutheran confessionalist distanced himself decisively from the Confessing Church and from Bonhoeffer, belongs with Bonhoeffer to the small number of theologians who saw through to the essence of National Socialism. Together, Bonhoeffer and Sasse worked out the Bethel Confession, which did not become known until 1959, when Eberhard Bethge included it in the collected writings of Bonhoeffer. This confession from 1933, along with the Altona Confession of 1932,[7] is one of the

---

7. "Das Wort und Bekenntnis Altonaer Pastoren in der Not und Verwirrung des öffentlichen Lebens" of January 11, 1933, is the first contemporary confession of the German Protestant Church in response to the challenge posed by the ideological movements of the early twentieth century. The writer of this confession was Hans Asmussen, at that time a thirty-four-year-old pastor in Altona. In 1934, Asmussen was not only an important contributor to the

"original sources" of the Barmen Declaration of May 1934. In this Bethel Confession, Bonhoeffer rejected the false doctrine "that Christ also testifies to Himself without the Scriptures and outside of the Scriptures, and that the Holy Spirit is also given without the word of the sermon grounded on the Scriptures and without the sacrament." In contrast to this, Bonhoeffer wrote: "only out of obedience to the Word of God in the Scriptures do we recognize the Creator, not out of some kind of interpretation of the events in the world. . . . The false doctrine that the voice of the *Volk* is God's voice . . ." must be rejected. For "the voice of the *Volk* cries 'Hosanna!' and 'crucify him!'"[8]

In this confession, Bonhoeffer did not yet consider an absolute separation of church and state. However, he very well did see that the secular authorities are to be put "within the bounds of their own order" through the proper proclamation of the Word, so that they do not become a "tool of the devil . . . who only seeks disorder, in order to destroy all of life." Thus, already at that time Bonhoeffer recognized that the ideological revolution of National Socialism was an immediate danger to law and order. The Bethel Confession distinguishes itself above all by the fact that it does not evade the Jewish question. It rejects the Aryan Clause, which forbade Jews to hold office in the church. It is well known that the Barmen Declaration does not take up this issue. In contrast, we read the following in the Bethel Confession: "The Christians whose ancestry is the Gentile world would have to give themselves over to persecution before they would voluntarily or under force relinquish the brotherhood with Jewish Christianity, which is founded upon the Word and Sacraments."[9] Precisely these words were not accepted as a confession by the Confessing Church—

Barmen Declaration, but his lecture on the declaration is considered to be the official commentary on this document.

The crucial passage of the Altona Confession, which critiques the radical political ideologies of the time, is the following: "Therefore, we categorically reject the dream of the coming earthly world-kingdom of justice, peace, and general welfare, and we reject it in all of its permutations. . . . Whether one believes in a coming earthly kingdom of peace and safety for all peoples, or in a classless society without hunger, hardship, or suffering, or in a future ethnic state of total justice and racial purity (*Artgemäßheit*), in any of these cases one thereby denies the boundary set by God, distorts political action, and teaches disdain for redemption through Christ. Any political party that sets such goals for itself becomes a religion." See Scholder, *Die Kirche*, pp. 234ff.

8. *GS*, 2:91ff.
9. Ibid., p. 117.

at least not in the clarity and unequivocality with which Bonhoeffer wrote them.

No Church Without Confession

How seriously Bonhoeffer judged the situation of the church in the late summer of 1933 can be seen in a letter he wrote to Barth on September 9 of that year. In this letter, Bonhoeffer seriously pondered whether or not the time had come to found an independent church, because the established churches lacked all understanding of heresy:

> To begin with we have drawn up a declaration in which we want to communicate to the church government that the Protestant Church of the Old Prussian Union has separated itself from the Church of Jesus Christ with the Aryan Clause. Then we will wait for an answer to this, that is, whether the pastors who sign this declaration will be fired or whether one can say something like what we say without having to be concerned about one's place in the church. Several of us are beginning to think seriously about an independent church. The difference between our situation and Luther's situation is probably that the Catholic Church expelled Luther for heresy whereas our church authorities cannot do that because they completely lack any concept of the heretical at all.[10]

We see that already in 1933, Bonhoeffer strove for a comprehensive answer to the challenge facing the church. Barth's answer was somewhat lame and procrastinating: by all means, we have to remain in the church. According to Barth, everything would have to be quite different and much worse in order to justify establishing an independent church. That Bonhoeffer was practically driven to desperation by this lame reaction within the Confessing Church will be touched on below. For now we observe that the issue of confession remained important to Bonhoeffer in the 1930s. In August 1935 he wrote the essay "Die Bekennende Kirche und die Ökumene." In this seminal essay Bonhoeffer stated: "The truth question, however, amounts to nothing other than the question of confession in a positive and limiting sense, of the *confitemur* [what is confessed] and the *damnatus* [what is anathematized]. It would be prudent if the Christian

10. *GS*, 2:126.

Churches of the Occident would choose not to overlook the experience of the Confessing Church that a church without a confession is defenseless and lost, and that a church has in its confession the only weapon that does not fall apart."[11]

Bonhoeffer wanted the other churches of the Occident (he was always concerned with the Occident) to assimilate the experiences that the German Confessing Church had in its ecclesiastical struggle. After all, Bonhoeffer saw the disaster of confessionlessness in Protestantism not only in Germany. His experiences worldwide had taught him that Protestantism in general threatened to collapse because of its loss of confessional conviction and identity.

That is why a church council was so important to Bonhoeffer at that time. He was deeply convinced of the necessity of a renewed reflection within European Protestantism. Already in the summer semester of 1932 he therefore appealed to the idea of a council in order to make clear that the integral relation of unity, truth, and confession may not be given up:

> The council has its authority through the worshipping assembly. Therefore the proclamation of the living Christ in the Body of believers forms, the parameters for the council. The properly proclaiming congregation can and, if necessary, must protest against the council. The congregation alone may do this. The concept of heresy is part of the concept of the council. False doctrine as such must be explicitly named in order to safeguard preaching and the confession. Today there are no longer any genuine councils because the concept of heresy has been lost. The "ecumenical assemblies" are anything but councils. They do not dare to make a judgment on doctrine. That is a heavy and substantial loss. The degeneration of theology that has been going on for two hundred years and the present-day crisis in our Protestant Church as a preaching church are intimately connected with this. Dogma and defense against heresy are necessary, extra-liturgical functions of the church.[12]

For Bonhoeffer at that time it was absolutely clear that the "church [must] not give the false impression of unity." "Good faith negotiation may not be mistaken for the truth of the content of faith. This seems

11. *GS*, 1:54.
12. *GS*, 5:260. See R. Mayer, *Was wollte Bonhoeffer in Fanö?*

to be happening in the ecumenical movement with its disregard for the question of heresy. Heresy in doctrine must be sharply fought. The church will have to do without depicting its torn and shattered unity as truth. The church must carry this disunity as its cross. It is possible to do that in the belief that God has called it as "one holy" *(una sancta)* church.[13]

Thus there can be no doubt: Bonhoeffer wanted the Confessing Church. He served it in an official status until the end of his life and during this whole time he held firmly to the conviction that the true church can only be a confessing church that condemns and excludes doctrinal error: "Whoever knowingly separates himself from the confessing church separates himself from salvation."[14]

The influence of the Bethel Confession on the Declaration of Barmen is clear. But as has been mentioned, Barmen did not include the statement about Christians of Jewish and Gentile ancestry. In this matter, only Bonhoeffer and a handful of co-workers were consistent. Of course, in May 1934 when the Barmen Declaration was drawn up, the signatories knew about the Bethel Confession as well as the threat against Judaism. Bonhoeffer was deeply wounded when the Bethel Confession was not accepted in this point. The to and fro of the discussion, the dearth of clear thinkers, the lack of courageous decisions—all of these were bitter disappointments for the young confessing theologian. From that time on, Bonhoeffer belonged to the so-called radical wing within the Confessing Church, and he was surely also one of the very few who were aware of the significance of this church struggle for the whole of the Western world. In the previously mentioned essay on the ecumenical movement he wrote: "The Confessing Church is carrying out and suffering through this struggle as a representative of the whole of Christendom, especially of Occidental Christendom."[15]

No Church Without Church Discipline

Doctrine and order, confession and congregational discipline, all irrelevant concepts to the established church in Germany of that time

13. Ibid., p. 272.
14. *GS*, 2:238.
15. *GS*, 1:243.

and of the present day, belonged together according to Bonhoeffer. In *The Cost of Discipleship* he emphasized church discipline, knowing that the communion of the saints is not an 'ideal' communion consisting of perfect and sinless men, but that a communion that will not call sin 'sin' will also be unable to arrive at faith. Therefore, the sinner in the congregation must be admonished and punished. In this connection a congregation must also have the courage to impose "exclusion from all community with the congregation." Thus Bonhoeffer defended the integral relation of doctrinal discipline and church discipline.

However, it was clear to him that false doctrine is more serious and injurious than lack of discipline. In complete contrast to today's theological modernism, Bonhoeffer found orthodoxy more important than orthopraxis:

> False doctrine corrupts the life of the Church at its source, and that is why doctrinal sin is more serious than moral. Those who rob the Church of the gospel deserve the ultimate penalty, whereas those who fail in morality have the gospel there to help them. In the first instance doctrinal discipline applies to those who hold a teaching office in the Church. It is always assumed that only those will be admitted to the ministry who are *didaktikoi*, able to teach. . . . Doctrinal discipline thus starts before the actual ordination. It is a matter of life and death for the Church that the utmost care be exercised with regard to ordinations.

Bonhoeffer expressed the relation between doctrinal discipline and congregational discipline as follows: "The discipline of the official ministry comes before ordinary church discipline. . . But both forms of discipline are essential to one another. St. Paul therefore rebukes the Corinthians for being so puffed up that they start schisms without exercising church discipline. It is impossible to separate doctrine and morality in the Christian Church."[16]

Doctrine, congregational discipline, and the governance of the church all belonged together for Bonhoeffer. When in 1933 a state commissar was temporarily appointed for the Prussian church, Bonhoeffer went so far as to call the pastors to refuse to perform funerals. His brothers did not follow him in this action. The consistent, the

16. *Cost of Discipleship*, pp. 330–31n.

"radical" Bonhoeffer experienced a Confessing Church that was not ready for the radicality of the church struggle.

Confessing Church—But No Church Struggle

In 1933, Bonhoeffer's will to opposition ran into a muddied mess of cowardliness, indecision, lack of principle, helplessness, and confusion. After just three months of "church struggle" Bonhoeffer saw himself alone in his position. Therefore he decided to leave Germany in order to take a post as pastor in London. His letter of October 24, 1933, to Barth is characteristic of his mood at that time:

> I felt that I had incomprehensibly come to a position of radical opposition to all of my friends; with my opinions on this matter I became more and more isolated, although I stood and remained in the closest personal relationship with these people—and all of that made me afraid, uncertain; I was afraid that I might lose myself in the arrogant certainty of being correct—and throughout all of this I could not see any reason at all why I should now see precisely these things better and more correctly than so many of the hard-working and good pastors whom I have always looked up to—and so I thought that it was probably time to go into the desert for a while. . . . On top of all of this, it seemed to me to be a symptom of what was happening that the Bethel Confession, on which I really worked passionately, was received with almost no understanding whatsoever.[17]

Bonhoeffer's modest mode of expression did not accurately reflect the situation. Bonhoeffer—not the moderates—had recognized the true state of affairs.

Bonhoeffer was to live through what he had experienced with his brothers in the Confessing Church in yet another arena. The ecumenical movement reacted to the problems in the German Protestant Church with an equally limp and insecure willingness to compromise. On April 7, 1933, Bonhoeffer wrote the following to Henry Louis Henriod:

> There comes a time when one simply has to decide. One cannot eternally wait for a sign from heaven that causes the solution to one's dif-

17. GS, 2:132f.

ficulty suddenly to fall into one's lap. The ecumenical movement too has to decide and thereby is subject to the general human fate of making mistakes. But not to act or take a position at all merely out of fear of making a mistake when others—namely, the brothers in Germany—daily must make infinitely difficult decisions anew, seems to me to go almost against the commandment of love. Postponed or missed decisions can be more sinful than wrong decisions which arise out of faith and love. . . . Christ is looking down on us and asking whether there is still anyone there who confesses Him.[18]

At any rate, on May 22, 1934, Bonhoeffer wrote the following to his grandmother, who had energetically opposed the boycott of Jewish-owned businesses on April 1, 1934, by entering a Jewish-owned store: "Unfortunately I too have no real trust anymore in the ecclesiastical opposition. I do not like the way they are proceeding at all and I am really afraid of the moment in which the responsibility falls to this opposition. I am afraid that we will then possibly have to look upon a terrible compromising of Christianity once again."[19] Already at that time, all of this led Bonhoeffer to the foreboding that he expressed in a letter to his brother Karl Friedrich, "that Christianity is coming to an end in the Western World, at least as it has been structured and interpreted up to now."[20] That is how Bonhoeffer felt inwardly—the same Bonhoeffer who lived, acted, and worked from 1935 until his death as an employee of the Prussian Council of Brothers of the Confessing Church—with a salary of 360 *Reichsmark* per month.

In spite of all of these doubts, reservations, and wounds, Bonhoeffer fought on bravely throughout the 1930s. A speech he made on January 10, 1935, before two hundred pastors in Stettin-Bredow shows how he fought: "The concern for the survival of the established church has already practically overrun the concern for the public word of truth. Instead of going forward we stop and ask who we really are: church or movement or group? Whoever sees the confessing church as a movement or as the moving force of a cause is lost; he sees only a pitiable bunch of self-willed, despondent people who are hardly worth being called a 'movement.' Indeed, he sees only an

18. Bethge, *Bonhoeffer*, p. 427.
19. *GS*, 2:181f.
20. Ibid., p. 158.

undisciplined crowd, disobedient, the antithesis to 'church.' But let us not be among those in this sad state! In stopping, everything breaks down; only in moving forward does the church exist."[21]

Thus, in this situation also Bonhoeffer understood church processually. The church is not, but rather the church becomes. The church is not an institution, but an event. That is a new and dynamic view of the church. It was the only view that could fit the situation—and that fits the modern situation as well.

At any rate the following is clear: the Bonhoeffer of the 1930s did not entertain any illusions about the Confessing Church. Therefore, we cannot call it a break in Bonhoeffer's thought, as Eberhard Bethge did, when in April of 1944 Bonhoeffer found himself thrown back to the "beginnings of understanding." This intellectual-spiritual drama had certainly taken place in Bonhoeffer's soul already in the 1930s. Looking back, Bonhoeffer wrote in 1943: "We have been silent witnesses of evil deeds; we have been drenched by many storms; we have learnt the arts of equivocation and pretence; experience has made us suspicious of others and kept us from being truthful and open; intolerable conflicts have worn us down and even made us cynical. Are we still of any use?"[22]

Lack of willingness to fight was not the only feature of the Confessing Church that Bonhoeffer found wanting. He also saw much stagnation, restorationism, and even reactionism. He saw how this church was trying somehow to save itself as an "institution of salvation." "The church must come out of its stagnation. We must move out again into the open air of intellectual discussion with the world, and risk saying controversial things, if we are to get down to the serious problems of life."[23]

Bonhoeffer saw the church struggle also as a struggle for a church that would be different than it had ever been:

> That is why the air is not quite fresh, even in the Confessing Church. To say that it is the church's business, not mine, may be a clerical evasion, and outsiders always regard it as such. It is much the same with the dialectical assertion that I do not control my own faith, and that it

21. Bethge, *Bonhoeffer*, p. 567.
22. *Letters and Papers from Prison*, p. 16.
23. Ibid., p. 378.

is therefore not for me to say what my faith is. There may be a place for all these considerations, but they do not absolve us from the duty of being honest with ourselves. We cannot, like the Roman Catholics, simply identify ourselves with the church. . . . Well then, what do we really believe?[24]

Thus Bonhoeffer was not a traditionalist. Neither was he a traditionalist in the church struggle. The struggle for discipline and confession was of foremost importance. Renewed reflection about the church in the modern world, the reality of Christian congregations in a world come of age—that was his other consuming concern.

24. Ibid., p. 382.

PART 10

Unity in the Church and Peace in the World

29

Peace and Justice

The Radicalism of Fanö—The Year 1934

How did things look in Europe, especially in Germany, when the ecumenical conference took place in 1934 on the island of Fanö? First of all a short look at the year 1933: On May 27, 1933, Martin Heidegger made his famous—or infamous—speech at his inauguration as rector of the University of Freiburg: "The oft-celebrated academic freedom is being cast out of the German universities, because this freedom was not genuine. . . . The German students' concept of freedom is now being brought back to its truth. In the future, the bond and service of the German student body will unfold out of this truth."[1] This bond was understood as the bond with the German *Volk*—the racial community. In the political mood of those years, the *Volk* became the saving bearer of truth about God and man. Intellectual and political (as well as ecclesiastical) life was to be a racially *(völkisch)* oriented life. Thus there was a racial revolution going on in Germany that made the year before the meeting in Fanö a dramatic year in Germany. In June 1933 the pastor of the military district of Königsberg, Ludwig Müller, took over the leadership of the Federation of Protestant Churches in Germany "in view of the state of emergency in the churches." In July

1. Martin Heidegger, *Die Selbsbehauptung der deutschen Universität*, 1933.

this German federation, which united the state-supported German established churches, accepted a new constitution in which the leader principle (*Führerprinzip*) was embodied in the office of the imperial bishop. The elections to the ecclesiastical committees resulted in a majority of seats for the movement that as German Christians wanted to bring National Socialist thought into the church.

The government was also able to stabilize itself in 1933. The number of unemployed sank below the 4 million mark. The job-creation program, which had been started up with a loan in the billions, made major projects possible that actually did lessen unemployment. In September 1933 the Prussian General Synod, in which the German Christians had a two-thirds majority, brought about a "new reality" that led to conservative and confessionally oriented Christians' having to leave the synod under protest. At that time pastor Martin Niemöller called for the establishment of an emergency alliance of pastors. In horror, a representative of the Swedish church observed at the Prussian General Synod of September 1933 that churchmen arrived at an ecclesiastical assembly in uniform with belt and dagger.

In October 1933 Germany left the League of Nations and openly admitted that it was rearming. On November 13, 1933, at a mass rally in the Sports Palace in Berlin the German Christians adopted such a radical tone that they discredited themselves and lost all opportunity to remain a significant movement in church life.[2] The elections to the *Reichstag* also took place in November 1933, and 92 percent voted the NSDAP's straight ticket. A law passed by this *Reichstag* then empowered the Reich government to change the constitutions of the individual provinces of Germany without the permission of any par-

---

2. In the Sports Palace in Berlin with its twenty thousand seats, the place where Hitler and Goebbels gave their speeches (this is where Goebbels gave his "Totaler-Krieg-Rede" ["Total War Speech"] in the winter of 1943), the German Christians, after a kind of introductory liturgy with music from SA-bands, propagated heroic piety and racially appropriate Christianity. The following changes were called for: the abolition of the Old Testament, the purification of the New Testament (especially of Paul and his "scapegoat theory"), the doctrine of the pure Jesus as opposed to the "exaggerated emphasis on the crucifixion" and victory over materialism (that is, capitalism). On this point, see Scholder, *Die Kirche*, 1:703ff. Neither the NSDAP nor the established churches were interested in this outrageous spectacle. The former did not want to mix their ideology with Christianity, and the latter wanted to preserve the organizational apparatus of the established church. Thus, the German Christians' rally in the Sports Palace marked the onset of their decline. From then on, they were no longer of significance.

liamentary committees. Also, the totally *Volk*-racial ideologue Alfred Rosenberg was charged with carrying out the ideological training and education of the Party. In January 1934 a sterilization law was passed under which people with hereditary diseases could be made sterile, if necessary against their will (in that case with a judicial ruling).

In May 1934 the confessing Synod of the German Protestant Church had formed and published the so-called Barmen Theological Declaration. In practical terms, this declaration brought about a split in the church, but not a schism. Then, in June 1934 the so-called Röhm Putsch was put down. In the same month the German Reich not only stopped paying the debt payments required under the Treaty of Versailles, but also stopped fulfilling the interest payment obligations under the Dawes and Young loans. In July 1934 the Austrian Chancellor Dollfuss was shot by National Socialists in his Federal Chancellery on Ballhaus Square in Vienna and bled to death without medical treatment. In August 1934, the month of the Fanö meeting, Reich President Paul von Hindenburg died at the Neudeck estate. Immediately a law that had just been prepared came into force under which the offices of Reich President and Reich Chancellor were united under Hitler who then, as "Führer and Reich Chancellor," took the fate of Germany into his hands backed up by an incomparable wealth of power. A plebiscite in the same month of August resulted in 89.93 percent approval of this ruling. Thus it was a dramatic year. Especially the murder of the Austrian Chancellor seemed to threaten the peace in Europe, because Mussolini had troops deployed at the Brenner Pass.

Bonhoeffer held the morning devotional on August 28 on the island of Fanö on Psalm 85:8: "I will listen to what God the Lord will say; he promises peace to his people, his saints."[3]

At that time Bonhoeffer was twenty-eight years old. His sermon was heard with breathless suspense. The listeners were upset by the radicality of his message and none of those present were ready at that moment completely to go along with Bonhoeffer's remarks. Bonhoeffer set the church of Christ, which is to be heard and united beyond all national borders, against the nationalism in Germany that was growing more and more radical every day. He set the proclamation of

3. *GS*, 1:216ff.

peace against the emerging inner and outer militarization in Germany. According to Bonhoeffer, the threatened world was still in existence only because of the church of Christ. Christians, said Bonhoeffer, may not train their weapons against each other. Christians who point their weapons at each other point them at Christ. Bonhoeffer wanted a peace that had to be risked in the readiness to give up security and to hand the peoples over to a perhaps dangerous peace without any advance concessions: "There is no way to peace on the way to security." The world should be forbidden to make war. The peace of Christ should be declared over the raging world: "The hour is hastening, the world is staring into gun barrels. . . . Who knows whether we will still be here next year?" When a Swedish woman asked Bonhoeffer what he would do in case of war, he answered: "I pray that God will give me the strength not to take up arms."[4]

In spite of strong objections from other participants, two resolutions were passed at the youth conference rejecting support by Christians "for any war whatsoever." There are no ifs, ands, or buts about these statements of Bonhoeffer. Completely in line with the World Federation of Interchurch Relations, he advocated a radical pacifism that surprised and astonished all participants. Not only the radicality of Bonhoeffer's statements is amazing, but above all it is amazing how he saw through the tense and dramatic situation of the year 1934.

Bonhoeffer was dissatisfied with the inner situation of Protestantism in Germany. He saw very well that crucially important things had been said in regard to doctrine at Barmen. But all of that was not enough for him. Bonhoeffer wanted Christians to intervene concretely in the events of their time.

The "Peace of Fanö" of 1934

The radical pacifism of Fanö in 1934 remained a lonely exception in the life and work of Bonhoeffer. Neither before nor after that did he ever express such radical pacifism. At the youth conference of the World Federation of Interchurch Relations in Cernohorske Kupele in Czechoslovakia in July 1932, Bonhoeffer had declared: "The order of international peace is God's commandment for us today." The church "will attempt in vain to disprove the nuisance of pacifist humanitari-

4. Bethge, *Bonhoeffer*, p. 451.

anism whenever the church does not itself already hear the command-ment of peace as the command of God." However, Bonhoeffer also remarked unequivocally "that the peace that is commanded of God has two limits: first, the truth and second, the law. The community of peace can only exist if it is not based on lies nor on unlawfulness." At that time it was very clear for Bonhoeffer: "Wherever a community of peace endangers or suffocates truth and law, the community of peace must be broken and battle declared against it. . . . Precisely because the peaceful order is a reality of the gospel, of the kingdom of God, truth and law can never be contrary to it." In opposition to tendencies in the theology of that time, however, Bonhoeffer also made clear that struggle and battle were not part of the creation order, but rather of the "preservational order in expectance of the coming of Christ, of the new creation."[5]

Completely in agreement with the European policies of the 1920s, which led to a real relaxation of tensions, Bonhoeffer saw in modern technological war a completely new type of war that was to be pre-vented at all costs: "Therefore, present-day war no longer falls under the concept of battle, because this type of war means the certain destruction of both sides. Therefore this type of war can simply no longer be characterized as an order of preservation in expectance of revelation, precisely because it is nothing but destructive . . . There-fore modern warfare, in other words the next war, must be declared anathema by the church."

It is significant in these remarks from Cernohorske Kupele in 1932 that peace is seen in connection with truth and justice and that there cannot be real peace wherever justice and truth are destroyed. In the proscription of modern technological warfare—which by the way was also done in the Kellogg Pact—Bonhoeffer took up arguments now used in today's nuclear pacifism. But if one sees the whole of Bonhoef-fer's argumentation, one cannot claim it as a foundation for nuclear pacifism.

"Peace" in Discipleship

In *The Cost of Discipleship* we do not detect the radical pacifism that Bonhoeffer had proclaimed at Fanö. Discipleship does not mean that

5. See the lecture "Zur theologischen Begründung der Weltbundarbeit," in *GS*, 1:41ff.

love of enemy can be made into a general principle in this world: "If we took the precept of non-resistance as an ethical blueprint for general application, we should indeed be indulging in idealistic dreams: we should be dreaming of a utopia with laws which the world would never obey. To make non-resistance a principle for secular life is to deny God, by undermining his gracious ordinance for the preservation of the world."[6]

The Christian lives in the love of Christ. Love is a gift of sanctification. Love of enemy, as such a gift of sanctification, occurs without the Christian himself being conscious of it. By the way, Bonhoeffer's argumentation here is just like Kohlbrügge's, for whom sanctification was an unconscious process. Bonhoeffer thought: "The good of Christ, the good in discipleship occurs without our being aware of it. The genuine work of love is always work which is hidden from me . . . Even his extraordinary love of his enemy remains hidden from the disciple. After all, he doesn't see the enemy as an enemy anymore, if he loves the enemy." These sentences show as well as any others that love of enemy can in no way be a "should," a political or even ethical program for improving or renewing the world. Thus love of enemy is possible only through sanctification. This sanctification can be experienced only in the community of Christians. In *The Cost of Discipleship* Bonhoeffer did not devote a great deal of attention to the life of the Christian with the secular authorities, the political existence of the Christian. Later on he realized that in *The Cost of Discipleship* he had too one-sidedly proclaimed "a holy life" secluded from the world. Later he was forced to experience that Christian life in the midst of political responsibility becomes a life of taking on guilt in facing up to conflict.

Bonhoeffer's Ethical Peace-Realism

The responsibility of the Christian in the midst of the realities of political life now caused Bonhoeffer to realize that "the sword can never bring about the unity of the Church and of the faith. Preaching can never govern nations. But the Lord of both kingdoms is the God who is made manifest in Jesus Christ. He rules the world through the office of the word and the office of the sword."[7] About war Bonhoeffer

6. *Cost of Discipleship,* pp. 160–61.
7. *Ethics,* p. 95.

now said: "In war, for example, there is killing, lying and expropria-
tion solely in order that the authority of life, truth and property may
be restored. A breach of the law must be recognized in all its gravity.
. . . Whether an action arises from responsibility or from cynicism is
shown only by whether or not, precisely in this violation, the law is
hallowed."[8] An absolute prohibition against killing another person
became unthinkable for Bonhoeffer: "One must speak of arbitrary
killing wherever innocent life is deliberately destroyed. But in this
context any life is innocent which does not engage in a conscious
attack upon the life of another and which cannot be convicted of any
criminal deed that is worthy of death. This means that the killing of
the enemy in war is not arbitrarily killing. For even if he is not personally guilty, he is nevertheless consciously participating in the
attack of his people against the life of my people and he must share in
bearing the consequences of the collective guilt."[9]

Thus the Christian in his actions is responsible to the commandment of God. Throughout all of this, the ethicist of responsibility Bonhoeffer defended himself against the reproach of double morality: "If
it is objected that in the world the Church demands the maintenance
of justice, of property and of marriage, but that from Christians she
demands the renunciation of all these things, if it is objected that in
the world retaliation and violence must be practised, but that Christians must practise forgiveness and unlawfulness, then these objections, which have as their goal a double Christian morality, and which
are very widespread, proceed from a false understanding of the word
of God."[10] Therefore, for Bonhoeffer the Decalogue and the Sermon
on the Mount are not two different "ethical ideals," but the one call of
God: "Neither the 'struggle for one's rights' nor the 'renunciation of
one's rights' is anything in itself, or can itself be, for example, a topic
of the Church's proclamation."[11] According to Bonhoeffer, one could
very well govern with the Sermon on the Mount, for a state leadership
also can honor God while fighting and destroying, and the church
must "oppose every concrete order which constitutes an offence to
faith in Jesus Christ."[12]

8. Ibid., pp. 261–62.
9. Ibid., p. 159.
10. Ibid., p. 358.
11. Ibid., p. 359.

When Bonhoeffer's brother-in-law, Hans von Dohnanyi, who himself was deeply involved in the resistance, reminded Bonhoeffer of the saying of Jesus that all who take the sword will perish by the sword (Matt. 26:52), Bonhoeffer said that whoever takes the sword for law and order will just have to accept that. This acceptance of burdens, suffering, and even guilt was a continual theme in Bonhoeffer's ethics of responsibility. To the question: who will withstand? he answered: "Only the man whose final standard is not his reason, his principles, his conscience, his freedom, or his virtue, but who is ready to sacrifice all this when he is called to obedient and responsible action in faith and in exclusive allegiance to God—the responsible man, who tries to make his whole life an answer to the question and call of God. Who are these responsible people?"[13]

Was Bonhoeffer a Pacifist?

It is unequivocally clear from Bonhoeffer's ethics that he recognized the political and intellectual necessity of the integral relation between law and power. In fact, for him power was even an exercising of the office of Christ. Does this new ethical orientation of Bonhoeffer mean that we have to forget his pacifism at Fanö?

In regard to the entirety of Bonhoeffer's statements on this subject we can say that for him war had no value in itself. War will always have to do with guilt. Peace, forgiveness, reconciliation, mercy will always be ultimate and crucial. Peace is the ultimate. And Bonhoeffer brought this ultimate to expression clearly and without compromise in his sermon at Fanö. However, he meant in this sermon peace among the brother peoples of the Occident—the Christian Occident. In that context a war would really have been a war between Christians, who then in the final analysis would have been shooting at Christ. Thus the Occidental dimension of the peace sermon at Fanö must necessarily be considered.

Peace in its extraordinary and ultimate importance is not possible when the normal divinely sanctioned order of life is destroyed. This penultimate of order also stands under the call of Christ. But the penultimate is always in relation to the ultimate and may never be absol-

12. Ibid., p. 360.
13. *Letters and Papers from Prison*, p. 5.

utized. It must always be the final goal to preserve and to cultivate the realm of law, order, and truth in the framework of peace. Only when this is not possible may force be risked and put to use as a last resort. Here also, one sees the dialectic in Bonhoeffer's thought. This dialectic of ultimate and penultimate, peace on the one hand and justice, truth, and order on the other hand, cannot be systematized. The Christian as one who acts responsibly will be able to resolve this dialectical structure of the integral relation of peace, law and Scripture only in and through a conflict. In this conflict situation, he must be ready to take guilt upon himself in responsible action. A "holy life" lived at the periphery of this world in order unconditionally to live out love of enemy and neighbor is not possible. Looking back, Bonhoeffer realized this, and he expressed his view on this in *Letters and Papers from Prison*.

30

No Unity Without Truth

Bonhoeffer as an Ecumenical

The University of Berlin of the 1920s and 1930s had a theological department that was very active ecumenically. Men such as Deissmann, Titius, Richter, Sigmund-Schultze, Hinderer, and Fabricius meant something in the world of international ecclesiastical and Christian cooperation. It is not necessary here to sketch Bonhoeffer's often depicted path within the ecumenical movement. At any rate he owed it to the Berlin theological department that he joined the "World Federation of Interchurch Relations" and soon became its youth secretary. This World Federation of Interchurch Relations was founded in Konstanz on August 1, 1914, at the verge of World War I amid the statement that "friendship between the churches shall be a means toward the reconciliation of the nations." Thus, from this standpoint the ecumenical movement stood in the service of peace. After all, it was a clear insight: in portraying their unity, Christians should contribute to the peaceful understanding between peoples that goes beyond national borders.

But when Bonhoeffer became involved, peace and international understanding by means of a church extending beyond all national borders was an offense in a country that was fully occupied with mobilizing a racial (*völkisch*), national and socialist orientation.

Already on July 26, 1932, in Cernohorske Kupele, Bonhoeffer felt compelled to state bitterly: "Whoever is involved in ecumenical work has to allow himself to be scolded as unpatriotic and untruthful, and every attempt at a reply is quickly shouted down."[1] But it was also the ecumenical contacts, the view beyond Germany's borders, that led Bonhoeffer to the insight that he expressed in a letter to Bishop Amundsen on August 8, 1934: "It must become clear—as terrible as it is—that the decision is just around the corner: National Socialist or Christian."[2] People outside of Germany did not see this fact nearly as clearly as Bonhoeffer saw it.

For the ecumenical movement outside of Germany, the ecclesiastical situation inside of Germany was very complicated. The unofficially sanctioned Confessing Church was faithful to the government but opposed its ideology (and had a complicated mix of factions within itself); the officially sanctioned Reich church was faithful to the government and accepted doses of racial (völkisch) ideology here and there (but was a complicated and differentiated mix of factions); and finally the great number of established provincial churches leaning this way and that brought about a situation that was confusing to people in and outside of Germany.[3] For this reason the question arose in the ecumenical movement as to who was to represent the Germany Protestant Christians in the ecumenical movement. Both German "church bodies" put forth effort to lay claim to this right. At that time, Bonhoeffer maintained with a fearless logical consistency that the Reich church had betrayed Jesus Christ as Lord and Savior. The ecumenical movement "Faith and Order" did not want to look at it that way at all. Neither was the other ecumenical movement for practical Christianity able to come to a clear position condemning the Reich church and recognizing the Confessing Church.

Thus for Bonhoeffer the immediate problem arose: "The Confessing Church and the Ecumenical Movement." When he wrote an essay

---

1. GS, 1:140ff.
2. Ibid., p. 205.
3. According to their own testimony, people who were assigned to church affairs in the Gestapo, the Nazi party, and the government could no longer adequately assess the totally confused situation of the Protestant Church in the Third Reich, nor the tensions within the Confessing Church. Scholder, in Die Kirche, has clearly brought out this state of affairs for the years 1933–35.

on this theme in 1935, the significance of the ecumenical movement had reached a low point for both the Reich church and the Confessing Church. Bonhoeffer wanted to make it clear to the ecumenical movement that the struggle of the Confessing Church in Germany was a struggle that was being fought for all Christians: "The Confessing Church is fighting and suffering this struggle as a representative of all Christendom, especially of Occidental Christendom."[4] Here once again, notice the significance that the "Occident" had at that time for Bonhoeffer. The Confessing Church had learned "that from the proclamation of the Gospel to the church taxes, the confession and this alone must define the church. Because there is no confessionless, neutral space in the church, it puts the question of confession to every discussion partner it encounters."

What did he mean by the issue of confession? Bonhoeffer meant the confession of the Reformation fathers, the crucial statements of *sola gratia, sola fide, sola scriptura*—by grace alone, by faith alone, by Scripture alone. The issue was the correct understanding of salvation, redemption, and reconciliation as opposed to an ideological view of man and a political salvation hope. Thus, in the confession the issue is the truth, and without truth there is no unity: "As true and as biblical the proposition may be that there is truth only in unity, it is just as true and just as biblical that unity is possible only in the truth." Unity and truth are this inseparable. And the truth must be confessed. That means *confitemur* (affirmation) and *damnatus* (condemnation). Thus, he who confesses the truth must also be ready to exclude and to condemn: "It would be prudent for the Christian churches of the Occident not to want to overlook the experience of the Confessing Church that a church without a confession is a defenseless and lost church."

Up to this point everything seems simple and clear. Now, however, the ecumenical movement brought its own problem into the situation. After all, various Christians and the representatives of various churches were united in the ecumenical movement. Thus, different confessions from different phases in the history of Christianity were living together in this movement. No one at that time could have

4. The essay "Die Bekennende Kirche und die 'Ökumene'" first appeared in the August 1935 issue of *Evangelische Theologie*. See *GS*, 1:240ff.

rightfully asserted that everything that was happening in the ecumenical movement was happening out of a unity of confession. Were there not even confessions represented that contradicted each other, such as the Reformed and the Lutheran, the Anglican and the Reformed, the Baptist and the Methodist? In the face of this dilemma Bonhoeffer arrived at the opinion that at certain times, ecclesiastical communities could live with dogmas, formulations, statements, or confessions that contradicted each other as long as the essential aspects of each church were not seriously threatened, opposed, or brought into question by this situation. Bonhoeffer was of the opinion that the church was threatened at its core not by traditional differences among various confessions, but by the contemporary challenge of a totalitarian state's ideology. Thus he wrote: "For the Confessing Church, the Antichrist is not located in Rome or even in Geneva, but in the government of the Reich church in Berlin."[5] Thus, the Confessing Church is a contemporarily confessing church. It takes up the challenges of its day and responds to them in a confession. And Bonhoeffer was of the opinion that such a contemporary confession, arising out of the challenge of the day, could bring the churches to lay their traditional differences aside for a while (not to forget them) in order to dedicate themselves to the most urgent task. Thus, the penultimate of traditional confessions was to submit to the ultimate of the contemporary confession. This is how one could formulate Bonhoeffer's dialectical understanding of the traditional and contemporary confessional situation.

Power in a Fallen World

Christians know that the human race lives in a world that has fallen away from God. Only the commandments of God and the law that derives from them can safeguard the human race from falling into the abyss. For a fallen human race law without power is senseless. The question can never be whether power is exercised, but how it is exercised. In this connection, power is subordinated to law according to Romans 13. This chapter of Romans expresses unequivocally that law cannot be without power, just as power must not be wielded without law. In this sense, Bonhoeffer did not desire a weak, but a strong state. But this state was conceivable for him only on the basis of the Chris-

5. *GS*, 1:255.

tian-Occidental order of law. Never, not even in Fanö, did Bonhoeffer consider being able to give up this Christian occidental order of law as the price for peace. Article 5 of the Barmen Theological Declaration, which was accepted by the confessing Synod on May 31, 1934, states: "The Scripture tells us that according to divine ordinance the state has the task of maintaining law and peace in the world not yet redeemed in which the church also is instituted; the state is to do so according to the measure of human insight and human ability by the threat and use of force." Thus, the integral relation of force, law, and peace in the fallen world is expressed very clearly here. No peace without power, but also no power that does not serve peace.

Unity and Truth

In *Church Dogmatics* Barth wrote: "Confessions are there for the purpose that one goes through them (not only once, but again and again anew). They are not there, however, for the purpose of returning to them, making one's home in them in order to bind and relate all of one's further thought to them . . . as if they were not based on belief in the coming Lord after all."[6] Undoubtedly, Barth's theology traveled beyond the traditional confessional limits. He got a taste of the wrath of the Lutherans as well as of the wrath of the Reformed camp—less so in Germany than in the Netherlands.[7]

At first, Bonhoeffer was a Lutheran and saw himself, especially in the ecumenical world, as a Lutheran theologian. Under the influence of Barth's theology, however, Bonhoeffer came under the suspicion of moving more and more toward the Reformed view of the integral relation between the state and the church and then toward the Reformed view of "sanctification" as well. Finally, Bonhoeffer was even labeled a radical millennialist. At the end of his life, in *Letters and Papers from Prison*, Bonhoeffer saw the relativity of all confessions. He saw that the traditional form of Christianity, and thereby the traditional confessional structure as well, were passing away. He did not believe that the heritage of the confessions had been used up once and for all or become superfluous. Rather, he thought that this heritage should be

---

6. Karl Barth, *Kirchliche Dogmatik*, 3/4, p. x (1951).
7. On the Dutch Reformed critique of Barth's theology, see G. Huntemann, *Die ideologische Unterwanderung in Gemeinde, Theologie und Bekenntnis*, 1985, pp. 70ff.

included in the new confession that had to be professed in the midst of the contemporary world. In just this way the Barmen Theological Declaration—to the later horror of the Lutherans—was such a confession, going beyond the confessional difference between Lutheranism and Calvinism in Germany. New challenges demand new answers. And in the presence of these new answers, the traditional answers, as they are harbored and cherished within the individual confessions, gain a different and new, but also all-embracing, place and value.

A New Confession Is Needed

The ecclesiastical landscape of both Europe and America has changed, to put it very carefully. We could use another image: a flood has deluged Western Christendom, and as Christians we now find ourselves in another landscape. This landscape is characterized by the end of the religious form of Christianity, as Bonhoeffer foresaw it. Christians cannot survive in this changed, newly churned up landscape without clarifying their identity in the form of a new confession. In formulating a new confession, the following areas will have to be clarified.

First, what does it mean to say "the Word of God"? The challenge of selective historical criticism must be answered. Barmen took a first step in this direction in order to make it clear that only God's Word can be the standard for the Christian body of believers. But the Barmen Theological Declaration could not and did not want to deal with the challenge of a modern analytical way of thinking that is being thrown out over the Bible like a net, binding its truth. This reflection on the nature of the Word of God, this Bible-believing response to the analytical-critical distortion of truth, is equally indispensable in all denominations. In a new confession, the Protestantism that has fallen into an "intellectual dead end" will have to take a stand on the *sola scriptura* of the Reformation fathers.

Second, feminism brings a matriarchal distortion of Christianity. Whether women may be ordained to the office of pastor is in dispute within Christendom. The contemporary feminization of the biblical view of God is a more important challenge to Protestants than the Mariology of the Roman Catholic Church. The changes in churchly habits and beliefs that have come in on the coattails of the feminization of Christianity—such as cheap grace, emotionalization, and electronic evangelization—must be thought through and answered. In this connection we see the necessity of professing and condemning.

Third, the present-day revolution as a rejection of parental authority, the weakening of sexual taboos and the denial of all biblical ordinances for sexual life, the doing away with the commandments (ordinances or mandates), and the permissive, hedonistic, purely emotionally oriented "new morality"—these are challenges that the church must not remain silent about because within Christendom itself there are representatives of ethical viewpoints that would adapt to this cultural and moral revolution. It must be made clear through professing and condemning whether and how much the law of God as revealed in the Old and New Testaments is still to have significance for the present day.

In these areas, the issue is the absolutely necessary clarification of the Christian conception of the Christian faith itself. This clarification will undoubtedly lead to a schism in contemporary Christianity. But in regard to what we have learned from Bonhoeffer, we must keep in mind that a future church will be possible, conceivable, and full of promise only as a confessing church under the Word.

Index